THE CRISIS OF CAREGIVING

THE CRISIS OF CAREGIVING

Social Welfare Policy in the United States

Edited by

Betty Reid Mandell

THE CRISIS OF CAREGIVING
Copyright © Betty Reid Mandell, 2010.

First published in 2010 by
PALGRAVE MACMILLAN®
in the United States—a division of St. Martin's Press LLC,
175 Fifth Avenue, New York, NY 10010.

Where this book is distributed in the UK, Europe and the rest of the world,
this is by Palgrave Macmillan, a division of Macmillan Publishers Limited,
registered in England, company number 785998, of Houndmills,
Basingstoke, Hampshire RG21 6XS.

Palgrave Macmillan is the global academic imprint of the above companies
and has companies and representatives throughout the world.

Palgrave® and Macmillan® are registered trademarks in the United States,
the United Kingdom, Europe and other countries.

ISBN: 978–0–230–62261–6

Library of Congress Cataloging-in-Publication Data

The crisis of caregiving : social welfare policy in the United States /
[edited by] Betty Reid Mandell.
    p. cm.
ISBN 978–0–230–62261–6 (hardback)
    1. Public welfare—United States. 2. United States—Social policy.
I. Mandell, Betty Reid.

HV95.C75 2010
361.6′80973—dc22   2009048757

A catalogue record of the book is available from the British Library.

Design by Newgen Imaging Systems (P) Ltd., Chennai, India.

First edition: June 2010

10 9 8 7 6 5 4 3 2 1

Printed in the United States of America.

Transferred to Digital Printing in 2011

*To all the caregivers who have been deserted
by the government.*

Contents

Introduction

Betty Reid Mandell

The United States could be called "the reactive welfare state." It does not take a preventive and noncoercive approach toward its members; rather it is reactive and largely coercive taking a "back-end" approach that responds to the destructive consequences of the relative neglect of the "front-end" approach and that is necessitated by such neglect.[1] The nation takes a preventive public health approach in ensuring that the population avoid diseases by drinking clean water and having adequate sanitation, yet it does not take a preventive approach in caring for people's health. Rather than enacting universal health insurance, the nation ignores the health needs of millions of its citizens. Illnesses that could have been prevented get worse, forcing people to seek expensive emergency or long-term care. The nation neither puts many resources into insuring that people are not poor nor insuring the physical and emotional health of children raised in poverty. It tries to patch up the consequences of poverty by taking children away from their parents rather than providing the resources to help families care for their children, putting homeless people in shelters rather than providing public and affordable housing and, finally, when all other systems have failed, building one of the largest prison systems in the world, with few resources for rehabilitation (as described in Marguerite Rosenthal's chapter on prisons).

The safety net, already thin before the current recession, has been stretched to the breaking point. Barbara Ehrenreich expressed it well:

> If nothing else, the recession is serving as a stress test for the American safety net. How prepared have we been for sudden and violent economic dislocations of the kind that leave millions homeless and jobless? So far, despite some temporary expansions of food stamps and unemployment benefits by the Obama administration, the recession has done for the government safety net pretty much what Hurricane Katrina did for the Federal Emergency Management Agency: it's demonstrated that you can be clinging to your roof with the water rising, and no one may come to helicopter you out.[2]

The shredding of the safety net has further exacerbated the crisis of caregiving. As I describe in chapter 1 "The Crisis of Caregiving," women's work of caring for children, the disabled, and the elderly has been devalued. When the work is paid, the pay is low. When it is done without pay, as in women's own families, it is considered a "labor of love," not worthy of financial reimbursement. Welfare "reform" has limited the time that low-income single mothers and their children can get help, has pushed them into low-wage labor without a guarantee of child care, and has prevented them from earning higher wages by forbidding them to get a college degree.

Some of the themes that run through all the chapters of this book are poverty, race, gender, social class, and the imposition of conservative morality on the poor. They are intertwined. As I describe in chapter 6 "Foster Care," most children separated from their parents and placed in foster care come from poor families, but poverty is not the only cause of their removal. Many children are removed because middle-class child welfare workers impose their own morality on poor families. Adding race to the equation, one finds that a disproportionate number of children of color are being removed because of the white child welfare workers' cultural insensitivity. In the "Adoption" chapter, I describe how race has been a hotly contested issue in the adoption system, with a continuing debate about preserving a culture versus assimilating to the dominant culture. Those who believe that we are, or should be, in a postracial culture may ignore the importance of maintaining one's cultural identity. Harsher treatment of people of color is glaringly evident in the prison system.

Racial discrimination was built into Social Security in 1935 by Southern Congressmen who did not include domestic workers and agricultural workers because they wanted cheap labor without government responsibility for the workers. The same discrimination occurred in the AFDC/TANF cash assistance program, which has always been stingy and punitive to maintain a supply of cheap labor.

The back-end approach to dealing with people's troubles sometimes leads to criminalizing people who need help. In the chapter "Shelters for the Homeless: A Feeble Response to Homelessness," I describe how drugs trigger conservative anxieties, causing some shelters for the homeless to test all of their residents for drugs whether or not they evidence drugged behavior. Anxieties about homeless people living on the street prompts officials to treat them like criminals.

Sex triggers conservative anxieties, leading legislators to punish TANF (welfare) recipients by not supporting children who are born while their mother receives TANF and to try to control teen's sexual behavior, in an effort to prevent pregnancy. Sexual anxieties sometimes prompt child welfare workers to take children from their parents because of the workers' perception of sexual abuse, when there has been no abuse.

Women's liberation and financial need have converged to send a lot of middle-class mothers into the wage labor market. (Poor mothers have always been there.) But supportive programs to help them juggle work and family responsibilities are scarce and grudging, as Randy Albelda and I point out in the chapter "Paid Family and Medical Leave." Few employers are willing to pay for family or sick leave, and the federal government grants only twelve weeks of unpaid leave. Only rich people can afford to pay for a baby sitter or a high-priced day care center. Women earn less than men, and they have a larger responsibility for the care of children and aged and disabled family members. The need for support of caregivers has reached crisis proportions. Conservatives blame the poor for their plight, typically describing them as lazy and irresponsible. This is evident in shelters for the homeless, where shelters give the impression that homeless people will not take the initiative on their own to look for work or housing, enroll their children in school, keep their living spaces clean, or budget their money properly. They must be forced to do so.

Society's helpers are also society's behavior enforcers. Michel Foucault wrote about the social control aspect of "helping," and the "judges of normality." His history of discipline and punishment traces the gradual widening of the function of the prison to incorporate the so-called helping professions, under the rubric of "normalization." He says,

> The judges of normality are present everywhere. We are in the society of the teacher-judge, the doctor-judge, the educator-judge, the "social worker"-judge; it is on them that the universal reign of the normative is based; and each individual, wherever he may find himself, subjects to it his body, his gestures, his behavior, his aptitudes, his achievements. The cerebral network, in its compact or disseminated forms, with its systems of insertion, distribution, surveillance, observation, has been the greatest support, in modern society, of the normalizing power.[3]

"Normalization" occurs in the adoption system, where workers give preference to white middle-class parents and discriminate against gays and lesbians, and in the foster care system, where there are heated debates about whether gays and lesbians should be foster parents. This occurs despite the pressing need for caring foster parents.

Normalization occurs in TANF and Head Start, when single mothers are pressured to get married because the two-parent family is more "normal," as Gwendolyn Mink points out in her chapter "Women's Work, Mothers' Poverty." Yet, as most low-income mothers know, getting married will likely make her family no longer eligible for the sets of government supports that are so vital to supporting their families on low-wage work.

Norman Mailer, observing Republicans at their 1968 presidential convention, commented on their self-righteousness in serving, and the lack of gratitude from the poor:

> In their immaculate cleanliness, in the somewhat antiseptic odors of their astringent toilet water and perfume, in the abnegation of their walks, in the heavy sturdy moves so many demonstrated of bodies in life's harness, there was the muted tragedy of the Wasp—they were not on earth to enjoy or even perhaps to love so very much, they were here to

serve, and serve they had in public functions and public charities (while recipients of their charity might vomit in rage and laugh in scorn).[4]

Middle-class people have built entire industries to serve, manipulate, and control the poor. Shelters for the homeless give temporary shelter to the homeless, but they also provide jobs for thousands of middle-class people. Rural communities resist attempts to close prisons because they provide jobs for people in the surrounding communities. The threat to close a military base arouses protests from residents in the community who work there or hope to work there. The foster care system employs thousands of middle-class people. Since the government pays more to place children in foster care than to support families in ways that prevent placement, the system continues. Thousands of middle-class people work in private adoption agencies to process the transfer of poor children, mostly babies, to middle-class families. Lawyers make money by brokering adoptions.

The Universal Declaration of Human Rights, which the United States voted to support when it was ratified by the United Nations in 1948, states that "everyone has the right to a standard of living adequate for the health and well-being of himself and of his family, including food, clothing, housing and medical care and necessary social services, and the right to security in the event of unemployment, sickness, disability, widowhood, old age or other lack of livelihood in circumstances beyond his control."[5]

Are we our brothers' and sisters' keeper, or do we say, "I've got mine, Jack. I'm pulling the ladder up. Too bad about you." Conservatives chant the mantra of "individual responsibility" to divert attention from the need for collective governmental solutions to our caregiving problems. Families have been told that caregiving is their private responsibility. As I describe in chapter 4, "The Privatization of Care," much of social welfare has been privatized. The first priority of private corporations is profit. Human needs too often take second place. Until we believe that human needs are top priority and there is a collective responsibility to meet those needs, we will continue to flounder around with the back-end approach.

NOTES

1. I am indebted to Leroy Pelton for this concept (Personal communication).
2. Barbara Ehrenreich, "A homespun safety net," *New York Times,* July 12, 2009, p. 9.
3. Michel Foucault, *Discipline and Punish: The Birth of the Prison.* New York: Random House, 1977, p. 304.
4. Norman Mailer, *Miami and the Siege of Chicago.* New York: The New American Library, 1968, p. 35.
5. United Nations General Assembly Resolution 217A (III), www. un.org/Overview/rights.

CHAPTER 1

Who Cares?: The Crisis of Caregiving

Betty Reid Mandell

Why should we care about caregiving? Because we are all involved. We have all been cared for as children. When our parents are old and unable to care for themselves, we care for them. We need someone to care for us when we are disabled, or we may need to care for a disabled relative or friend.

JUGGLING WORK AND FAMILY

One of the casualties of unfettered capitalism is caregiving. The needs of children, the aged, and the disabled for sensitive and reliable care take a back seat to the needs of capital. Conservatives say the family is crumbling and in crisis; feminists say the crisis is in the lack of caregiving provisions for working parents and lack of cash support for unemployed parents. Conservatives want a return to the male breadwinner type of family where men make the living and women stay home to care for their children. Irving Kristol believes that this would solve problems such as illegitimacy and male irresponsibility.[1] Francis Fukayama hopes that women will rediscover their biologically imprinted nurturing capacities and realize that taking a few years off work to stay with young children is best for their families. When this happens, he says, "day care will become the lot of the children of 'working class or welfare mothers' only."[2]

Conservatives call for a moral regeneration to restore the patriarchal nuclear family and the breadwinner father who earns the "family wage," yet they favor economic policies such as deregulation, a flexible labor market, and lowered wages, which, along with rising expectations, create the need for both parents to work. Feminists, on the other hand, call for "family friendly" state and employment policies that will make it possible for parents to combine work and child care without sacrificing their careers or neglecting their children, their aged parents, or disabled family members.

Since colonial times, women have done most of caregiving, both paid and unpaid. They care for their own children, and they care for other people's children. They are the primary caregivers of aged and disabled relatives, both their own relatives and their husband's relatives. And they are the primary caregivers of other people's aged and disabled relatives. Approximately 93 percent of caregivers in long-term care facilities for the aged are women, many of them immigrants. Caregiving for one's own children is not defined as work, and it is not paid.

The only federal program to give cash for caregiving is the program that most people call "welfare." It began as part of the Social Security Act of 1935, during the Depression. Unemployment was high during the Depression, and Aid to Dependent Children (ADC) helped to keep women out of the labor market so that men could have the available jobs. It was only for children; mothers were not included until 1950. It was modeled after the Mothers' Pension programs that had been enacted earlier in some states. These programs were based on the "family wage" assumption, for example, that the male parent would be the breadwinner while the female parent stayed home to care for the children and the home. The male's wage was supposed to be adequate to care for the entire family. The "family wage" theory has gradually eroded as more women entered the wage labor market. It has not completely faded away for the middle class, but it has faded away for parents dependent on public assistance. Middle-class women are often praised for getting out of the wage labor market to care for their children at home, but poor women are now expected to work for wages as well as to care for their children.

CAREGIVERS FOR FAMILY MEMBERS

In 2007, approximately 34 million people who care for their own family members provided care at any given point in time, and approximately 52 million provided care at some time during the year. The estimated economic value of their unpaid contributions was approximately $375 billion in 2007, up from an estimated $350 billion in 2006.[3] Nearly three-quarters of these caretakers are women. They provide an average of 50 percent more hours per week of informal care than men.

A substantial number of adults who provide care to a parent, aged 65 or older, report symptoms of depression. Two out of three informal caregivers are in ill health. Routine caregiver tasks can cause acute and chronic physical strain, particularly when caregivers lack appropriate training. Although most caregiving is short-term, prolonged responsibilities take a toll on the emotional and physical health of caregivers. Caregivers worry about not having enough time to spend with their spouse, partner, or children, or by themselves.[4]

Home care services can relieve some of the stress, but these are being cut back by cash-starved states. A Massachusetts study found that more of the state's elderly are being abused or neglected, as economic stresses push family caregivers to the breaking point and the social service programs that once helped them are cut back. An agency that handles Boston's protective services program reports that they received 134 reports of alleged elder abuse and neglect in January 2009, the highest for any month in the agency's 32 years of running the program.[5]

Caregivers for older people spend an average of $171 a month on out-of-pocket expenses—or approximately 1.5 billion per month—for groceries, medications, home modifications, and the like, for their family member. "This is the equivalent of an IRA each year for many women who may not have a pension through their workplace."[6] A MetLife study estimated that the cost to "intense" caregivers over a caregiving and working "career" was nearly $600,000 in lost pensions, wages, and Social Security.[7] "As a result of all this, women are more likely than men to face poverty in retirement: 12 percent vs. seven percent. As the number of women who provide informal caregiving increases, the number of poor older women will inevitably increase."[8]

The recession has made the problem more severe. A survey of 1,005 caregivers in 2009 by the National Alliance for Caregiving and Evercare found that one in six said they had lost a job during the downturn, and 21 percent said they had to share housing with family members to save money. One of these unemployed caregivers, Carol Szalega, quit her job to care for her parents. She has been unable to find part-time work that she could do at home. She said, "For people who quit their jobs to take care of their parents, there's no stimulus plan for us."[9]

The Costs of Caregiving

Women's caregiving responsibilities result in lower wages and inability to advance in a career. Economists call this the "motherhood penalty." In 1991, by one estimate, it accounted for more than 60 percent of the difference in men's and women's wages in the United States.[10]

When women stay out of the labor market they not only give up their wages, but they also are left behind in professional advancement, sacrificing the higher wages they could earn at the top of their field. Ann Crittenden documents this in her book *The Price of Motherhood: Why the Most Important Job in the World Is Still the Least Valued*. Economists, most of whom are men, ignore or downplay the importance of domestic activity. "One current economics text, for instance, argues that 'in the most advanced industrial economies, the nonmarket sector is relatively small, and it can be ignored.'"[11] Nancy Folbre comments on this:

> Economists have been profoundly uncomfortable—even resistant—to the notion that time devoted to children is economically important. What they really resist is the idea that altruism might be one of the engines of economic growth. This would destroy their model that self-interest drives everything.[12]

Economics textbooks usually measure economic success by Gross Domestic Product and family income. They imply that increases in productivity and income will increase human happiness. Yet, when people are asked what increases happiness, they say that the pleasure of increased income dissipates relatively quickly. Strong family and community relationships seem to have a larger and more lasting impact.[13]

Mothers who have stayed home to care for the children are also disadvantaged when they divorce. Crittenden argues that when a couple have agreed that the wife should stay home to care for the children, the man's wages should be a true "family wage," equally shared with his wife as an equal partnership. Courts, however, consider the man's wages to be entirely his property and issue support orders that favor the man. Research shows that even high-income husbands pay a much lower percentage of their income for support of their children than do poor or middle-class men.[14]

In 1991, Carol Lees, a single mother of three in Canada, refused to answer the census question because it did not contain a question about her unpaid labor of caregiving. She went on to organize a campaign calling on Canadian women to boycott the 1996 census unless it counted their unpaid labor. Despite much conservative opposition, the government relented in 1995 and added three new questions to the census. People are now asked how many hours in the previous week they spent on (1) home maintenance, housework, and yard work; (2) supervision of children, either their own or others'; and (3) care or assistance of the elderly.[15]

The sociologist Jesse Bernard argued more than 30 years ago that what family caregivers need more than anything else is an economic base that reflects their very real value to society. She described women's unpaid work as the infrastructure on which the entire superstructure of the economy rests.[16]

Most corporations have not changed their expectations or structures to accommodate employees' caretaking responsibilities. Rosanna Hertz, who studied women and men in dual-career marriages found that "Career women postpone childbearing until they have been promoted to higher ranks in their firms."[17] Furthermore, the corporations prevent women from taking collective action against policies that impede their progress "by making individual deals and special arrangements with the few women who are seen as indispensable to the organization."[18] To advance in highly paid careers at large corporations, women often work from 60 to 70 hours a week. They frequently complain of ulcers, fatigue, and stress.[19]

Women in highly paid careers have to hire help to be freed to advance in their careers. Thus, progress for some women is bought at the expense of equal progress for other women. "Dual career couples have an indirect but material interest in maintaining an unstable, low-wage pool of labor."[20] There is a small boom in the employment market for unskilled labor due to the increasing numbers of career women.

Most workers are not in highly paid careers. When they take time off from work because of caregiving responsibilities, they feel the pinch. Three-quarters of caregivers for older people work full or part-time, and half of those who work are making some sort of work-related adjustment. The most frequent adjustment is to go to work late, leave early, or take time off from work. Other adjustments include taking a leave of absence, dropping back to part-time or taking a less demanding job; losing job benefits; turning down a promotion, choosing early retirement, or giving up work entirely.[21]

Fathers as Caregivers

The belief that women should be primary caregivers is deeply imbedded in custom and in people's psyches. The main thrust of the women's movement was to achieve equality in the work place, as well as to exercise choice in whether to have children. There was less emphasis on achieving equality with men in caretaking and homemaking.

One of the reasons that mothers stay home to care for the children while fathers work outside the home is that men generally make more money than women, so it often makes economic sense for the woman to stay home. But has equal pay led to equal caretaking? Do dual-career couples share the caretaking and housework equally? The American Time Use Survey gave some insight on this question. It found that when women lose their jobs, they spend twice as much time on child care and housework. When men lose their jobs, they spend the same time sleeping, watching TV, and job searching.[22]

Still, attitudes are changing, as documented by many studies.[23] An Association of Retired People (AARP) survey found that almost 40 percent of caregivers for older people are men, compared to 27 percent in 1997.[24] A 1996 survey asked whether husbands and wives should share household tasks according to individual interests and abilities (rather than according to "men's work" and "women's work"). Approximately 94 percent agreed with the statement.[25] Over the past few decades, women have been doing less care and house work, while men have done more. Yet, while fathers may be pitching in more these days, women still do the lion's share of caring and cleaning. University of Massachusetts economists Jooyeouyn Suh and Nancy Folbre estimate that, on average, from 2003 to 2007, women spent 4.5 hours a day on housework and care of children or elders compared to men's 2.8 hours.[26]

Many conservatives believe that men should not be expected to be caregivers.

> Wade Horn, former president of the National Fatherhood Initiative and ... assistant secretary for children and families in the Bush administration, warned fathers against acting like mothers, saying the "new nurturing father ideal," in which a man "shares equally in all childrearing activities from the moment of birth," is "of course, nonsense."[27]

Sweden has been concerned with the gender inequality in childrearing and has enacted paid family leave policies to encourage fathers' participation in childrearing. However, officials have been disappointed by the small number of fathers who took advantage of the paid leave. In 1992, they appointed a special government commission to investigate why men were not opting for more childrearing. The commission discovered that the single most important factor in determining how much time a father spent with his children was the mother's attitude. The key variable was the mother' education—a proxy for her position in the labor market. The more money she earned and the more fulfillment she found outside the home, the more space she was willing to create for the father within it.[28]

Many nations do not provide paternity leave. A study of 173 nations found 169 providing paid maternity leave, but only 66 had paid paternity leave.[29]

THE VALUE OF CARE WORK

The reproduction of the labor force, while essential for continued production, has been treated as a private family matter that does not require pay. This reliance on unpaid care work has saved money for both employers and the government, but it has put a heavy burden on women. Until fairly recently, there has been little theoretical discussion of this. Deanne Bonnar sums up this theoretical vacuum:

> The problems of care, if they were addressed at all, were to be absorbed into the market (Marx), were the consequence of intrapsychic conflicts (Freud) or resulted from personal failing (family values moralists). The reality of the intensity of the work, its multifaceted nature, and the skills and supports needed to do even adequate care work have not been understood.[30]

In 1995, the World Bank started to include estimates of human capital in measuring countries' wealth. They estimated that 59 percent of the wealth in developed countries is embodied in human and social capital (i.e., educational levels, skills, a culture of entrepreneurship).

> The remainder consists of natural resources (25 percent) and manufactured capital (16 percent). Since most natural resources are a given—you can't create more oil or arable land—this means that in the wealthiest countries, human capital accounted for three quarters of the producible forms of wealth.[31]

The economist Marilyn Waring argues that we need to rethink basic economic concepts such as gross domestic product in ways that take community well being into account. When she was a member of the New Zealand Parliament, Waring became a proponent for determining economic policy based on time and use rather than on money. Economists consider women to be unemployed as unpaid workers. However, if the boundaries of what is considered production were extended to include unpaid household work, all people engaged in those activities would be considered self-employed. She said,

> If unpaid labor were considered based on the equivalent pay scale of people who do that work for pay, unpaid household work would constitute the single largest service and production sector. It would be the equivalent of 571,000 full-year, full-time jobs. This work includes child-care and senior care. Expenses for these services are paid out of the workers' own pockets with no tax deductions and no incentives.[32]

Waring helped to pressure the government of New Zealand to implement a national Time Use Survey in 1998. The survey was designed to "Show up which sex gets the menial, boring, low status and unpaid invisible work which in turn highlights oppression and subordination."[33]

The AARP has issued a report, which provides an estimate of the value of family caregiving for long-term care for people with disabilities. They found that "the economic value of caregiving exceeded total Medicaid long-term care spending in all states, and was more than three times as high in 36 states. Compared with Medicaid home- and community-based service spending, the economic value of family caregiving was at least three times as high in all states, and more than 10 times as high in 19 states. The costs of caregiving to caregivers themselves are more than a simple accounting of hours. They include direct out-of-pocket expenses, economic insecurity caused by changes in work patterns, and health effects."[34]

DIRECT CARE WORKERS

More than three million people are employed as direct care workers in the United States. They include nursing assistants, home health aides, and personal and home care aides.[35] Most direct care workers receive very low salaries and few benefits. They work under high levels of physical and emotional stress. Low wages and poor working conditions lead to a high turnover rate—more than 70 percent in nursing homes, and between 40 and 60 percent in home care agencies annually. This costs long-term care employers at least $5 billion annually. The median hourly wage for nursing assistants is $11.14, $9.62 for home health aides, and $8.89 for personal and home care aides.[36] Home care for the elderly is one of the fastest-growing areas within the health care field. It is also one of the lowest paid and most exploitable. Outdated labor rules from 1975 allow home care aides to be defined as companions, which exempts their employers, usually private agencies, from federal standards governing overtime and minimum wages. A *New York Times* editorial expressed outrage at this:

> It is unconscionable that workers who are entrusted with the care of some of the nation's most vulnerable citizens are themselves

unprotected by basic labor standards. It is also unwise, because poor pay for long hours leads to high turnover, which undermines the quality of care. Turnover also drives up the cost of providing home care—a needless drain on Medicaid, which pays for many home care services. And that is not the only way that poor quality home care jobs end up costing taxpayers. Nearly half of home care workers rely on food stamps or other public assistance, so taxpayers ultimately compensate for their low pay and inadequate benefits.[37]

NANNIES

Rich people often hire nannies to look after their children. Some of these nannies are from a similar social class and race as the employer, but most of them are not. Nannies who come from middle-class homes are sometimes paid a good salary because some affluent parents want a nanny similar to themselves in terms of education and social status. Some employers try to entice the nanny to stay by establishing emotional ties, trying to incorporate the worker into the family. This can be satisfying to both parties, but it has the pitfalls of exploiting the worker by holding out family-like expectations.

Most nannies are poor women, many with children of their own. Many are of a different ethnicity than their employers and many are immigrants, some of them undocumented. Some high-level political figures have made the news because they hired undocumented immigrants. Perhaps the most publicized case occurred in January 1993 when incoming President Bill Clinton nominated Zoë Baird for attorney general. Baird, a highly successful corporate lawyer, and her husband, a Yale law professor, had hired an undocumented Peruvian couple to look after their three-year-old son. When they hired them they were aware that the couple were in the country illegally and they did not pay required taxes on them. After being grilled for days by senators, Baird became the first Cabinet nominee to withdraw in 120 years.[38]

After the Baird incident, the public became interested in the women who cared for the children of rich dual-career couples, and the media began to cover the story. The dominant theme of the story was exploitation. A *Wall Street Journal* reporter wrote, "There is a dirty little secret in middle- and upper-middle-class America: Nannies are among the most exploited workers in the country."[39] Two young women published a fictionalized account of their experiences as nannies to rich New York City couples,[40] which featured narcissistic, materialistic parents who thoughtlessly, and sometimes cruelly, exploited their nannies and ignored their children.

The nannies in the Hertz study were drawn from three principal sources: women less than the age of 25, older women, and recent female immigrants (legal or illegal). These women generally have fewer skills and fewer employment opportunities than do men or citizens, and they are easier to exploit. Most employers hire a series of workers. The 11 couples in Hertz's study had hired a total of 29 childcare workers during a 3-year period.[41]

Some employers rely on external pressures, such as labor market competition or worker vulnerability, to exert control over a worker's performance.[42] The most egregious form of this is to use an undocumented worker's illegal immigrant status to control her, which happens fairly often. One example of this is a woman from Uganda who had been imprisoned and beaten by military police in Uganda and who escaped by coming to the United States. She ended up as a virtual slave in the home of a woman who lived in a Boston suburb, working constantly to care for the woman and her three children and four boarders, and being yelled at by her employer. She never received any money for her work. She never left the house and one day, after living there for three months, she discovered her passport was missing. After five months, she left with the four boarders and was helped by a church to apply for asylum. She said, "I felt trapped, but I had to take it because I had no place to go."[43]

The rich people whom Hertz studied did not want to place their children in franchise day care centers because they understood business practices and knew that the day care center would probably make a profit at the expense of their children. They would not consider public day care because they associated that with the stigma of poverty and welfare. Some would not put their children in day care because of worries inspired by highly publicized and controversial cases of alleged sexual abuse by day care workers. If their children went to a day care center at all, it was to a high status one where their children would get a "leg up" on admission to high status elementary and high schools and an Ivy League college.

There is a global movement of caregivers from poor countries to industrialized countries. Large numbers of women from Ecuador go to Spain to care for children. In Italy, there is a large influx of women carers (called "badanti") from Eastern European countries such as Moldavia, Rumania, and the Ukraine. They are middle aged and leave a family behind. A priest is often the broker for them. They, along with couples living in as domestic servants from the Phillipines, Sri Lanka, and so on, got special treatment in recent immigration legislation, compared with other workers such as factory and building workers. However, as usual, this legislation purported to legalise their position with the employers paying the taxes, while in fact the employers often took it out of the immigrants' pay packet.[44]

Julia Wrigley studied caregivers in Los Angeles and New York and found that the 79 employers she interviewed had hired caregivers from 29 different countries, including 10 in Latin America, 5 in the Caribbean, 11 in Europe, and 3 in Asia. Employers often prefer a caregiver of a lower class because they feel this gives them more right to control them and to underpay them. One experienced employer told a friend that "sometimes it was better to accept 'dumb' employees who were under the parents' control rather than deal with cocky ones."[45] But control is hard to achieve, since the caregiver works in the privacy of the home without direct supervision (unless the employer chooses to install a hidden camera, which some do). The caregivers often have to submit to tyrannical control because they have no other options (particularly if they are undocumented immigrants). Those who have other options often leave. There is a high rate of turnover.

Historically, large numbers of women of color have gone into domestic work, including African Americans in the North or South, Mexican Americans in the Southwest, or Japanese- and Chinese Americans on the Pacific coast. "As late as 1940, almost 60 percent of African-American women worked as domestics."[46] Very few African American women now enter domestic work; most of those who do it are older women. One agency director who hires workers said, "I once asked a friend of mine who's black and she said that her mother did that already. American black people have been slaves and domestics for years. And after they scrub somebody's floor, they get up saying 'My child will never do this.'"[47]

Parents who employ caregivers seldom admit to racial prejudice, but owners of domestic employment agencies say that many parents refuse to accept black workers. If they do accept them, they expect to pay them less than white workers.[48] Since few African Americans apply for domestic work, this prejudice mainly affects Caribbean women. Different parents have different prejudices. One mother said she would accept Salvadoran women, but not Guatemalans. One lawyer refused to hire any Latinas, and insisted that the caregiver's native language had to be one she liked. She said, "I like French. I don't want Spanish. It's not going to be Castilian Spanish. Actually, I would probably say that it's limited to French."[49]

These prejudices about class and race create tensions in the relationships between employer and employee, and instill elitist attitudes in the children who are cared for. Even employers with egalitarian ideologies worry that their own status as personal "dictators" cannot help influencing their children. Even an employer's egalitarian attitude cannot keep the children from growing more distant from the caregiver as they grow older. One Mexican caregiver said that the boy she looked after included her in the pictures of his family that he drew in kindergarten, but he stopped doing this when he went to first grade. She said, "The closeness he felt for me has grown cold. He sees me as an employee."[50] The child's distance led the caregiver to withdraw in turn, and to regard him as just another employer. Children whose parents do not enforce respect toward the caregiver develop even more callous attitudes. As children get older, they come to see caregivers as their personal servants and can become quite tyrannical toward them.[51]

The quality of care suffers when caregivers are underpaid and disrespected by both their employers and the children they care for. Caregivers work in conditions where they have no peer companionship. They are often given little or no autonomy by their employers and work in "aching isolation and boredom."[52] These harsh working conditions can lead to depression. A substantial minority of the caregivers whom Wrigley interviewed seemed sad.[53]

Media discussions about the "supermom" who has it all—a highly paid and satisfying career and well cared for children—are almost always talking about white and at least middle-class women. In reality, that supermom is having trouble juggling career and children. But the vast majority of working women cannot afford to pay for a nanny and they are having even more trouble. They are often the maids, au pairs, baby-sitters, and housekeepers for the supermoms. Most maids and baby-sitters also stay in their occupations for life. Women hold the majority (59 percent) of low-wage jobs. Women who work in service occupations are disproportionately low paid. "Fifty-eight percent of those working within private household services, as well as 74 percent of those working in all other personal-service jobs, are low paid."[54] The majority of minimum-wage workers in the United States are women. The typical woman earns 77 cents for every $1 earned by a man and has fewer financial resources to withstand unemployment.[55]

Day Care

Robert Kuttner writes that "now the Wall Street scandals have reached all the way into the nursery schools."[56] A stock analyst at Citicorp, Jack Grubman, upgraded his rating of sagging AT&T stock to do his boss a favor, so that the boss, Citicorp chairman Sandy Weill, would use his influence to help Grubman get his twins into a prestigious nursery school. (AT&T's chairman served on Citicorp's board, and was a Citicorp client.) The nursery school, the 92nd street Y in Manhattan, "has a terrific record at graduating its tots into elite private grammar schools, which in turn feed prestigious prep schools and then, of course, the Ivy League. But what about the rest of America?"[57]

The larger story, Kuttner says, "is the absence of any decent pre-school or after-school places for millions of working Americans who aren't buddies of the chairman of Citicorp."[58] The large scale influx of working women into paid labor has not been accompanied by a corresponding increase in day care facilities or help with paying for day care. Welfare reform has pushed millions of low-income women out of the home into waged jobs, but neither the federal government nor the states have provided enough day care for these women. The shortage of day care is so severe that four child-care providers in the City of Boston were exempted from a city living-wage ordinance, the first exemption of Boston's living-wage law, which was enacted in 1998. Even the low $10.54 an hour mandated by the living wage law is far more than day care teachers make. Child care workers frequently earn wages only slightly above minimum wage. The child care providers said that they would have to cut spaces in programs for children of low-income families if they were not granted an exemption from the law.[59]

The lack of access to day care and after-school care has led to neglect of many children while mothers work, and sometimes to horror stories. A woman in Atlanta, Nakia Burgess, appeared in an Atlanta court on October 3, 2002, charged with murder. Her three-year-old daughter, Ashante, died after being left in Burgess's sweltering car. Her attorney said Burgess left Ashante in the car because she could not find affordable day care.[60] In his movie *Bowling for Columbia*, Michael Moore tells the story of a six-year-old child who shot and killed another six-year-old child at his school. The child's mother, a welfare recipient, had been forced into a workfare program. She got up at 6:00 a.m. to take the workfare bus, which drove her 40 miles to her work. She left her son in the care of her brother, where the child discovered a gun and took it to school. Moore interviewed several officials in the area who are indignant at the policy that forces a mother to be in a workfare program instead of caring for her son.

Some public day care is offered in prekindergarten programs. In the United States, approximately 1.1 million American preschoolers are in state-financed prekindergarten classes and approximately 900,000 are in Head Start—only a small percentage of those who could benefit. In April 2009, $2 billion from the stimulus package was earmarked for states to support child-care services for families where parents are working, seeking employment, or getting job training.[61]

According to the National Association of Child Care Resource & Referral Agencies, a nonprofit organization of community family-support agencies, the number of preschoolers with working parents exceeds the number of child-care slots by an average of 41 percent in 30 states.[62]

ORGANIZING CARE WORKERS

The countries with strong welfare provisions have strong unions. Improvements in this country's caretaking provisions will depend partly on union organizing, as well as on feminist organizations and other advocacy organizations. We list those organizations in the appendix B.

There have been some promising beginnings. Service Employees International Union (SEIU) has organized thousands of health care workers at hospitals. They have also organized home care workers, some of them who care for their own aged or disabled family member. Organizing employees of the nonprofit agency New Health Services (NHS) was the first large-scale organizing in Milwaukee at the low end of the wage scale since the 1997 launch of "W-2," Wisconsin's welfare reform system initiated by then-governor Tommy Thompson (later to become the director of U.S. Department of Health and Human Services). Many former welfare recipients are employed by NHS. These workers were paid at the rate of $7.10 an hour, with no benefits of any kind. After their union was certified, they went on to negotiate a contract for higher wages, improved training, health insurance, and pension benefits.[63]

During the 5-year period between 1997 and 2002, union organizing of home care workers in San Francisco County doubled, from $5.00/hour to $10.00/hour. During that same period, the percentage of workers who stayed in their job for more than a year increased from 39 percent to 74 percent.[64] Moreover, consumers' demand to employ unionized workers in their homes has increased, due largely to the fact that consumers can now hire a worker they know and trust to provide that care (because the person can now afford to give it) whereas before consumers may have gone without adequate levels of care at all times. Employing care workers from one's personal network (family, community, etc.) increases the likelihood of ethnic and racial matching.[65]

There has been a bitter fight between SEIU and one of its locals, the Union of Health Workers (UHW). After Andy Stern, the president of SEIU, placed UHW in trusteeship, rank-and-file leaders of UHW at 100 worksites with some 9,000 nursing home workers signed up a majority of their coworkers to decertify from SEIU and become an independent union. Their complaint was that SEIU had made an agreement with a group of nursing home operators in exchange for organizing rights to new facilities. The agreement stipulated that the union could not support or sponsor any legislation, could not file grievances on nursing home practices, and could not speak up about patient care issues or publicly campaign for increased patient-staffing ratios. They said that Andy Stern has kept long-term workers divided from hospital workers and created a "ghetto" union for low-wage workers outside of hospitals who are doing the same work, contrary to the principles of industrial unionism. UHW wanted to combine nursing homes and hospitals in their organizing.[66]

Farm workers, housekeepers, nannies, and other domestic workers have no legal protection and are among the most highly exploited workers in the nation. An organizing campaign called "Labor Justice" aims to organize those groups. It was launched by two veterans of United Farm Worker union campaigns, LeRoy Chatfield and former UHW attorney Jerry Cohen. By 2009, they had won the backing of labor, political, civil rights, academic, religious, and community leaders and organizations in more than 30 states. The Labor Justice campaign leaders call the exclusion of farm workers and domestics from the protections of the Labor Relations Act "one of our nation's last vestiges of slavery and segregation."[67]

Domestic workers are beginning to organize for better working conditions. In New York, Jobs with Justice and Domestic Workers United introduced a bill in the New York legislature called "Bill of Rights for New York's Domestic Workers." It is the first attempt in the nation to set labor standards for domestic workers and would set a precedent for labor standards for domestic workers around the country.[68] The bill calls for severance and overtime pay, advance notice of termination, one day off a week, holidays, healthcare, and annual cost of living increases, among other fundamental rights. The bill had strong support.[69]

The Reluctant Welfare State

Some societies take collective responsibility for their citizens' care needs. Others leave it up to individuals or families. The United States has historically been more reluctant than other industrial nations to take collective responsibility for its citizens' care needs. Yet in response to people's struggles, the government has developed some social welfare systems. The Social Security Act of 1935, enacted during the Great Depression, provided the basic framework for a safety net. It was enlarged in 1995 by the addition of Medicaid and

Medicare. The federal government directly administers Old Age, Survivors, and Disability Insurance (OASDI), work-related pensions for the aged and their survivors and the disabled, and the means-tested Supplemental Security Insurance (SSI) for the disabled, through local Social Security offices. Administrative costs are low, compared to the high administrative costs of welfare. The federal government also directly administers tax credits, through the Treasury Department. Rules are clearly spelled out for these federal programs. Once eligibility has been established for Social Security, the claimant simply receives a monthly check in the mail. There are no behavioral requirements such as welfare imposes. However, Social Security benefits go only to people who have done paid work, not to unpaid caregivers.

Medicare is financed by the federal government, but contracted out to private organizations to administer. The rules are uniform, in contrast to the various rules that states make for welfare.

Finding Help in the Bureaucratic Maze

The rest of the safety net is an uneven patchwork of programs funded and administered by different bureaucracies. Welfare (TANF, Temporary Assistance to Needy Families) and Medicaid reside at the Department of Health and Human Services, but are administered by states. The food stamp program (now called Supplemental Nutrition Assistance Program, SNAP) is funded by the Department of Agriculture but administered by the states. Federal rent subsidies are provided by the Department of Housing and Urban Development, but some states give rent subsidies and some cities build low-income housing. The Department of Labor oversees unemployment insurance, but states administer it and have differing rules.

With such a jumble of agencies and states, it is no surprise that people are often confused about what help they are entitled to, and have trouble getting it. Much of the administration of safety net provisions is arbitrary, capricious, and coercive. In the recession, more people are turning to the safety net for help because they have lost their jobs. The *New York Times* conducted a study of what kind of help people are getting and found a Byzantine patchwork of programs, with many roadblocks to access and wide variations between states. Here are two examples:

When the recession cost Erika Nieves of Bridgeport, Conn., her job with a wrestling promoter, she did get unemployment benefits. But that caused her to lose a welfare-to-work grant and her child care subsidy. Now Ms. Nieves is months behind on her rent and is job hunting with a 2-year-old. "They took away my aid when I need it the most," she said.

With a high-risk pregnancy at age 35, Jewell French-Allen left a $40,000 a year job in Massachusetts and applied for jobless benefits. But the state denied the request, ruling that she had quit by choice. She then took a sales job at much lower pay, and was laid off. Had she never held the first job, Ms. French-Allen could have gotten unemployment benefits, but because her earlier request had been denied, the state added a test—and disqualified her because the weekly pay from the second job was less than the benefits she would have gotten from the first. Two days after she was rejected again, she went into labor and delivered a boy who weighed less than two pounds. "I am bitter—if I had gotten unemployment, he wouldn't have been born prematurely," she said. "When you can't support yourself financially, it puts incredible stress on your body."

Just 50 percent of people eligible for food stamps receive them in California, compared with 98 percent in Missouri. Approximately 19 percent get jobless benefits in South Dakota, compared with 67 percent in Idaho.

Nationwide, approximately two-thirds of people eligible for food stamps receive them. But just 21 percent of poor children get cash welfare; 30 percent of eligible households get subsidized housing; and 44 percent of the unemployed get jobless benefits.[70]

When states have to pay for safety net programs with their own money, rather than federal money, they are likely to be stingy. Most states have eliminated their general relief programs for the able-bodied childless unemployed, which was entirely state funded. This has led to more people becoming homeless, an example of the "back end," reactive, approach to welfare. The amount of the TANF grant in all states is below the poverty line, but the grant is even less in poor southern states, which have historically been stingy in the amount of welfare grants they give to families because states bear the cost of expanded welfare rolls. States that are cash-starved because of the recession give priority in cutting those programs that do not bring in federal money.

In 2009, Massachusetts lawmakers proposed to eliminate health care for legal immigrants, including people seeking asylum from war-ravaged regions such as Iraq, Somalia, and the Sudan. The proposal was voted down. Some immigrants do not qualify for matching federal subsidies and so are more expensive for the state to insure. Many people who lose insurance coverage put off going to the doctor until they are seriously ill and then end up in the emergency room with catastrophic and expensive illnesses. Emergency rooms must treat all comers, and the state often foots the bill for those who cannot afford the care. Dr. Michael Grodin, director of medical ethics at Boston University's School of Pubic Health, said the immigrants who would be affected by the cuts have serious health problems. Approximately 70 percent have a torture history, 30 percent of the women have been raped, and 5 to 10 percent of the men have been raped in prison.[71] Again, the "back end," reactive, approach to providing care.

Social Welfare and the Labor Market

Social welfare provisions have always been tied to the labor market. Welfare scholars have coined the phrase "the principle of less eligibility" to describe the principle that welfare grants should always be lower than low wages, so that people will take any job rather than go on welfare. The reason that domestic workers and agricultural workers were not included in the original Social Security law was that segregationist Southern Congressmen wanted low-paid domestic and agricultural workers. They created barriers to the ADC program, such as "unsuitable home" provisions, which kept African American mothers from getting benefits. During the War on Poverty, welfare rights activists struck down some of these restrictive requirements.

Those Southern Democrats also insured that domestic workers and farm workers were not included in the National Labor Relations Act, which was enacted in 1935 as part of President Franklin D. Roosevelt's New Deal. Therefore, they have no legal protection against unfair employment practices.

The title of the TANF program signals that help is only temporary, and the law that enacted it, the Personal Responsibility and Work Opportunity Reconciliation Act (PRWORA), aims to get recipients off welfare and into waged work as soon as possible. When Congress enacted the ADC program in 1935, there was widespread support for mothers to stay home to care for the children, at least until the children were school age. But as more mothers entered the paid work force, the program gradually lowered the age of children who could be supported. In 1988, the Family Support Act tightened the regulations on child support and work requirements. The work rules exempted parents whose youngest child was less than the age of three, or at states' option, a child younger than three years but not younger than one year. The present TANF law requires mothers to go to work when the youngest child is one year old.

Government safety net provisions sometimes supplement employees' wages, thereby enabling the employer to keep wages low. At present, food stamps and Medicaid supplement the low wages of many Wal-Mart employees.

Recently, several conservative governors spurned money from the stimulus act to expand unemployment insurance, saying the move would raise business taxes and kill jobs.[72] The stimulus act of February 2009 contained more than $100 billion in safety net provisions, but much of the aid consists of financial incentives the states are free to reject.

SHREDDING THE SAFETY NET

Conservatives oppose government welfare programs, arguing that the free market and private philanthropy will meet people's needs. The Reagan administration began to shred the safety net, and the shredding continued through the Bush administration. In 1996, President Clinton eliminated the entitlement status of welfare when he signed the PRWORA. It was the opening salvo by conservatives to get rid of all entitlements. Money to administer the program was given as a block grant to states, which can administer it in any way they choose, as long as they comply with the restrictive federal requirements. Eligibility standards vary between states.

The politicians who created TANF would rather have parents caring for other people's children for low wages than caring for their own children in their own homes. And since the law did not guarantee child care to those parents, many children are unsupervised while their parents work at their low-wage jobs.

POLICING THE BEHAVIOR OF THE POOR

Conservatives are alarmed by what they see as the crumbling of the nation's morals and the demise of the patriarchal nuclear family. They oppose women getting pregnant without being married, particularly teen pregnancy. They oppose permissive sexuality, and want to force men to marry the mother of their children and support the children. But rather than creating programs that would prevent many pregnancies such as sex education in high schools, including giving contraceptive information and making contraceptives easily available, they fund abstinence programs, which do not work. Rather than provide employment for fathers so they would be able to support their children and perhaps marry the mother, they prosecute poor men for nonsupport. Again we see the backward, reactive, approach to caring for people's needs.

TANF has had devastating consequences for parents and their children. The Center for Budget and Policy Priorities reported that as states have imposed tighter restrictions on welfare, only 40 percent of poor families who qualify for public assistance receive it, compared with 80 percent in the recessions of 1981–1982 and 1990–1991.[73] Even before the economic meltdown, a large number of single mothers were trying to make ends meet with neither earnings nor cash assistance.

> In an average month in 2005—the last year for which comprehensive data are available—690,000 single mothers and 1.3 million children lived in families that received neither earnings nor government cash income support (from TANF, SSI, unemployment insurance, or Social Security) and consequently had monthly income below half of the poverty line. This represented a sharp increase from 1996, when 303,000 single mothers fell into this category.[74]

A 2008 study by the *New York Times* found that "despite soaring unemployment and the worst economic crisis in decades, 18 states cut their welfare rolls last year, and nationally the number of people receiving cash assistance remained at or near the lowest in more than 40 years."[75] States have pushed people off the rolls for various reasons, often for failure to attend work programs. A research and advocacy group in Texas said, "We're really just pushing families off the program."[76] Rising unemployment has been particularly hard on women without a high school degree. "Joblessness among women ages 20 to 24 without a high school degree rose to 23.9 percent last year, from 17.9 percent the year before."[77]

Applicants for TANF feel demeaned when workers treat them like criminals who intend to defraud the system. According to Kaaryn Gustafson, an associate professor at the University of Connecticut Law School, "applying for welfare is a lot like being booked by the police." Some states take mug shots and require fingerprints.[78]

The safety net has been shredded in many other ways. Federal housing subsidies have been cut by nearly two-thirds since the 1980s. Job training has been cut back. Some cash-strapped states have cut back on Medicaid. Few states have any public assistance program at all for single unemployed people or married people whose children are beyond the eligibility age for welfare. Some people may be eligible for food stamps, but people between the ages of 18–50 are eligible for only 3 months of food stamps in any 36-month period. There are severe restrictions on food stamp eligibility for immigrants. Most are ineligible unless they have some special status, although their children are eligible if born in the United States.

GETTING SOMETHING FOR NOTHING

Means-tested benefits are likely to give rise to resentment toward the people who receive the benefit. There is a widespread belief that people should not get something for nothing. And there is also widespread resentment of people who are considered "undeserving" to receive benefits they have not worked for. There should be no "free loaders." This opprobrium is most often directed to low-income people who are thought to be cheating. Until recently, little attention has been focused on the financial wheeler-dealers whose get-rich Ponzi schemes have led to the present financial meltdown. Michael Lewis, writing about "the end" of Wall Street in *Portfolio* magazine, says, "Something for nothing. It never loses its charm."[79]

Racism has played a part in white people's resentment about what they perceived as giving black people an unfair advantage, as we have seen in the fights over affirmative action. Racism also causes some white welfare clients to believe that black people are getting preferential treatment for welfare benefits, as documented in a study of welfare recipients in Philadelphia's Kensington district.[80] But it is not just racism that causes recipients to believe that they are more "deserving" than the next fellow. I do outreach in the Dudley Square Department of Transitional Assistance (welfare) office in the predominately black neighborhood of Roxbury in Boston. Clients, both black and white, often tell me that they are not like those "other people" who abuse the system. They have worked, want to work again, but have fallen on hard times and need a little help to tide them over until they find work. Immigrants now seem to be the scapegoat du jour. One man angrily ranted to me about "all the benefits going to immigrants." I told him that the law prohibited benefits from going to any illegal immigrants, and most legal immigrants. He continued his rant unabated until his wife told him to shut up and let me talk so that I could tell him about the benefits and resources that were available to him and his family. He reminded me of a statement that Frances Fox Piven once made: "I am continually amazed by how little facts matter in the welfare debate."

One of the most significant accomplishments of the welfare rights movement of the 1960s was to remove what William Blake called the "mind forg'd manacles" of welfare recipients who had been brainwashed to believe they should be ashamed to ask for help. Through collective action, they came to believe that they were *entitled* to help. President Reagan's budget director David Stockman declared, "There are no entitlements. Period." Welfare activists challenged that, and still challenge it.

The membership of the National Welfare Rights Organization (NWRO) was predominately African American, and their work helped black people to get AFDC, a program that had in the past been dominated by white families. This in turn created a public impression that equated welfare with black people and gave rise to the conflation of stereotypes about black people with stereotypes about welfare recipients. Senator Long labeled NWRO activists as "brood mares" and asked who would iron his shirts if women received welfare. And we are all familiar with President Reagan's "welfare Cadillac."

Some middle-class feminists, who believed that being in the paid work force was the path to liberation and self-fulfillment, thought that it was good for welfare mothers to be required to work to receive benefits. But they themselves had professional jobs, which were more satisfying than most of the work that welfare recipients found. It is not liberation to spend a lifetime doing unchallenging and alienating work.

Although most Americans favored welfare reform, surveys show that they would not consider it a success if it did not reduce poverty. Yet, if Americans had looked more closely at welfare reform, they would have realized that it would not reduce poverty because parents had to take any low-wage job, and had no chance of getting better ones because the law prevented them from going to a four-year college. By flooding the low-wage labor market, welfare reform was destined to lower the wages of the bottom third of the work force, as predicted by the Urban League. And it was another blow at entitlements.

Public assistance began in Britain after the public commons were enclosed and people no longer had the right to use the commons to raise food on the commons. The commons were distributed to the landowners and fenced. This allowed the landowners to develop commercial crops and forced landless country people to hire themselves out to the owners. "The Poor Laws permitted owners to replace many of their permanent workers with day laborers hired for the duration of indispensable work, and then send the day laborers home to live on the minimum subsistence that the parish was obliged to give the poor."[81]

Universal versus Means-Tested Programs

Care work is valuable work that should be adequately reimbursed. The first requirement for a program that pays for care work should be that it be a universal, rather than a means-tested, program. As the late great British social welfare scholar Richard Titmuss said, "Programs for the poor are poor programs." Means-tested public assistance programs stigmatize the recipients and pay amounts that do not provide an adequate standard of living. They require voluminous documentation and investigation of recipients to insure that they are not cheating, resulting in high administrative costs. Universal programs such as Social Security pensions do not stigmatize claimants and have low administrative costs because they do not check on recipients after the initial determination of eligibility. People who receive Social Security pensions are called "claimants" because they are claiming what rightfully belongs to them. People who receive public assistance are called "recipients" because they are receiving what officials have decided they "deserve." People who receive public assistance are required to behave in a certain way.

The 1935 Social Security Act established pensions that were work-related. Some people argued for a means-tested pension, but FDR insisted that it be work-related to protect it politically. He knew that means-tested benefits were always the first to be cut. On the other hand, ADC, Title VII of the Act, was means-tested.

COMPARISON TO OTHER COUNTRIES

Most other developed nations have much more extensive welfare provisions than the United States. Northern European welfare states provide universal medical and dental care, high quality child care, housing subsidies, assistance to college students, and well-funded social service agencies. Cash grants include stipends to the unemployed, pensions to the old and disabled, and child allowances to parents or guardians. Some countries provide lengthy paid leaves for new parents.

France has a universal day care system that is a model for the world. Public nursery school is available for every three year old. Virtually every French child is enrolled in one of the world's best preschool systems, free of charge. Every French mother receives a cash allowance for each child. The allowance can be spent in any way she wants, including hiring help at home. If she hires a licensed nanny, the government will even cover the costs of her contributions to the nanny's pension program. France also gives parents a year long paid maternity leave, and it provides free universal health care.[82] The French government also finances a licensed network of subsidized crèches, where 20 percent of young children are cared for in a family setting.[83]

Sweden provides generous family benefits that assures mothers and fathers financial security at childbirth or adoption, and allows parents to combine work, education, and family life. Parental leave compensates new parents for time away from work for a total of 13 months, at 80 percent of their previous earnings. A universal child allowance pays approximately $135 a month for the first child and progressively more for each additional child. Families with an absent parent receive an advanced maintenance payment, a public grant to the custodial parent that is even more generous than the child allowance that these families also receive. Compensation for the grants are collected from the absent parents by the authorities whenever possible. The amount per child per month is approximately $170.

Sweden has been a leader in policies for the disabled that aim to enable them to live like others. Most with serious disabilities have returned to community settings, both in small supervised group homes and in independent living situations. Tremendous efforts have been made to provide employment, even for severely disabled people.[84]

Long workweeks make juggling work and family especially difficult. Sweden had addressed this problem by allowing parents to work a six-hour day until their children are eight years old. In the Netherlands, the official workweek is 36 hours, and workers have a right to a 4-day week. The legal workweek in France was reduced from 39 to 35 hours in 2000, and pressure is rising for the rest of Europe to follow suit.[85]

Norway provides paid family leave for a year for new mothers at 80 percent of their previously salary. They can take a second year at less pay. Parents who do not choose to take the second year at home can go back to work and put their child in subsidized day care.[86]

Finland gives each new mother a choice of either a complete layette or approximately $150. Parents with a stroller or carriage who board a bus in Helsinki get on the back of the bus to a special section reserved for them and are not required to pay a fare. Finland's National Health Insurance provides compensation, in the form of a sickness allowance, for loss of income due to incapacity for work. It also provides a compensation for loss of income to the parents of a sick child during the treatment and rehabilitation of the child.

Unemployed people in Finland receive benefits for 500 days. Employed people who are sick receive a sickness allowance for up to 300 workdays. A maternity allowance is payable for 263 working days. For the first 105 days, it is paid to the mother ("maternity allowance"); for the next 150 days it can be paid alternatively to the mother or the father ("parental allowance"). In addition, fathers are eligible for a "paternity allowance," which is payable for up to 18 weekdays at any point during eligibility for maternity/parenthood allowance. They need not be legally married; a cohabiting father qualifies. Entitlement to the benefit begins on the 155th day of pregnancy. A family allowance is payable to each child less than the age of 17. A child maintenance allowance is payable if the person who has been ordered to provide child support has failed to do this or if the court has not established maintenance liability.[87]

WHERE DO WE GO FROM HERE?

Can we build a better system than TANF? Or is antiwelfare sentiment too strong? There has been a steady drum roll of pundits proclaiming that welfare reform is a success. Harvard professor Elaine Kamarck wrote in the *Boston Globe*, "America's public assistance system has made great strides in helping the poor."[88] In the face of all this opposition, what chance do we have of achieving anything progressive on the welfare issue? Is it futile to even try, considering the current economic situation? It is certainly a formidable challenge, but what does it gain us if we succumb to hopelessness and give up our vision of a better world? Paul Krugman expressed it well:

> Some people say that our economic problems are structural, with no quick cure available; but I believe that the only important structural obstacles to world prosperity are the obsolete doctrines that clutter the minds of men.[89]

These are the "mind forg'd manacles" that William Blake wrote about in his poem "London":

> In every cry of every Man,
> In every Infant's cry of fear,
> In every voice, in every ban,
> The mind-forg'd manacles I hear.[90]

We may not get to the promised land of a compassionate system that takes collective responsibility for people's welfare, but we need a vision of what such a system would look like to even begin the journey toward our goal.

Clearly we need a more humane work and welfare system than we have now. What are the alternatives? There have been many visions of a better way, and many alternative proposals. Some proposals would change the existing safety net programs in an incremental way; others suggest an entirely new approach. I describe the current safety net programs in the appendix A, and I discuss alternative proposals in chapter 9.

The PRWORA is due to be reauthorized by Congress in 2010. The workfare program's contingency fund for extending the poor emergency help during recessions seems certain to run out of money next year. A *New York Times* editorial urged Congress to deal with that. It goes on to say, "And there already are sensible calls to repair workfare as we know it, by allowing more cash assistance and easing mandates for work, at least until there's work again."[91]

It is very important to end the time limits on TANF, and advocates are gearing up for that struggle when the bill comes up for reauthorization in Congress. A Boston area group called the Care Caucus that I helped found is focusing on TANF reauthorization, and has made ending the time limits their first priority.

When Barney Frank was interviewed for a profile in the *New Yorker*, he said, "Someone asked Harold Macmillan what has the most impact on political decisions. He said, 'Event, dear boy, events.' "[92] The financial meltdown and rising unemployment will force policy makers to take a fresh look at the work requirements and the time limits of TANF. It may even be an opportune time to introduce a completely new approach to helping parents to care for their children. The middle class has fallen into the ranks of the poor and is beginning to understand the need for welfare. When middle-class people are affected, then we can begin to talk about universal, not means-tested, benefits. Barbara Ehrenreich says it best:

> If that sounds politically unfeasible, consider this: When Clinton was cutting welfare and food stamps in the 90s, the poor were still an easily marginalized group, subjected to the nastiest sorts of racial and gender stereotyping. They were lazy, promiscuous, addicted, deadbeats, as whole choruses of conservative experts announced. Thanks to the recession, however—and I knew there had to be a bright side— the ranks of the poor are swelling every day with failed business owners, office workers, salespeople, and long-time homeowners. Stereotype that! As the poor and the formerly middle class Nouveau Poor become the American majority, they will finally have the clout to get their needs met.[93]

Only time will tell whether the people who have lost their middle income and status will shed their "mind forg'd manacles" about welfare and join with the rest of the poor to demand a collective humane solution to their needs.

NOTES

1. Irving Kristol, "A conservative perspective on public policy and the family," in *The family, civil society, and the state*, ed. by C. Wolfe. Oxford: Rowman and Littlefield, 1998, pp. 257–264.
2. Rosemary Crompton, "Gender restructuring, employment, and caring," *Social Politics*, vol. 8, no. 3, Fall 2001, p. 269. Citing Francis Fukuyama, *The Great Disruption*, and London: Profile, 1999.
3. Ari N. Houser, "Valuing the invaluable: The economic value of family caregiving, 2008 update," AARP Public Policy Institute, November 2008, http://www.aarp.org/research/housing-mobility/caregiving/i13_caregiving.html. Accessed January 30, 2010.
4. Laura Young, *Women and Aging: Bearing the Burden of Long-term Care*. Testimony at Joint Hearing before the Special Committee on aging of the committee on Health, Education, Labor, and Pensions of the U.S. Senate. U.S. Government Printing Office: Washington, D.C, p. 41
5. Kay Lazar, "Mass. elder abuse on rise," *Boston Globe*, February 9, 2009, p. A6.
6. Ibid.
7. Ibid.
8. Laura Young, p. 36.
9. John Leland, "Downturn puts a chokehold on those caring for family members," *New York Times*, June 7, 2009, p. 19.

10. Jane Waldfogel, "Understanding the 'Family Gap' in pay for women with children," *Journal of Economic Perspectives*, vol. 12, no. 1 (1998), pp. 1137–1156.
11. Ann Crittenden, *The price of motherhood*. New York: Henry Holt, 2001, p. 76.
12. Ibid., p. 77.
13. Nancy Folbre, *Economies of care*, unpublished manuscript, 2008.
14. Ibid., p. 184.
15. Ibid., p. 82.
16. Jesse Bernard, *The future of marriage*. New York: World Publishers, 1972, pp. 43–44.
17. Rosanna Hertz, *More equal than others: Women and men in dual-career marriages*. Berkeley and Los Angeles: University of California Press, 1986, p. 206.
18. Ibid.
19. Ibid., p. 35.
20. Ibid., p. 195.
21. Gail Gibson Hunt, Executive Director, National Alliance for Caregiving. Testimony for a Joint Hearing of the United States Senate Special Committee on Aging and the Health, Education, Labor, and Pensions Subcommittee on Aging, February 6, 2002, p. 51.
22. Ellen Goodman, "The curse of an equal workforce," *Boston Globe*, February 13, 2009, p. A17.
23. John F. Sandberg and Sandra L. Hofferth, "Changes in children's time with parents, U.S., 1981–1997, unpublished paper, Population Studies Center, University of Michigan, April 2000; Suzanne M. Bianchi, "Maternal employment and time with children: Dramatic change or surprising continuity?" 2000 presidential address, Population Association of America, revised June 2000.
24. Cathie Gandel, "The new face of caregiving: Male caregivers," *AARP Bulletin today*, January 23, 2009. http://bulletin.aarp.org/yourhealth/caregiving/articles/the_new_
25. Ibid.
26. Randy Albelda, "Up with women in the downturn," *Ms.*, Spring 2009, p. 36.
27. Ibid., p. 20.
28. Crittenden, p. 244.
29. Jody Heymann, Alison Earle, and Jeffrey Hayes, "The work, family, and equity index: How does the United States measure up?" Boston: The Project on Global Families, 2007. Accessed January 30, 2010.
30. Deanne Bonnar, "The wages of care: Change and resistance in support of caregiving work," *New Politics*, Summer 2006, p. 18.
31. World Bank, *Monitoring environmental progress*. Washington, D.C., 1995.
32. Marilyn Waring, *If Women Counted*. London: Macmillan, 1989.

33. Ibid.
34. Ari N. Houser, "Valuing the invaluable," Ibid.
35. Direct Care Alliance, Inc. "Direct care alliance policy brief no. 1," March 2009. pdf accessed at Direct Care Alliance Policy Brief No. 1, Accessed January 30, 2010.
36. Ibid.
37. *New York Times*, January 28, 2009.
38. Julia Wrigley, *Other people's children*. New York: Basic Books, 1995.
39. Joanne Lipman, "The nanny trap," *Wall Street Journal*, April 14, 1993, p. 1
40. Emma McLaughlin and Nicola Kraus, *The nanny diaries*. New York: St. Martin, 2002.
41. Hertz, pp. 165–166.
42. Ibid., p. 179.
43. Cindy Rodriguez, "Up from 'slavery,'" *Boston Globe*, November 18, 2002, p. B4.
44. Janet Kilkenny, personal communication.
45. Wrigley, pp. 5–6.
46. Ibid., p. 10.
47. Ibid., p. 11.
48. Ibid., p. 10.
49. Ibid., p. 11.
50. Ibid., p. 128.
51. Ibid., pp. 128–129.
52. Ibid., p. 134.
53. Ibid., p. 135.
54. Ibid., p. 28.
55. Sharon Johnson, "Union women eager for Solis to start her work," *Women's e News*, January 27, 2009. http://www.womensenews.org/story/labor/090127/union-women-eager-solis-start-her-work. Accessed January 30, 2010.
56. Robert Kuttner, "The rich-poor gap in decent preschools," *Boston Globe*, November 20, 2002, p. A19.
57. Ibid.
58. Ibid.
59. Sarah Schweitzer, "City gives first-ever wage law waivers," *Boston Globe*, November 18, 2002, p. B7.
60. *Boston Globe*, October 4, 2002, p. A3.
61. Leslie Bennetts, "The new push for quality child care," *Boston Globe Parade Magazine*, July 19, 2009, p. 4.
62. Ibid.
63. D. Glenn, "I thought you said she worked full time," Dissent, Summer 2001, pp. 101–105.
64. Candace Howes, "Upgrading California's Home Care Workforce: The Impact of Political Action and Unionization": University of California Institute for Labor and Employment, 2004.

65. Candace Howes, "The impact of a large wage increase on the workforce stability of IHSS Home Care Workers in San Francisco County," University of California Institute for Labor and Employment, 2002.
66. Meredith Schafer, "The NUHW Revolt," *Against the Current*, July/ August 2009.
67. Dick Meister, "A last vestige of slavery and segregation," moderator@ portside.org, May 28, 2009.
68. Jobs with Justice, "Now is the time to stand with domestic workers," jwjnational@jwj.org, May 28, 2009.
69. Lizzy Ratner, "The new domestic order," *The Nation*, September 28, 2009, p. 13.
70. Jason DeParle, "For recession victims, patchwork state aid," *New York Times*, May 10, 2009, p. 1.
71. Kay Lazar, "Senate's health cuts stir outrage," *Boston Globe*, May 15, 2009, p. 1.
72. DeParle, Ibid.
73. Sharon Parrott, "Recession could cause large increases in poverty and push millions into deep poverty," Center on Budget and Policy Priorities, Washington, DC, November 24, 2008.
74. Ibid.
75. Jason DeParle, "Welfare aid not growing as economy drops off," *New York Times*, February 2, 2008.
76. Ibid.
77. Ibid.
78. Barbara Ehrenreich, "A homespun safety net," *New York Times*, July 12, 2009, p. 9wk.
79. Cited by Frank Rich, "Two cheers for Rod Blagojevich," *New York Times*, Week in Review, December 14, 2008, p. 12.
80. Carol Cleaveland, " 'A Black Benefit': Racial prejudice among white welfare recipients in a low-income neighborhood," *Journal of Progressive Human Services*, vol. 19, no. 2, 2008.
81. André Gorz, "(S)He who doesn't work shall eat all the same," *Dissent*, 1987, pp. 179–187.
82. Crittenden, p. 90.
83. Ibid., p. 264.
84. Information about the Swedish welfare state has been taken from the article "The ups and downs of the Swedish welfare state," by Helen Lachs Ginsburg and Marguerite Rosenthal, *New Politics*, Summer 2006, pp. 70–78.
85. Ibid., p. 260.
86. Crittenden, pp. 191–192.
87. Information about Finland is from *Kela: Statistical Yearbook of the Social Insurance Institution, Finland*, 2001, and from a personal interview with the international representative of the Social Insurance Institution in Helsinki.
88. Elaine Kamarck, "Look to the Internet to fight poverty," *Boston Globe*, November 29, 2008, p. A11.

89. Paul Krugman, "What to do," *New York Review of Books,"* December 18, 2008, p. 10.

90. William Blake, "London," in A. J. M. Smith, *Seven centuries of verse.* New York: Charles Scribner's Sons, 1967, p. 285.

91. "Welfare as we knew it," *New York Times,* December 25, 2008.

92. Jeffrey Toobin, "Profiles," *New Yorker,* January 12, 2009, p. 47.

93. Barbara Ehrenreich, "Rich get poorer, poor disappear," *Huffington Post,* January 12, 2009.

CHAPTER 2

Women's Work, Mother's Poverty: Are Men's Wages the Best Cure for Women's Economic Insecurity?

Gwendolyn Mink

In the 2008 Democratic Party platform, the only provision with women in the title was one promising "Opportunity for Women." The provision pledged "that our daughters should have the same opportunities as our sons,"[1] confining measurement of women's equality to our access to men's jobs and men's wages. The nomination, then election, of the first African American presidential candidate portended and promised great change. But through its platform, the Democratic Party looked backward to an equality agenda drawn by women's exclusion from men's world. This agenda finds singular and transformative power in direct comparisons between women's and men's status, earnings, and opportunities. But to focus only on such comparisons misses many of the persistent inequalities imposed on women.

Certainly, women who enter men's world encounter signal inequalities: Hillary Clinton's presidential campaign and Lilly Ledbetter's unequal wages are just two high-profile examples. But women who do the work historically assigned to women, whether in the labor market or in the family, face inequalities, as well—inequalities rooted in the low value ascribed to work performed primarily by women.

The low valuation of women manifests, whether women are labor market workers or caregivers in families. In the labor market, a gender-based earnings gap disfavors women and leads inextricably to a gender-based distribution of poverty that breeds misery for mothers and their children. In families, the lack of economic compensation for caregiving means inevitable poverty for mothers who cannot earn or depend on a male wage. Both the earnings gap in the labor market and the earnings vacuum for caregivers follow from the value we assign to women's work, whether it is performed for wages or for families.

WOMEN'S WORK AND WOMEN'S POVERTY: EVIDENCE OF THE LOW VALUE OF WOMEN'S WORK IN THE LABOR MARKET

Data on the wage gap document the depressed value of women's work in the labor market: work that is performed mostly by women earns low pay; work that usually is performed by men earns less pay when it is performed by women; and work that usually is performed by women earns more pay when it is performed by men.

Women who worked in the labor market full-time, year-round in 2007 earned only 78 cents for every dollar earned by men. Twenty-two cents is the wage differential for women as a whole in comparison to men as a whole. The Cadillac of all wages belongs to white men, however, so we really should measure wage inequality in terms of white men's wages. In comparison to each dollar earned by white men, white women earned approximately 73 cents; Asian/Pacific women earned 70 cents; African American women earned 62 cents; American Indian and Alaska Native women earned 57 cents; and Latinas earned only 51 cents (see table 2.1).[2]

In 2007, the median annual income for full-time, year-round women workers of all races was $34,278—as compared to $44,255 for their male counterparts of all races (an income gap of $10,000). Among men, whites earned the highest median income of $50,139. White women earned $14,000 less than white men in 2007—or $36,398. Asian/Pacific women earned $15,000 less than white men, or $35,249. African American women earned even less: their median wage was $31,035—$19,000 less than white men's. Meanwhile, the earnings gap for American Indian and Alaska Native women was $22,000 and for Latinas was $25,000 (see table 2.2).[3]

Educational disparities do not explain these wage inequalities: the wage gap tracks within and across all educational levels (see table 2.3). In 2007, the median income for women who completed high school was $21,219, while for men it was $34,435. A 2-year associate's degree garnered women

Table 2.1 Women's earnings as a percentage of white men's earnings (full-time/full-year workers, 2007)

White	Asian Pacific	Black	American Indian	Latina & Alaska Native
73	70	62	57.5	51

Table 2.2 Median annual income (dollars) (full-time/full-year workers, 2007)

White Men	White ♀	API♀	Black ♀	AI&AN♀	Latinas
50,139	36,398	35,249	31,035	28,837	25,454

Table 2.3 Median annual income by education (full-time/full-year workers, 2007)

	All Men ($)	All Women($)
HS degree	34,435	21,219
AS degree	41,035	34,435
BA degree	57,397	38,628

$27,046, but got men $14,000 more ($41,035). A $19,000 wage gap takes hold at the bachelor's degree level: women with BA's earned $38,628 in 2007 as compared to $57,397 for men. These income figures are for women and men of all races. If we compare white men's income to everyone else's, the gaps are even wider. In fact, in 2006, white men with just a high school diploma made almost as much ($36,539) as white women who had graduated from college ($39,006).[4]

The wage gap data takes a snapshot of wage differences in a single year. If you compare men's and women's wages longitudinally—across time—the income gap is much larger than the 22 percent reported by the Census Bureau. The Institute for Women's Policy Research (IWPR) compared the income of female and male full-time/full-year workers over a 15-year period. Over 15 years, the earnings gap favored men by 36 percent overall—that is, men's income was 36 percent higher than women's income. When the sample was broadened to look at everyone who was employed at all—not only those who were employed full-time/year-round, but also those who were part-time and part-year workers—the gap was substantially larger, at 62 percent.[5]

Across a lifetime, these disparities add up to huge losses. Among full-time/full-year workers, a woman with a high school diploma loses $700,000 in earnings as compared to a man with a high school diploma. A woman with a BA loses $1.2 million over her lifetime. A woman with an advanced degree loses $2 million.[6]

Not surprisingly, the cost of inequality follows women into retirement, especially unmarried women. The retirement income gap averages approximately $8000 each year for single women.[7] Overall, single older women—widows and divorcees, as well as those who never married—share a poverty rate of approximately 20 percent.[8]

WOMEN'S POVERTY

The wage statistics show that women in general have lower incomes than men. Women's lower earnings, in turn, mean that women are more likely to be poor than men.

Today, more than 37 million people live below the poverty line—live on less than $16,530 per year for a family of three.[9] Sixteen million people—slightly less than half of all those in poverty—live in what is called "extreme" poverty, meaning that they live on less than half the poverty line income, or $8250 a year for a family of three. Another 15 million people live just above the poverty line (up to 125 percent of poverty, or approximately $20,000 a year for a family of 2). Altogether, 50 million people are almost poor, officially poor, or extremely poor. Women figure disproportionately among them.[10]

There has been a gender poverty gap every year since the official poverty line was drawn in the 1960s. Although poverty statistics consistently have shown that women in general are somewhat more likely to be poor than men in general, they also reveal deep poverty gaps based on the race and marital status of women. Women of color are much more likely to be poor than white men and white women (see table 2.4). Women whose family incomes do not include a male wage are disproportionately poor, as well: only 20 percent of women in poverty are married.

Among women, single mothers (with children under age 18) carry the greatest risk of poverty (see table 2.5). In 2007, more than 1 in 3 single mothers was officially poor—for a poverty rate of 37 percent. In contrast, the married parent poverty rate was 6.7 percent—or one-sixth the poverty rate of single mothers. For the population as a whole, the poverty rate was 12.3 percent.[11] Race exacerbates the disproportionate poverty of single mothers: while white single mothers' poverty rate was 29.2 percent in 2007, for African American single mothers the poverty rate was 43.9 percent and for Latina single mothers it was 46.6 percent.[12]

Table 2.4 Poverty rates by sex and race/ethnicity, 2007

	Women (%)	Men (%)
All	13.8	11.1
African American	26.5	22.3
Latina/o	23.6	19.6
Asian American	10.7	9.7
White	11.6	9.4

Table 2.5 Poverty rate and median income by family type, 2007

	Poverty rate (%)	Median income ($)
Single mothers (all)	37	33,370
White	29.2	
Black	43.9	
Latina	46.6	
Single fathers (all)	17	49,839
Married parents (all)	6.7	72,785

Sources for all tables: U.S. Census Bureau, Current Population Survey, *2008 Annual Social and Economic Supplement*; American Community Survey; *Historical Poverty Tables, 1959–2007.*

In 2007, 62 percent of poor families with children were single mother families, as compared to just 15 percent of nonpoor families. In 83 percent of single mother families, at least one person (usually the mother) was in the labor force. Yet, even when single mothers are wage earners, the poverty rate for their families is 27.2 percent—more than twice the poverty rate of the general population.

FEDERAL POLICY AND WOMEN'S IMPOVERISHMENT

Employment and Wages

If families that must survive on a woman's wage alone are more likely to be poor, then women's low wages must have something to do with women's disproportionate poverty. If poverty implicates low wages, both implicate employment inequality.

Forty-five years ago, Congress enacted Title VII of the Civil Rights Act, which forbids discrimination in employment, including sex discrimination. Over the years, Title VII has helped to open up the labor market to women—it ended job classifications based on sex, for example, and enabled women to challenge hiring, firing, and promotion decisions based on sex. But although Title VII has been a powerful weapon against workplace exclusion and abuse, it has provided relatively weak mechanisms for achieving income fairness for women workers.

Title VII is concerned with letting women into the labor market, and in ensuring that being female will not disadvantage a woman in her struggle to survive in the labor market. Title VII insists that women have access to employment and prohibits workplace discrimination, including wage discrimination. But Title VII does not insist that employment itself change to respond to the perspectives and circumstances women bring into the labor market. Nor does it recognize gender-based wage differentials as discrimination unless it can be proved that the differential was imposed deliberately "because of" a worker's sex.

Where wages are concerned, Title VII works in conjunction with the Equal Pay Act, which avows that women and men shall receive the same wages for the same work. This has turned out to be a very constrained guarantee, as courts have interpreted the Equal Pay Act to protect women against wage discrimination only where their jobs are identical to men's, and only in single workplaces or establishments, at that.

Even so, women who do perform the same job as men—as welders or engineers or gardeners, say—do not receive the same pay as men. This is because the Equal Pay Act allows pay differentials based on "factors other than sex"—which usually turn out to be factors related to sex, such as negotiating skills, or family interruptions, or unstated biases against women.

Wage gaps based on sex (and race) within job categories attest to wage discrimination that Title VII and the Equal Pay Act are supposed to prevent. But for various reasons, wage discrimination persists despite the law. Heinous as they are, discriminatory wage decisions do not by themselves account for the scale of the earnings gap I have just outlined.

Another factor that contributes to sex-based income inequality is sex-based occupational segregation. Occupational segregation manifests as the disproportionate clustering of women or men in particular jobs: most pilots are men, for example, while most nurses are women. Studies show that the more female a job, the lower the pay in comparison to similar jobs that require similar training but are performed mostly by men. So, for example, maids and housecleaners (mostly women) earn approximately $3000/year less than janitors (mostly men).[13] At all levels of employment, from the best jobs to the least desirable ones, female jobs earn less pay.[14]

Some people argue that the only way around the wage impasse that arises from occupational segregation is to get women into men's jobs, where they can earn men's pay. Women who want those jobs certainly should be able to get them; but I am afraid that is not necessarily going to get them men's pay. Movement into traditionally male jobs is happening, if slowly; but unequal pay follows women into those jobs.

Take the legal profession, for example: in 2007, the median salary for men in law jobs (paralegals, attorneys, judges) was $105,233. For women, the median salary was $53,790. That is a nearly 50 percent gap! Among judges, there is a 36 percent wage gap, with male judges earning a median $108,100 while female judges earned a median $69,500. Looking just at lawyers narrows the gap, but a gap remains: $120,400 median annual income for men, as compared to $93,600 for women.[15]

Focusing on wages attached to particular jobs reveals significant sex-based disparities. But focusing exclusively on the wage gap misses the bigger picture. Women's poverty does follow from the wage structure: women are more likely to earn low wages and low wages keep women poor. Two-thirds of minimum wage workers are women; and a full-time/year-round minimum wage income—$13,624—barely brings a family of 2 to the poverty line. Approximately 31 percent of full-time, continuously employed women earn less than $25,000 per year.[16]

If we compare women's and men's earnings longitudinally, we can see gross disparities that exceed the disparities linked to particular jobs. According to the IWPR study, among workers who had earnings in all 15 years reviewed, men's average earnings were 57 percent higher than women's—$49,068 to $29,507.[17] This income differential widens for the majority of women (52 percent, as compared to just 16 percent of men) who spend at least one calendar year without any earnings. Women who take time out of the labor force usually do so to care for children, parents, or a sick spouse. Among women who do not leave the labor force altogether, large numbers work part-time or part-year to accommodate similar care needs of their families. Even the most persistent women workers are in the labor market for fewer hours each year than are male workers—21 percent fewer hours (1,766 for persistent women workers vs. 2,219 for male workers overall). Overall, women workers spend a third less time in labor market jobs each year, widening income disparities between women and men.[18]

These income disparities are due in part to discrimination in the valuation of women's work, as well as of women themselves. But they also reflect longstanding conflict between the time demands of labor force participation, on the one hand, and the care needs of families, on the other. The "work-family" conflict for women is not just psychological or emotional. It is tangibly economic, a fact that is most apparent when we consider the degree to which mothers are employed. In the IWPR study, whether married or single, all mothers with children in the home were employed on average for about 1,331 hours per year—which is approximately 820 hours less than the average for fathers.[19] Needless to say, fewer hours of employment mean less income. Lower wages for the jobs women do compounds the impoverishing effect of the current "work-family balance."

So far, policymakers have been reluctant to do what it will take to make the labor market friendly to the care concerns women bring into it. What it will take is, for starters: (1) universal, subsidized child care so that parents do not have to worry about meeting the routine care needs of children; (2) paid family leave and paid childbirth leave so that caregivers and pregnant women do not have to trade an income for a family; and (3) liberal leave policies at work—so that workers can take an occasional sick day or care day, or take time to deal with personal issues.

We came close to comprehensive child care in the early 1970s, but Nixon vetoed the legislation. We have been fighting over whether poor people deserve child care ever since. In 1996, welfare reform ended the child care entitlement for low-income families. So unless a family can afford $1000 to $2000 a month for child care, somebody in the family has to take responsibility for children's supervision and nurturance. Partly by default and partly by choice, that "somebody" usually is a woman.

The federal government enacted a family leave law in 1993, but 40 percent of workers are not covered because their firms employ fewer than 50 workers. For those who are covered by this law, many cannot avail themselves of leave because the leave is unpaid. The Family Medical Leave Act does not provide income assistance to workers who leave jobs under its terms; nor does it require employers to do so. Our unemployment insurance system does not recognize family considerations as legitimate reasons to lose or leave a job, so unemployment compensation is not available when a worker takes family leave. It is not surprising that 78 percent of the workers who have not been able to take family leave report that the reason is that they could not afford to go without an income.[20]

Poverty and Policy

The discrimination and unfairness I have described affect all women who need an earned income. But they affect some women more than others— low-wage women workers more than elite women workers; women of color more than white women; and single mothers more than either single women or married mothers.

Women in general have a slightly higher poverty rate (13.8 percent) than men (11.1 percent), as measured by family income.[21] But women who are single mothers have a whoppingly high poverty rate of 37 percent.[22] All women face inequality in the labor market; the wage gap straddles the entire economy. So why are single mothers disproportionately poor?

Because they are single mothers.

That is, because they are raising children without a man's wage. According to the Census Bureau's income and poverty statistics (see table 2.4), in 2007 the median family income for married couples was $72,785 and for male-headed households (no wife present) was $49,839. For female-headed households, by contrast, the median income was $33,370.[23] The IWPR longitudinal study confirms that marriage vastly increases the family income and standard of living of women, cushioning them from the harsh reality of life on a woman's wage. According to the study, only 5 percent of consistently married women experienced chronically low family incomes, while 35 percent of single women did.[24]

The income benefit of marriage for mothers is even more pronounced when there are children under age 18 in the family. Single mothers with children have the lowest of all individual earnings and an increased likelihood of living on a family income of less than $25,000/year for a period. Worse, the average income deficit for poor families—the dollar difference between a family's income and its poverty threshold—is highest for single mother families, at $9,059. Although income deficits afflict all types of families in poverty, single father families and married families fare better than single mothers, with average income deficits of $7,780 and $7,937, respectively.[25]

Raising kids on a woman's wage means economic hard times. Low and unequal wages are just part of the problem. The widespread assumption that employment and caregiving are trade-offs (rather than complementary aspects of family responsibility) contributes significantly to mothers' poverty both in the labor market and in families. The idea that "working mothers" trade caregiving for employment when they enter the labor market permits employers and government to refuse support for child care, paid family leave, and flexible personal days. At the same time, the idea that "at-home mothers" trade employment for caregiving permits employers and government to regard family work as part of a private economic calculus worthy of no public economic support at all.

Welfare

Powerful and consistent empirical evidence shows that the devaluation of women's work in the labor market and in families destines women's families to economic insecurity. Public policy has responded to that insecurity primarily by goading mothers into low wage jobs and marriage. Rather than revalue and support women's work, the public policy designed to mitigate the economic insecurity of mothers' families actually disdains single mothers as labor market workers, as caregivers, and as unmarried women.

That public policy is what we call welfare—or what antiwelfare reformers of the mid-1990s named Temporary Assistance for Needy Families (TANF). At the time welfare reform policy was enacted, it was widely hailed for transforming single mothers into breadwinners by forcing them to take low wage jobs in the labor market. While compulsory labor market work is a feature of welfare reform, the reform equally emphasized the compulsory introduction of fathers into single mother families.

Indeed, the guiding principle of welfare policy is that the economic security of families requires mothers to have relationships with fathers. This is a privatizing move, tying the economic well-being of families to the presence of fathers' wages. It is also a patriarchal move, conferring economic security only to those mothers who conform to traditional father-mother norms.

The pro-patriarchal attributes of welfare policy are not accidental. The 1996 welfare law was rife with condemnation of single mothers and was concerted in its efforts to insert fathers into low-income single mother families. The preamble to the law began with the assertion that "marriage is the foundation of a successful society." It then proceeded to blame numerous social ills—among them child abuse, truancy, and crime—on nonmarital childbearing and single motherhood.[26]

The law went on to tie the purposes of welfare to promoting marriage, preventing nonmarital childbearing, and fostering two-parent (heterosexual) family formation.[27] Although the law declared that one goal of welfare is to "provide assistance to needy families" with children, it conditioned assistance on reform of the reproductive and family decisions of such families. Program rules regulating teenage mothers, discouraging illegitimacy, promoting abstinence, and compelling mothers to identify biological fathers and cooperate with child support enforcement—all advance these goals.

The welfare reform law enacted in 1996 was revised and extended in 2006.[28] The renewed welfare program fastens the economic security of single mothers ever more tightly to the end of single motherhood. The principal addition to welfare policy was the creation of funding streams dedicated to promoting married fatherhood: $1.5 billion over 5 years ($750 million each year) for pro-marriage, pro-father activities. Beyond dedicated federal spending, the renewed welfare law gives states incentive to spend their TANF block grants and their own state funds to support federal pro-marriage, pro-father activities.[29]

Although married fatherhood promotion is a distinctive feature of the renewed welfare program, welfare is not the only federal policy arena to fund marriage and fatherhood promotion activities.

The Office of Child Support Enforcement has offered grants to promote married fatherhood, as well as to teach unmarried biological fathers that if they pay child support they can get access to their children. The

Office of Refugee Resettlement also sponsors marriage promotion—to the tune of $4.4 million in 2006.[30] Even Head Start has gotten involved—since 2004, the federal Head Start agency has encouraged local Head Start facilities to promote fatherhood. A federal Head Start bulletin tells program workers to make sure fathers feel welcome at Head Start centers by, among other things, removing posters and other materials about domestic violence, as well as by creating comfort zones for dads through events such as "Guys Night Out" and masculine activities such as "Dads' Day at Home Depot."[31]

THE EASY WAY TO GET A WOMAN A MAN'S WAGE: FIND A MAN

It should certainly come as no surprise that the Bush administration used federal money to promote patriarchy. But the emphasis on marriage and the focus on fathers are not the provenance of conservatives alone. Indeed, marriage promotion got its start before Bush, when the Clinton administration promoted marriage through incentive payments to states. Beginning in the late 1990s, many Democrats sponsored fatherhood promotion legislation; as Senator and now as President, Barack Obama energized the cause. No longer monopolized by Dan Quayle and the "family values" lobby, marriage and fatherhood are now widely regarded—by progressive and conservative alike—as the keys to ending poverty.

Many progressive antipoverty advocates are uncomfortable with conservative-inspired marriage promotion, to be sure; but they have been equally uncomfortable with feminist arguments that single mothers should be able to bear and raise children on their own. In fact, I cannot think of a single nonfeminist progressive policy advocate or policymaker who affirms single mother family formation as the right of women—not the hard luck of such women—or as good for children. On the left as on the right, it is axiomatic that single motherhood is a bad thing. Liberals might pity single mothers, while conservatives chastise them; but either way, single mothers are defined as a social problem.

Some progressive antipoverty advocates have even adopted the frame drawn by conservative proponents of the traditional married family. Some antipoverty advocates now publicly endorse the claim that helping fathers enter mothers' families should be a goal of government and a cornerstone of antipoverty policy.

The liberal Center for Law and Social Policy (CLASP), for example, espouses "marriage-plus" to encourage two-parent family formation among the poor. While CLASP wants to "ensure that public policy helps all parents—whether never married, cohabiting, separated, divorced, or married," its bottom line is that married biological parenthood is a desirable public goal that should be advanced by government. As CLASP put it in a 2005 report, "public policy should try to help more children be born into, and grow up with, two biological married parents, who have a reasonably healthy, cooperative relationship."[32]

This position continues to stigmatize single mothers as deficient and single mother families as disadvantaged—not because of economic status but because mothers are single. What's more, the emphasis on biological parenthood heightens the preferred status of heterosexual parents and supports longstanding impediments to gay and lesbian adoption and/or legally recognized de facto parenthood for nonbiological mothers or fathers.

To foster biological married parenthood, some antipoverty advocates have called for programs focused on low-income men. The purpose of these programs is to make low-income men more marriageable father material, and so to advance the goal of heterosexual, biological family formation. For example, at a poverty summit convened by John Edwards in November 2005, several prominent antipoverty advocates and researchers complained that "welfare reform focused on everybody but adult men" and argued that "we need to put men back on the agenda...and...support men in the same way that we do women." According to several antipoverty advocates and researchers who spoke at the conference, we need to focus on men as fathers because "the growth of single [mother] families is a major cause of poverty." One speaker also justified investing in men as a way to get mothers to "play by the rules"—especially the "rule" against bearing and raising children outside marriage.[33]

Progressive antipoverty advocates differ from their conservative counterparts in that most do not argue that "Life with Father" is intrinsically morally superior to growing up in other family forms. Nonetheless, the pro-father, "marriage-plus" approach does advance a heterosexist, two-parent essentialism in the name of what is best for children.

For progressive and mainstream marriage proponents, what makes married families "better" for children is that married families have more money—so children are better off financially when raised by married parents. This is empirically true: as I pointed out earlier, the median income for married families was $72,785 in 2007, as compared to $28,832 for single mothers. Pro-marriage poverty advocates reason that because children are financially secure when parents are married, children in married families do better in school and behave better than they do in single mother families.

Although advocates of this position claim to "follow the data"—their faith in married fatherhood produces cherry-picked data that evades important questions. For example, the number of single father families has risen exponentially since 1970 (from half a million to 2 million) just as has the number of single mother families (from 3 million to 10 million). But no one singles out father-only families to show the harms of one-parent childraising and the benefits of married parenthood.

There is a huge income disparity between single mother and single father families (approximately $15,000/year). This is a gap we should expect from what we know about gender-based wage disparities. It is a gap that illuminates women's inequality, not women's inferiority either as workers or as parents.

Approximately 37 percent of single mother families have incomes below the poverty level, as compared to 17 percent of single father families. Single mothers are 106 percent more likely to be poor than single fathers. This poverty arises not because single mothers refuse to work for wages in the labor market. Single mothers are in the labor force: in fact, they work at greater rates and for longer hours than single mothers anywhere in the advanced capitalist world; and they are employed at greater rates than are married mothers, especially married mothers with children under the age of six.[34]

So the problem is not that single mothers are lazy or have less of a work ethic than married parents, or than single fathers. The problem is not intrinsic to the structure of single mother families but to the low economic value assigned to women—both in the labor market and as caregivers in their own families.

Marriage promotion may indeed improve economic circumstances for many women. But it will not move us closer to equality for women, and it will not improve options for women and children whose safety and well-being is endangered by the presence of particular men in their families. Binding family economic security to men's earning power, not women's, may force wage-poor women to stay in abusive relationships; exposes mothers to poverty at divorce; and assures disproportionate poverty to mothers who never marry. Even for mothers who eke through these dependencies and disparities, economic inequality comes home to roost later on when fewer retirement assets and lower pension income spell high rates of poverty for elderly women who are on their own.

In their 2008 platform, Democrats congratulated themselves for "eighteen million cracks in the highest glass ceiling," yet economic equality for women seems like a wistful dream. Despite the new demographics of official power, the demographics of inequality persist. The Obama administration retained marriage and fatherhood promotion funding in its first budget request; its Department of Health and Human Services continues marriage and fatherhood initiatives undertaken by the Bush administration; and the new Office of Faith-Based and Community Initiatives makes supporting fathers "who stand by their families" one of four key priorities.[35] The Obama economic recovery plan stresses work supports to the exclusion of direct poverty mitigation for poor families, such as the repeal of time limits on welfare eligibility and participation. The White House Web site's brief on poverty notices poor mothers only once, when it calls for "home visits to low-income, first-time parents by trained professionals."[36]

Emblematic of incorrigible disregard for women's work in families and in the labor market, marriage and fatherhood promotion is the nail in the coffin of hope, the defeat of equality for women. Comparable worth for women? Raise the minimum wage to a living wage? Change unemployment insurance to take women's work patterns into account? Paid family leave? Universal child care? Provide income support to caregivers in economic recognition for the work of raising children and caring for family members? Why fight poverty the hard way when all women need is a man with a family wage?

Notes

1. Report from the Platform Committee, *Renewing America's Promise*, presented to the 2008 Democratic National Convention, August 13, 2008, p. 16.
2. U.S. Census Bureau, American Community Survey, S2002 "Median earnings in the past 12 months (In 2007 Inflation-Adjusted Dollars) of workers by sex and women's earnings as a percentage of men's earnings by selected characteristics," 2007, http://factfinder.census. gov/servlet/STTable?_bm=y&-qr_name=ACS_2007_1YR_G00_ S2002&-geo_id=01000US&-ds_name=ACS_2007_1YR_G00_&-_ lang=en&-format=&-CONTEXT=st.
3. Ibid.
4. Ibid.; U.S. Census Bureau, Current Population Survey, 2007, "Annual social and economic supplement, table PINC-03: Educational attainment—people 25 years old and over, by total money earnings in 2006, Work experience in 2006, age, race, hispanic origin and sex," 2007, http://pubdb3.census.gov/macro/032007/perinc/ new03_000.htm.
5. Stephen J. Rose and Heidi I. Hartmann, *Still a man's labor market: The long-term earnings gap*, Institute for Women's Policy Research, Washington DC, 2004.
6. The WAGE Project, http://www.wageproject.org/ files/costs.php. Accessed February 3, 2010.
7. National Women's Law Center, "Congress must act to close the wage gap for women," April 2008, p. 3.
8. Rose and Hartmann, *Still a man's labor market*, p. iv.
9. U.S Census Bureau, Current Population Reports, *Income, poverty, and health insurance coverage in the United States: 2007*, August 2008.
10. U.S. Census Bureau, Current Population Survey, *Historical Poverty Tables*, Table 4, "Poverty status of families, by type of family, presence of related children, race, and hispanic origin: 1959 to 2007," August 2008, http://www.census.gov/hhes/www/poverty/histpov/famindex.html. Accessed February 3, 2010.
11. Ibid.
12. Ibid.
13. National Women's Law Center, "A platform for progress: Building a better future for women and their families," 2008, p. 5.
14. "The gender wage gap by occupation," Institute for Women's Policy Research Fact Sheet, April 2009.
15. Debra Cassens Weiss, "Being a lawyer and male makes you a top earner, census report shows," abajournal.com, September 10, 2008; U.S. Census Bureau, 2007 American Community Survey, Table S2002. "Median earnings in the past 12 months (in 2007 inflation-adjusted dollars) of workers by sex and women's earnings as a percentage of men's earnings by selected characteristics."

16. Rose and Hartmann, *Still a man's labor market*, p. 18.
17. Ibid., p. iii.
18. Ibid., ch. 3.
19. Ibid., Table 13, p. 28.
20. National Women's Law Center, "Platform," p. 8.
21. U.S. Census Bureau, Current Population Survey, Detailed Poverty Tables, "POV01: Age and sex of all people, family members and unrelated individuals iterated by income-to-poverty ratio and race: 2007: Below 100% of poverty—all races," http://www.census.gov/hhes/www/macro/032008/pov/new01_100_01.htm. Accessed February 3, 2010.
22. *Historical Poverty Tables*, Table 4.
23. U.S. Census Bureau, *Income, poverty, and health insurance*, p. 7.
24. Rose and Hartmann, *Still a man's labor market*, p. 25
25. U.S. Census Bureau, *Income, poverty, and health insurance*, p. 17.
26. P.L. 104–193, *Personal responsibility and work opportunity reconciliation act*, Title I, Sec. 101.
27. Ibid., Title I, Part A, Sec. 401.
28. P.L. 109-171, *Deficit Reduction Act of 2005*. For TANF provisions see Department of Health and Human Services, Administration for Children and Families, "Reauthorization of the temporary assistance for needy families program: Interim final rule," *Federal Register*, vol. 71, no. 125 (June 29, 2006).
29. Ibid., Sec. 7103, "Grants for healthy marriage promotion and responsible fatherhood."
30. http://www.acf.hhs.gov/healthymarriage/funding/orr_projects.html. Accessed February 3, 2010.
31. *Head Start Bulletin*, "Father involvement," (June 2004).
32. Paula Roberts and Mark Greenberg, "Marriage and the TANF rules: A discussion paper," Center for Law and Social Policy (Washington DC, 2005).
33. "Panel 1: Confronting poverty: What role for public programs?," and "Panel 2: Family structure, poverty and family well-being," Proceedings of the University of North Carolina at Chapel Hill, Center on Poverty, Work and Opportunity Summit, *Chicago-Kent Employee Rights and Employment Policy Journal*, vol. 10, no. 1 (2006).
34. In the mid-1990s, before punitive welfare-to-work policies took effect, 76 percent of single mothers in the United States were employed at least 10 hours per week, as compared to 20 percent in the Netherlands, 27percent in the United Kingdom, and 72 percent in France and Austria. See Libertad Gonzalez, "Single mothers and work," *Socio-Economic Review* (2004), pp. 285–313.
35. http://www.whitehouse.gov/the_press_office/ObamaAnnouncesWhiteHouseOfficeofFaith-basedandNeighborhoodPartnerships/ Accessed February 3, 2010.

CHAPTER 3

Paid Family and Medical Leave

Randy Albelda and Betty Reid Mandell

How many people can afford to take time off from work without being paid? Not many. When a worker gets sick or a child or parent gets sick; when a woman is giving birth or when a parent needs to go to a conference with a teacher, leaving work can not only cost a day's pay, but it can also cost advancement in a career. Women, who do most of caregiving, are particularly disadvantaged.

There is intense interest in paid family and medical leave. Activists have been working for years to get it in their states, cities, and nation. A Google search of "Paid Family Leave" on March 3, 2009 showed 16,400,000 entries. The need is great.

Activists won a partial national victory in 1993 with the passage of the Family and Medical Leave Act (FMLA). The precursor of the FMLA, the Alternative Work Schedules Act (AWSA)[1] was originally intended as an energy conservation measure to decrease the traffic and the gasoline used in downtown Washington, DC, but the efforts of advocates turned it into a family-friendly act.[2] The act won the support of conservationists as well as work-life advocates.[3]

The FMLA provides 12 weeks of unpaid leave for workers in companies that employ at least 50 employees. The leave is for the birth and care of a newborn child, for placement of a child for adoption or foster care, to care for an immediate family member with a serious health condition, or to take medical leave. In 2008, Congress amended it as the National Defense Authorization Act to permit a spouse, son, daughter, parent, or next of kin to take up to 26 workweeks of leave to care for a member of the Armed Forces who is undergoing medical treatment, recuperation, or therapy.[4] Importantly, however, the FMLA does not provide paid leave.

Activists have succeeded in getting paid family leave legislation in only three states: California, Washington, and New Jersey. They have fought to get it in many other states.[5] In addition, three cities have passed paid sick days legislation (San Francisco, Washington, DC, and Milwaukee).[6]

Five states (California, Hawaii, New Jersey, New York, and Rhode Island) and Puerto Rico use their mandatory Temporary Disability Insurance (TDI) programs to provide paid sick leave for own health illnesses. In addition to the already established leave for one's own disability (including up to 10 weeks of maternity disability), California and New Jersey have added programs that provide employees up to six weeks a year of paid leave to care for a seriously ill child, spouse, parent, domestic partner, or a new child.[7]

The federal FMLA was an important first step, but it is only a partial remedy to a larger problem of managing family and medical leaves that workers face. A Department of Labor study in 2000 found that 38 percent of workers are not eligible under the provisions of the FMLA due to their employer size or their recent work history.[8] In addition, some workers who need leave to take care of family members are excluded because they are not a spouse, child, or parent of the person who needs their care. And millions of U.S. workers are excluded from coverage because they cannot afford unpaid leave. A study of paid leave by Robert Drago showed that "welfare policies, and particularly work requirements under Temporary Assistance to Needy Families (TANF), are serving to reduce parental time investments in childcare for infants, and doing so for groups that have few resources and have historically experienced discrimination in the workplace and community."[9] Expansion of paid leave "would disproportionately help the working poor, women with lower levels of education and lower status jobs, and women of color."[10]

> Single mothers may not be able to afford to use either paid leave or reduced hours options if they involve even a minimal loss of income or, worse still, the loss of health insurance coverage. The resources provided to single mothers need to be enhanced if we desire an equitable distribution of policy utilization.[11]

The benefits to employees of paid medical and family leave are obvious. At some point in all of our work lives, we need to take time off from work because of our own illness or the need to care for family members, including newborns. Being paid for that time off eases our anxieties and improves both our psychological and physical health. The benefits to family members are also obvious. In 1997, American pediatricians recommended that new mothers breast-feed for a full year. Ann Crittenden commented on this:

> This was a sick joke in a country that entitles new mothers to no paid leave at all. American mothers are guaranteed only three months' maternity leave without pay—forcing most working mothers to return to their jobs within a few weeks after giving birth, because they can't afford to take three months off without a pay check. As a consequence, poor mothers are far less likely to breast-feed than their better-off

sisters, and infants as young as six weeks are going into day care, with some spending as many as ten hours a day in group settings.[12]

Crittenden recommends that mothers be granted at least one year of paid leave so they can breast-feed at home. Some people argue that working mothers who breast-feed do not need to stay home; they can use a breast pump when at work to save the milk for the infant. Many women do this, but they often have a problem with employers who do not want them to the take time off from work, or do not provide a private space for them to use the breast pump.

COMPARING THE UNITED STATES TO OTHER COUNTRIES

The United States is one of very few industrialized countries that do not have some form of universal, mandatory sick leave and paid maternity leave. Among 21 high-income economies, only Australia and the United States do not have legislative requirements to provide paid maternity leave and only the United States does not have paid time off for extended own-health leaves.[13] Half of the other of these 21 countries offer paid paternity and/or sex-neutral parental leave as well.[14] Several nations have implemented "right to request" policies. These permit employees to ask for flexible work arrangements or reduced hours employment. Twelve of the European Union nations provide for part-time employment upon return from parental leave, and those policies are limited to caregivers.[15]

Sweden guarantees 11 months of generous paid maternity leave, followed by the statutory right to work no more than 30 hours per week until the child reaches the age of 8. Each local district has a list of child care crèches that provide family care for children less than the age of 2, and federal housing assistance increases after the baby is born.[16]

Programs for paid leave in Europe are financed by social insurance, usually payroll taxes paid for by some combination of employee and employer contributions. "They are then pooled across enterprises, industries, and generations and between men and women, so when a worker goes out on leave, the bill isn't footed by the employer other than through a diffused tax burden."[17] Some discussions of paid leave in the United States have proposed that the employer pay the full cost. Janet Gornick says, "I think that would be catastrophic; employers would protest, and rightly so, and their incentive to discriminate against young women would be quite intense."[18]

In their study of parental leave policies in 21 countries, Janet Gornick and Rebecca Ray noted 5 best practices:

1. The most important element is that the leave needs to be paid, and at a generous rate.

2. Men and women need to have their own, nontransferable entitlements.
3. The coverage and eligibility should be broad.
4. Collective financing is crucial because it reduces the financial burden on individual employers which, in turn, reduces political opposition to these programs as well as the incentive to discriminate against young women.
5. The best-practice cases enabled parents to flexibly draw the benefits to which they are entitled. This flexibility in terms of timing is important, but no one argues that workers should have unlimited flexibility. Employers do need a reasonable notification period before employees take leave and, ideally, before they return. That is fair.[19]

EMPLOYER BENEFITS

Some employers provide workers with paid leave for family or medical reasons through benefits such as sick leave, vacation time, parental leave, or medical leave, but they are not legally required to do so.[20] Just more than one-third of all those who took any type of family or medical leave received no pay.[21] Fewer than half of all employed women received any paid leave during the first 12 weeks of their children's lives and only 7 percent of employers offered any paid paternity leave.[22]

A national study of employers showed that 79 percent of employers say that they provide paid or unpaid time off for employees to provide elder care without jeopardizing their jobs.[23] Only 6 percent provide direct financial support for local elder care programs. In general, there has been only a modest increase for employer support for family care assistance or flexible workplace policies over the last several years. "Small increases in policy adoption are being seen in the availability of elder care, adoption assistance, and access to long-term care insurance, which are now available to about 1 in 10 workers."[24]

There are gaps in the implementation of FMLA. The National Study of Employers survey found that approximately a quarter of organizations offer less than 12 weeks of unpaid leave for maternity leave, paternity leave, adoption or foster care leave, and to care for a child with a serious illness.[25] A 30 percent of organizations that fall under the FMLA do not offer the federally mandated 12 weeks of leave,[26] and they are breaking the law. Another problem with FMLA is the lack of education for employees regarding their rights. Many employees did not know how the FMLA applied to their situation.[27]

The limitations of our current voluntary income replacement programs are increasingly apparent. Typically, few if any family members are available to provide unlimited free care. Ironically, paid health providers want to keep patients in care facilities for less time than they did when unpaid care was more plentiful, requiring families to find and/or provide alternative care. Paid family and medical leave is a step toward acknowledging the way our families work.[28] The vast majority of U.S. workers

(85 percent) lack access to any formal paid work-family policies.[29] We have a long way to go.

Benefits and Costs to Employees and Employers

Numerous studies document the benefits of paid family and medical leave to employees and to society: Employees who have paid family and medical leave are more likely to return to work and stay longer in jobs.[30] Even unpaid leave has a large positive effect on the psychological well being of employees with elder care needs.[31] Countries with longer parental leave have a more egalitarian gender division of housework,[32] and lower wage gaps between women and men.[33] Research bears out that full recovery from childbirth typically takes six months or longer.[34] Longer leaves improve the quality of mother-infant interactions and reduce marital instability.[35] Children whose mothers returned to work early (less than nine months after childbirth) scored less on child-cognitive scores than other children, even after adjusting for home environment.[36] One study found a detrimental effect on children's cognitive development when mothers are employed in the first 12 weeks of a child's life, only somewhat mitigated by the increased income associated with employment.[37] Being able to take time to deal appropriately with one's own health problems or the illness of a child, spouse, or parent is likely to speed recovery and reduce the need for relying on government-provided caregiving or health care. A study of 16 European countries over the years from 1969 to 1994 found that more generous paid leaves reduced deaths among infants and young children.[38]

The Internet advocacy organization Moms Rising speaks to the antipoverty effects of paid family and medical leave:

> Having a baby is a leading cause of "poverty spells" in this country (times when income dips below what's needed for basic living expenses like food and rent). Paid Family Leave helps families bridge the income gap caused by folks being unable to go to work because they have to care for a new baby or a sick parent or spouse. In fact, nearly half of working people report that an illness or injury in their family caused them to get behind on their bills, including mortgage payments. We need Paid Family Leave to help families stay out of poverty—especially in this time when so many families are already vulnerable.[39]

Employers resist mandatory family and medical leave, both paid and unpaid. Yet they overestimate the costs and underestimate, or refuse to consider, the benefits. When paid family and medical leave legislation was introduced in the Massachusetts legislature in 2006, Randy Albelda and Alan Clayton-Matthews, economists at the University of Massachusetts Boston, studied the costs and benefits of the plan. Using a simulation model, they estimated the current employer and employee wage costs when employees take paid and unpaid family and medical leaves, and the new and redistributed wage-replacement costs of the proposed program. They estimated the current situation in Massachusetts as follows:

- There are already significant costs borne by employers and employees of family and medical leave taking. In Massachusetts, just under 357,000 of 3.2 million employees take 442,570 leaves (some workers take more than one leave annually) and forego $1.36 billion in annual wages. Employers provide $372 million in wage replacement for a total wage cost of $1.73 billion. The average cost to the worker who takes a leave is just more than $3,000 annually while the average cost to his or her employer is close to $1,300.
- Approximately 50 percent of current leaves in Massachusetts are for own-health reasons, 22 percent are for prenatal leave (including maternity disability) and 23 percent of leaves are for tending to an ill relative.
- The average length of leave for all leaves is 5.4 weeks.
- Currently 33.8 percent of all family and medical leaves are without any wage replacement.

When Albelda and Clayton-Matthews applied their simulation model to the proposed paid family and medical leave program that allowed for 12 weeks of paid leave, replacing all of weekly earnings up to $750/week, they estimated:

- The total number of family and medical leaves taken increases by just under 25,400 to a total of 467,962, a 5.7 increase. The total number of leaves using the proposed program will be 183,981 (assuming two-thirds of all eligible workers taking leave actually use it).
- The total cost of the proposed program is $389 million. Averaged across all employees, the annual cost is $120 per worker and the weekly cost is $2.31.
- Total costs of leaves (including lost wages, employer benefits, and the program costs) rise to $1.84 billion, an increase of 6.4 percent over current costs. The amount of employer wages foregone and employer benefits paid decrease with the proposed program. The new program results in some costs being shifted from employers to employees, and from individual workers taking leave to all workers.
- The average length of leave increases by one-half day from 5.4 weeks (based on a five-day week) to 5.5 weeks.
- The percentage of leaves with no wage replacement decreases to 24.0 percent.
- While the percentage of all leaves without pay decreases for all workers, the proposed program will disproportionately decrease the percentage without pay for leaves taken by workers in low-income households,

nonwhite, younger, and less educated, helping to level a very unlevel employment playing field.

These estimates refute the arguments that paid leave programs are too costly. The estimates should also dispel fears about lengthy extensions of leave-taking due to a paid leave program. Indeed, there are important gains for employees and employers with paid family and medical leave. As a social insurance program, paid leave provides all covered workers the right to receive wage replacement for a limited amount of time when they need it at a relatively small annual price to individual workers. Employers will benefit by reduced use of employer-paid time off and reduced turnover. Furthermore, a universal paid leave program will provide some workers who currently do not have paid leave—typically those with the lowest wages—some form of wage replacement.[40]

Albelda and Clayton-Matthews point out that paid job-protected leave might encourage workers to return to their jobs once the need for leave is over, instead of leaving the labor force altogether or finding work in a new workplace—just as the FMLA reinforces workers' job attachment now. This could have several effects:

- Returning to work reduces turnover, lowering employer costs—both the direct costs of advertising, interviewing, orientation, training, and processing (of both the exiting and the in-coming employee) and indirect costs associated with losing employees who understand internal networks, specific customers, or coworkers' abilities, and decreased morale or efficiency associated with working with inexperienced new employees.
- Workers who stay with their employers might see improved future earnings, since quitting a job can decrease workers' future earnings potential. In addition, workers will benefit from the continuation of any employer benefits offered.
- There might be government savings as well, since workers who quit instead of returning may need to rely on government support (like Unemployment Insurance, TANF, or Medicaid) for longer than if they had retained their job because of using a paid leave program.

Because the plan would be financed by employee payroll deductions, "a paid leave program—beyond administrative costs—will only marginally increase the current cost of leave taking. With an employee-based plan the largest share of the cost of leave taking will be borne by the workers who take those leaves; however, a portion of those costs will be shifted onto workers not taking leave."[41]

Employer Opposition to FMLA

Employers and employees have fought each other over FMLA since it began. Some employers have a "give-them-an-inch-and-they'll-take-a-mile" attitude about workers' use of the benefit. Companies accuse workers of using the act to take time off for vague and chronic maladies and are doing so intermittently, which makes scheduling harder. Some workers contend that companies are making it more difficult to qualify for leave and are requiring second or third opinions from doctors.[42]

Companies have spied on workers whom they suspect of fraudulent claims. The seventh U.S. Circuit Court of Appeals in Chicago has twice sided with employers who used surveillance to observe employees suspected of abusing the FMLA. On July 21, 2008, they handed down a decision on the case of Diana L. Vail, who worked a night shift at the Raybestos Products Co., a car parts manufacturer in Crawfordsville, Ind. She was approved for 33 days of intermittent medical leave from May through September 2005 because of migraines. As the summer progressed, Ms. Vail's use of her leave became more frequent. Her supervisors became suspicious because they knew her husband had a lawn mowing business and that she would help him. Raybestos hired an off-duty police sergeant to investigate. Ms. Vail took medical leave on Oct. 6, 2005, was observed mowing a lawn. She was terminated, and then filed suit, claiming, in part, that the termination violated FMLA. A lower court dismissed her case and a three-judge panel reviewing the case said that "the information gleaned from the reconnaissance was sufficient to give Raybestos an 'honest suspicion' that Ms. Vail was not using her leave for its intended purpose. While conducting surveillance of an employee 'may not be preferred employer behavior, employers have certainly gone further' and hired investigators to videotape employees on FMLA leave, the appeals court said in its ruling."[43]

The second case before the Chicago appeals court was Harold Crouch versus Whirlpool Corp. Mr. Crouch had been working at Whirlpool in Benton Harbor, Mich., since 2000, while his fiancée had been there since 1969. The couple attempted to coordinate their vacation times, which are based on seniority. While his fiancée received all of her requested vacation time, Mr. Crouch was denied most of his. In both 2002 and 2003, he filed for disability leave for the same periods for which he had unsuccessfully sought vacation time, both times claiming a knee injured during yard work. A supervisor noticed this and the company hired a private investigator, who videotaped Mr. Crouch doing yard work during the period he was out on disability. Mr. Crouch was terminated and sued, claiming violation of the FMLA. "Whirlpool's honest suspicion forecloses Crouch's FMLA claim," said the three-judge panel, which upheld a lower court ruling dismissing the case.[44]

According to a *Business Insurance* article, businesses have become emboldened by these court suits and "a growing number of employers are turning to surveillance to catch employees suspected of abusing the Family Medical Leave Act."[45] However, lawyers warn employers to respect privacy concerns and not become "overzealous and overreaching in their invasion of an employee's privacy."[46] The FMLA regulations contain a prohibition against using aggressive surveillance or treating an employee on FMLA differently than other employees. The lawyer who successfully represented the employer in the Vail case, Matthew S. Effland, advised employers to hire trained private investigators or off-duty police officers rather than sending out someone from the security department with a video camera.[47] Carl C. Bosland, managing director of the Denver-based Bosland Consulting Group, advised employers to be cautious about interpreting the results of surveillance. He said employees are eligible for FMLA leave if they are unable to perform a particular essential job function. This means they may still meet FMLA's technical requirement even if they are seen engaging in activities that make it "look like they're just malingering."[48]

A coalition of business groups lobbied to tighten the regulations. A spokesman for the National Association of Manufacturers said, "Our employers don't have any problem with employees using the leave for something like chemotherapy treatment or a pregnancy, but you can get it for a cold or migraine headaches. And that causes enormous scheduling and productivity problems."[49] In support of their campaign to tighten regulations as proposed by the Labor Department in February 2008, employers claimed that employees as well as employers thought the FMLA was being misused. A group called the National Coalition to Protect Family Leave, which included the U.S. Chamber of Commerce and National Retail Federation, conducted a national telephone survey of 1,000 registered voters, which said that more than 60 percent of Americans thought the FMLA needed tightening to eliminate misuse. Some of the questions in the survey gave a worst-case scenario that was aimed at alarming people, such as: "vulnerable citizens, such as children waiting for a school bus or people in need of emergency 9-1-1 services, are left to themselves."[50] Lisa Horn, a representative of the coalition, said that the potential for FMLA misuse is widely seen by Americans, particularly when it comes to sporadic, unscheduled leave. For example, she said, one in three workers say they cannot get their job done when a coworker takes unscheduled leave.[51]

Debra Ness, president of the National Partnership for Women and Families, opposed the Labor Department's proposal to tighten regulations. She said, "For 15 years, the FMLA has worked well. Now, with the economy in trouble and families struggling, workers need its protection more than ever."[52]

The Bush administration had issued regulations that watered down the FMLA just before President-elect Barack Obama was sworn in. In November 2008, the Department of Labor issued the new rules, which took effect January 16, 2009. The new rules allow employers to demand recertification of a medical condition every 30 days. If the employer has reason to doubt an employee's need for leave, the rules would require the employee to get a second opinion.[53] A Human Resources department can directly contact an employee's health care provider. Employees taking leave must tell their supervisors the same day or the following day. Previously, notice could be delayed. Employers can deny "perfect attendance" awards to workers on FMLA leave and do not have to grant it in increments smaller than they allow other leave.

Under the new rules, the time an employee spends in "light duty" work does not count against FMLA. Also, a company must explain in writing why it is denying leave. While they won some victories, employers did not get everything they wanted, because the changes did not define "serious health condition," or iron out problems with intermittent leave.

Sharyn Tejani, senior policy counsel at the National Partnership for Women and Families, criticized the Department of Labor for not doing an empirical FMLA study, rather than just asking for comments. "You shouldn't change regulations for the entire country based on employer complaints," she said.[54] A Congressional advocate of FMLA, Rep. Carolyn Maloney, D-New York, wrote a letter to Obama's chief of staff Rahm Emanuel requesting "that the president-elect's transition team take a close look at how we may expeditiously redress any new regulations that undermine access to FMLA leave."[55]

Employees worry about increasing employer scrutiny of their use of FMLA. They are concerned that the direct contact with medical providers would violate medical privacy. One employee asked the advice of Lily Garcia, who writes a column about employment law for the *Washington Post*.

I have been certified for Family and Medical Leave Act time off for an ongoing problem that requires frequent tests and treatments (leaving an hour early twice a month, on average). My supervisor is not happy about this and is requiring me to submit proof that I attended the appointment and that I had the appointment. When I talk to the human resources department about this, they don't understand where she is coming from, but they are also not willing to get in the middle of it because it's a doable request. It is doable, but I am feeling harassed. Should I just be grateful that I have FMLA and jump through these hoops, or should I start tracking this as a hostile work environment? It feels hostile.[56]

Garcia advised her that if her employer has reasons to doubt her need for leave, the law could require her to obtain a second medical opinion. "What your employer may not do is administer the FMLA in such a way that it amounts to retaliation against those who take advantage of the law."[57] Since the employer's request was doable, she advised the woman to comply with it but to keep good notes of her employment relationship for possible future use.

THE ROAD AHEAD

The opposition against paid family and medical leave is strong. Business lobbies are well organized and have lots of money. The Bush administration was strongly allied with business interests. During the presidential campaign, Democratic candidates indicated support for family leave. Barack Obama proposed expanding the 1993 family leave law to include businesses with fewer than 25 workers. He also proposed to give states $1.5 billion in incentives to start paid family leave programs,[58] and he supported a federal guarantee of sick leave, saying he would "require that employers provide seven paid sick days per year."[59] Michelle Obama has said that she is concerned about the problems of juggling work and family life.

In 2009, a bill was proposed in the U.S. House to grant Paid Family Leave for all federal workers, sponsored by Rep. Carolyn Maloney. The Internet advocacy group Moms Rising was working hard for its passage. They argued that policies for Federal employees can lead the nation.

This bill was passed by the House on June 4, 2009 and awaited action by the Senate. Republicans opposed it. Republican Pete Sessions of Texas said, "Maybe we just ought to let federal employees take 16 years off. Hello! Hello! Wake up, Washington! We're in a recession, and somebody is going to have to pay for this."[60]

In March 2009, the Family Leave Insurance Act of 2009 was introduced in the House, cosponsored by Representatives Pete Stark (D-CA), Lynn Woolsey (D-CA), and Carolyn Maloney (D-NY). It would provide 12 weeks of paid benefits to workers who need to take time off to care for an ill family member, a new child, or because of their own illness. It would work like Unemployment Insurance and would be funded by individuals and their employers paying 0.2 percent of employee's wages into an insurance fund. It would include employers who have two or more employees for 20 or more weeks during the year. Rep. Stark, Chair of the House Ways and Means Health Committee, said,

If we want to help people through the recession, we need to make sure that workers can maintain their incomes without sacrificing their families' needs. The Family Leave Insurance Act will provide paid family leave for workers, which will mean healthier children, stronger families, and more competitive businesses.[61]

Rep. Stark expected to have a fight on his hands. He said, "Employers didn't step up on Medicare or Social Security. We made them do it and now it's part of the system."[62]

Moms Rising is urging people to work for the federal Family Leave Insurance Act.

A congressional act to provide sick leave to employees, called the Healthy Families Act (HFA), was introduced in May 2009 by Senator Kennedy, in the Senate, and Rosa DeLauro, in the House.[63] It would require employers of 15 or more employees to provide up to 7 job-protected sick days each year.

As usual, business groups mobilized to block the legislation. Some employers cynically referred to HFA as the Paid Vacation Act because a doctor's certificate is not required unless the employee is out for three or more consecutive days.

There is also a campaign to get more flexibility in work hours, to accommodate caregiving responsibilities. In 2007, the Working Families Flexibility Act was introduced in both the Senate and the House of Representatives. This act allows an employee who works for an employer with at least 15 employees to request a change in his or her scheduling, place of work, or number of hours worked. The employer is permitted to refuse the request as long as it provides a reason for doing so—such as a loss of productivity or the effect of the change on the employer's ability to meet customer demand.[64]

Most countries with paid leave policies finance them through payroll taxes, although Canada uses its unemployment insurance system. A federal paid leave program could adopt similar mechanisms. For example, Heather Boushey from the Center for American Progress recently proposed a plan for paid family and medical leave through the already existing Social Security program, which is funded by payroll taxes.[65] It could be funded either by adding a small increase to the payroll tax (approximately three-tenths of a percent), lifting the earning cap beyond its 2009 level of $106,800, or by allowing workers to trade future Social Security benefits for paid time to provide care during their working years. The bureaucracy to finance the system and to deliver checks (although they would have to be sent out quicker than the system currently functions) is already in place, and Social Security already provides benefits to workers who become disabled and a worker's surviving family members. There is already a structure in place to establish the criteria for eligibility that consider a variety of circumstances.[66]

Boushey believes that this is a good time to push for this plan, suggesting that "we leverage populist outrage over Wall Street bailouts to overcome past hurdles to secure family leave insurance for all workers, including low-wage workers. When corporate executives with tin ears whine about cuts to their multimillion-dollar pay packages amid a deep recession, now is the time for progressives to focus on inclusive labor-market solutions for all American families."[67]

Federal legislation that establishes uniform policies for all the states is the best possible outcome. It is unfortunate that Obama's proposal would leave it up to the states, rather than enacting uniform federal provisions. Even though activists have had notable success in winning and proposing state legislation, many states have no policy at all and those that do vary in their coverage.

Part-time workers are generally not covered by paid family and medical leave. For many of them, welfare also serves as family leave. Ellen Bravo, co-ordinator of the Multi-State Working Families Consortium, recommended that, in addition to using stimulus funds to expand Unemployment Insurance, Congress should use stimulus funds to help states set up Family Leave insurance funds for part-time as well as full-time workers.[68]

The swine flu (H1N1) virus highlighted the dilemma of parents across the nation who found themselves in a bind when hundreds of schools closed. Nearly half of all workers—59 million people—and 86 percent of food service workers do not have the right to paid sick days. President Obama was slow to acknowledge the problem, and only requested that parents and businesses think about "contingency plans" if kids get sick and must stay home. He urged employers to "allow infected employees to take as many sick days as necessary." Yet there is no penalty for employers who choose not to pay workers in this situation, or for those who refuse workers any time off at all.

The times seem ripe for expansion of paid family and medical leave. Middle-class people as well as poor people are affected by it, which gives it more political clout. Unions have crafted strategic plans to fight for legislation. Many academics are doing research and publicizing it. Many advocacy organizations are fighting for it. Moms Rising is using the Internet creatively to organize. Public awareness is high. Activists have formed strong coalitions in their states and nationally. Activists need to just keep on keepin' on, in their long march for good federal legislation.

NOTES

1. Formally known as the Federal Employees Flexible and Compressed Work Schedules Act of 1982. The act does not require agencies to use the recommendations, but in 1994 President Clinton recommended each executive department and agency to establish procedures that encourage the expansion of family-friendly work arrangements.

2. Janet M. Liechty and Elaine A. Anderson, "Flexible workplace policies: Lessons from the Federal Alternative Work Schedules Act," *Family Relations*, 2007, vol. 56: 304–17.

3. Ellen Ernst Kossek and Brian Distelberg, "Work and family employment policy for a transformed labor force," in Ann C. Crouter and Alan Booth, *Work-life policies* (Washington, DC: The Urban institute Press, 2009), p. 22.

4. U. S. Department of Labor, March 2, 2009. http://www.dol.gov/esa/whd/fmla/index.htm/ Accessed February 3, 2010.

5. In 2009, paid sick days legislation had been proposed in 13 states—Arkansas, California, Connecticut, Illinois, Massachusetts, Maine, Minnesota, North Carolina, Ohio, Pennsylvania, Tennessee, Vermont, and West Virginia. Paid family leave legislation was proposed in six states—Arizona, Massachusetts, Minnesota, New Jersey, New York, and Pennsylvania.

6. Julia Weber, "Policy mini-brief series," Alfred Sloan Foundation, Boston College, 2009. Accessed at http://wfnetwork.bc.edu/topic.php?id=43

7. Randy Albelda and Alan Clayton-Matthews, *Sharing the costs, reaping the benefits: Paid family and medical leave in Massachusetts* (Boston, MA: Labor Resource Center), June 2006, and New Jersey Department of Labor and Workforce Development, March 30, 2009. http://lwd.dol.state.nj.us/labor/fli/content/fli_fact_sheet.html

8. David Cantor, Jane Waldfogel, Jeffrey Kerwin, Mareena McKinley Wright, Kerry Levis, John Rauch, Tracey Hagerty, and Martha Stapleton Kudela, *Balancing the needs of families and employers: Family*

and *Medical Leave surveys* (Washington, DC: U.S. Department of Labor), January 20, 2001. http://www.dol.gov/whd/fmla/toc.pdf. Accessed February 3, 2010.

9. Robert Drago, *What would they do? Childcare under parental leave and reduced hours options* (University Park, PA: Penn State Population Research Institute), April 2009, p. 21.
10. Ibid., p. 22.
11. Ibid., p. 23.
12. Ann Crittenden, *The Price of Motherhood* (New York: Henry Holt, 2001), pp. 258–259.
13. Rebecca Ray, Janet C. Gornick, and John Schmitt, *Parental leave policies in 21 countries: Assessing generosity and gender equality* (Washington, DC: Center for Economic and Policy Research), September 2008 and Jody Heymann, Hye Jin Rho, John Schmitt, and Alison Earle, *Contagion nation: A comparison of paid sick day-policies in 22 countries* (Washington DC: Center for Economic and Policy Research), May 2009.
14. Ray, Gornick and Schmitt, *Parental leave policies.*
15. Drago, p. 2.
16. Jennifer Glass, "Work-life policies," in Crouter and Booth, p. 232.
17. Judi Casey and Karen Corday, "Parental leave policies in 21 countries: Assessing generosity and gender equality," An interview with Janet C. Gornick and Rebecca Ray, *The Network News*, vol. 11, no. 3, March 2009. http://wfnetwork.bc.edu/The_Network_News/57/experts.htm.
18. Ibid.
19. Ibid.
20. Albelda and Clayton-Matthews, *Sharing the costs*, p. v.
21. U.S. Department of Labor, *Balancing the Needs of Families and Employees: FMLA Survey Report*, Washington, DC: U.S. Department of Labor, 2000, Table A1–4.4.
22. U.S. Office of Personnel Management, "Paid parental leave," 2001. http://www.opm.gov/oca/leave/HTML/ParentalReport.htn. Accessed February 4, 2010.
23. James T. Bond, Erin Brownfield, Ellen Galinsky, and Stacy S. Kim, "The national study of employers," 2005. http://familiesandwork.org/site/research/reports/2005nse.pdf.
24. Kossek and Distelberg, p. 34.
25. The exact percentages are as follows: 22 percent for maternity leave; 29 percent for paternity leave; 22 percent for adoption or foster care leave; and 21 percent to care for a child with a serious illness.
26. Bond, et. al., p. 25.
27. U.S. Department of Labor, *Family and Medical Leave Act Regulations: A report on the Department of Labor's Request for information—2007 Update* (Washington, DC: U.S. Department of Labor), 2007. http://www.dol/gov/esa/whd/FMLA2007Report/2007FinalReport.pdf. Accessed February 4, 2010.

28. Albelda and Clayton-Matthews, *Sharing the costs*, p. 3.
29. Kossek and Distelberg, p. 14.
30. Sunhwa Lee, "Women's work supports, job retention and job mobility: Child care and employer provided health insurance help women stay on jobs." Washington, DC: Institute for Women's Policy Research, 2004; Colleen Henry, Misha Werschkul, and Minita Rao, "Child care subsidies promote mothers' employment and children's development." Washington DC: Institute for Women's Policy Research, 2003.
31. Elisa K. Pavalka and Karhryn A. Henderson, "Combining care work and paid work: Do workplace policies make a difference?" *Research on aging* vol. 28: 359–79, 2006.
32. Makiko Fuwa and Philip N. Cohen, "Housework and social policy," *Social Science Research* vol. 36, no. 2: 512–30, 2007.
33. Jane Waldfogel, "Understanding the 'Family Gap' in pay for women with children," *Journal of Economic Perspectives* vol. 12, no. 1 (1998), 137–156.
34. Lorraine Tulman and Jacqueline Fawcett, "Maternal employment following childbirth," *Research in Nursing and health* 13: 181–188, 1990.
35. Roseanne Clark, Janet Shibley, Marilyn Essex, and Marjorie Klein, "Length of maternity leave and quality of mother-infant interactions," *Child Development* vol. 68, no. 2: 364–383, 1997.
36. Jeanne Brooks-Gunn, Wen-Jui Han, and Jane Waldfogel. "Maternal employment and child cognitive outcomes in the first three years of life: The NICHD study of early child care." *Child Development* vol. 73, no. 4: 1052–1073, 2002.
37. Charles L. Baum, "Does early maternal employment harm child development? Analysis of the potential benefits of leave taking." *Journal of Labor Economics* vol. 21, no. 2: 409–448, 2003.
38. Christopher Ruhm, "Parental leave and child health," *Journal of Health Economics* vol. 19, no. 6: 931–960, 2000.
39. momsrising@mail.democracyinaction.org
40. Albelda and Clayton-Matthews, *Sharing the Costs*, pp. v–vi.
41. Ibid., p. 16.
42. Kris Maher, "Is family leave act too soft or too tough?" *Wall Street Journal Abstracts*, November 21, 2007, D1.
43. Judy Greenwald, "Appeals court rules twice for employers with 'honest suspicion' of workers on leave," *Business Insurance*, September 1, 2008, p. 28.
44. Ibid.
45. Judy Greenwald, "Firms use private eyes to track FMLA abuse; Experts urge caution as privacy concerns rise," *Business Insurance*, September 1, 2008.
46. Ibid.
47. Ibid.
48. Ibid.

49. Susanna Schrobsdorff, "Family leave under fire? *Newsweek*, March 26, 2007, p. 8.
50. Hsin-Yin Lee, "Poll finds most seek reform of family, medical leave law," *Washington Times*, March 9, 2008, p. A04.
51. Ibid.
52. Ibid.
53. Lily Garcia, "When your supervisor wants a doctor's note every time," *Washington Post*, December 28, 2008, p. K01.
54. Mark Schoeff Jr., "Opponents of FMLA changes seek redress," *Workforce Management*, December 15, 2008.
55. Ibid.
56. Garcia, "When your supervisor."
57. Ibid.
58. Sue Shellenbarger, "Family time: Lawmakers push to expand paid leave," *Wall Street Journal Abstracts*, November 19, 2008, p. D1.
59. Ibid.
60. Katharine Mieszkowski, "House passes paid leave for some new parents," http://www.salon.com/mwt/broadsheet/2009/06/05/family_leave/, June 5, 2009. Accessed February 4, 2010.
61. *American Chronicle*, "Stark introduces Paid Family Leave legislation," March 28, 2009. http://www.americanchrnicle.com/articles/view/96339. Accessed February 4, 2010.
62. Eve Tahminciogler, "Paid Family Leave becomes hot workplace issue," msnbc.com.contributer, June 3, 2008.
63. National Partnership for Women and Families, "Nations top work/family expert applauds introduction of paid sick days legislation, urges Congress to quickly pass bill," May 19, 2009. http://www.nationalpartnership.org/site/PageServer?pagename=newsroom_pr_PressRelease_090519. Accessed February 4, 2010.
64. Chai R. Feldblum, "Policy challenges and opportunities for workplace flexibility," in Crouter and Booth, p. 256.
65. Heather Boushey, "Helping breadwinners when it can't wait," Center for American Progress, June 8, 2009. http://www.americanprogress.org/issues/2009/06/fmla.html Accessed February 4, 2010.
66. Ibid.
67. Ibid.
68. Ellen Bravo, "Letter to the editor," *New York Times*, February 13, 2009.

CHAPTER 4

The Privatization of Care

Betty Reid Mandell

Selling Uncle Sam is the title of a book on how to do just that, for entrepreneurs eager to make some money off of Uncle Sam.[1] Sitting close to it on the library shelf is a book sponsored by the World Bank and the Fleming Bank, advising corporations worldwide on how to make money by privatizing their government's various ventures.[2] Both the World Bank and the Fleming Bank fund privatization ventures throughout the world. In their analysis of what has already been accomplished through privatization, they like most of what they see.

For the past three decades, businesses have been eager to take over every government function that shows promise of making a profit. Corporations are increasingly taking over basic services such as hospitals, prisons, crime prevention, sanitation, and even water. Libraries are starting to be privatized, while more city parks are operated by private services. Corporations are forming charter schools to compete with public schools, and vouchers are given to parents to allow them to pay for a private school. Over the same period, both neoliberals and neoconservatives have been trashing government while exalting the beauty of the free market, touting it as more efficient, productive, higher quality and cost effective than government because it is competitive. In contrast, government is described as monopolistic, bureaucratic, inefficient, and staffed with overpaid featherbedding functionaries. The solution, they say, is to farm government services out to private businesses.

"Privatization" implies an adversarial relationship between government and business. A more commonly used term now is "public-private partnerships," which posits government and business as cooperative partners focusing on efficient management techniques. Stephen Linder suggests that the Labor government in Britain preferred to use the term "partnership" to distance themselves from the worst excesses of privatization under the Thatcher government.[3]

As capital searches for investment opportunities, privatization has become globalized, and no country is exempt from this. Chile was one of the first developing countries to privatize, following the overthrow of Salvador Allende. The World Bank is fulsome in its praise of Chile's "innovative" privatization of pension funds:

> This move created a sizable and stable base of institutional investors for Chile's equity market, allowing a number of large privatizations to be absorbed domestically. Pension funds acquired some 23 percent of the shares in divested state enterprises. Chile's move toward private management of pensions has been emulated by other Latin American countries, including Argentina, Bolivia, Mexico, and Peru.[4]

The World Bank does not mention that since privatizing its pension funds, administrative costs in Chile ran to more than 15 percent of the funds, as compared to 0.8 percent for administrative costs of Social Security in the United States.[5] Conservatives in the United States have been trying for years to privatize Social Security. It would be an enormous windfall for stockbrokers and a disaster for nearly everyone else.

PRIVATIZATION IN THE UNITED STATES

The U.S. government has been contracting out social services to private entities for a long time. Privatization in this country generally refers to expanding this practice, especially on the state and local levels. Government has also been privatized by withdrawing government funds from a service, as has been done with welfare, Medicare and Medicaid, the National Endowment for the Arts, and National Public Radio. When government funds are withdrawn, people are forced to pay for goods and services from private sources, or rely on private charity. This form of privatization is closely related to the conservative push for voluntarism and charitable choice. Vouchers are another form of privatization. Instead of building houses, the federal government gives Section 8 vouchers to families to subsidize their rent for private housing. Vouchers are sometimes used to allow customers to "shop around" for services such as providing training services under the Workforce Investment Act.[6]

One of the top priorities of privatization advocates is to break the back of unions, and especially the public unions, which have been gaining strength even as unions in the private sector decline. Closely related to this priority is their desire to lower wages for all workers. The relatively high wages for public workers at the lower end of the wage scale have been eroded by welfare reform, which has forced millions of welfare recipients into the low wage labor market and lowered wages for workers in the lowest third of the pay scale.

CORRUPTION

Privatization often lends itself to corruption by both private and public officials. Since this is done in secret, it is hard for the public to find out about it.

To avoid corruption in contracting, privatization must be placed under strict supervision. Proponents of privatization resist this, as they want less public regulation. Despite their singing the praises of competition, they are even happier if they can get the contract without bidding for it. More than half of the federal government's purchases in 2002 were done without bidding or with procedures that auditors say are noncompetitive.[7] Corruption can also be a public-private partnership. A particularly shocking example of this involved two judges in Wilkes-Barre Pennsylvania who took bribes from private companies to sentence juveniles to detention centers. Two judges were charged with taking $2.6 million in kickbacks to send teenagers to two privately run youth detention centers. Some of the teenagers were locked up for months for stealing loose change from cars, writing a prank note, and possessing drug paraphernalia. Many of them had never in trouble before. Some were imprisoned after probation officers recommended against it. Many appeared without lawyers, despite the U.S. Supreme Court's 1967 ruling that children have a constitutional right to counsel.[8]

When the Personal Responsibility and Work Opportunity Act was passed in 1996, many private companies contracted with states to manage welfare programs. Lockheed was the largest business in the welfare reform market. It launched a major "welfare reform/self-sufficiency initiative."[9] Its Information Management Services Division had child support contracts in 16 states and contracts in 20 states to convert various welfare benefits to electronic debit cards.

Lockheed has a long history of bribery of public officials, price-fixing, "and the art of defiantly pleading no contest to such charges when they become public."[10] They were caught twice during the 1980s for using illegal influence with New York City public officials to get a contract to privatize their parking enforcement activities. Mayor Guiliani barred Lockheed from any business dealings with the city for four years. Still Lockheed tried to get a contract from the city by lobbying at the state level to privatize the management information system of public transportation in the city.

The Welfare Warriors, a welfare rights group in Milwaukee, Wisconsin, documented the corruption in welfare contracts in Wisconsin, describing it as "Wisconsin's Bloated Welfare Empire." Six private, for-profit companies received contracts to administer the city's Temporary Assistance to Needy Families (TANF) case welfare program. Under welfare reform, Wisconsin's welfare costs increased from $548 million for 299,700 individuals to $710 million for less than 20,000 individuals. During the first 2 years of welfare reform, these corporations earned $65.1 million in profits. Some of those earnings were achieved by denying cash to families, sanctioning them, or kicking them off the rolls.

An audit of Wisconsin's welfare program, called "W-2," was conducted in April 2001. They found that two of these companies, Goodwill and Maximus, admitted to "improperly spending" a half million dollars each in projects in other states, parties, promotional schemes, meals, and concerts. "Neither corporation was prosecuted for felony welfare fraud. Nor did Tommy

Thompson, then governor of Wisconsin, terminate their lucrative W2 contracts."[11]

In 2007, the Justice Department brought criminal charges against Maximus for Medicaid fraud. Maximus was under contract with the Washington DC Child and Family Services Agency (CFSA) to manage foster care cases, and admitted responsibility for causing the city to submit Medicaid claims for children who may not have received foster care. Maximus agreed to pay $30.5 million to settle the false claims lawsuit and $12.2 million that had been recovered from CFSA after a federal investigation found that it could not support 35 percent of the claims it had submitted.[12]

In 2008, Maximus was told by the Department of Public Services of Los Angeles County that their $32-million contract would not be renewed, as another company's bid was better. Maximus spent $124,000 to hire two lobbying firms to get their contract renewed, and later they hired two more lobbying firms. In addition, Maximus gave $1,000, the maximum allowed, to the campaigns to reelect two county supervisors.

County officials had previously complained about the work that Maximus did, and in 1993 did not renew a Maximus contract to provide welfare-to-work services. "Seven years later, Maximus won a smaller contract after a bruising political battle over whether the job of helping welfare recipients enter the workforce was best done by public or private employees."[13] When a vote was held on the Maximus contract in 2000, one county supervisor who had previously been allied with labor and antipoverty activists, voted for the contract. "On the day of that vote, union members filled the supervisors' meeting room shouting 'shame.'"[14]

SOCIAL SERVICES AND THE PUBLIC INTEREST

Advocates of the free market assume that the public interest will be automatically served if each individual follows his or her economic self-interest. It has not worked out that way for the poor and the vulnerable. Private companies have increasingly taken over the social services. To make a profit in business, they prefer to serve clients who will help them do that, which leads to "creaming" the clientele. The people whom private organizations find too difficult or intractable are left for the government to serve directly, if they are served at all.

Social services (e.g., foster care and adoption, counseling, rehabilitation, private charity) have long been dominated by the nonprofit sector. Private charity began before public charity, most often under the auspices of religious groups or religious-minded individuals. Catholic Charities, the Federation of Protestant Welfare Organizations, United Jewish Appeal Federation and the Salvation Army, for example, are large providers of private charity. However, voluntary agencies are not really "private" any more because much of their funding comes from federal, state, and local governments in public-private partnership arrangements. Nonprofit agencies have, in effect, become "paid agents" of the government to an extent that no one in the nineteenth century would have dreamed possible. They have increased their contracting with both state and federal governments since the 1980s. Many voluntary service agencies receive more than 70 percent of their funds from federal and state sources. Child welfare agencies received 59 percent of their income from governmental sources in 1986; in 1960, that figure was 28 percent.[15]

The Welfare Warriors, campaigning against the child welfare department that took children from their parents, conducted a bus tour of the private agencies in Milwaukee, which had received contracts from the Bureau of Milwaukee Child Welfare (BMCW). They found that BMCW, like the W-2 program that administered welfare, had been mostly privatized. They reported that the BMCW "empire" had received "$125 million to fund 850 Bureau and private staff; 169 private agencies and therapists; and 98 lawyers, who take and keep 2774 children away from their moms each year on *unproven* allegations of abuse and neglect."[16]

Nonprofit agencies are no longer exclusively concerned with the poor; in fact, they have increasingly disengaged from the poor. A study by the Urban Institute in the 1980s showed that more than half of nonprofit human service agencies had few or no poor clients and only 27 percent had mostly poor clients. Research shows that

Charity benefits the relatively advantaged rather than disadvantaged groups, well-established organizations rather than new, grassroots activities, community organizing, issue advocacy, or controversial public policy initiatives. Social and class elites are overrepresented on boards and have disproportionate power over priorities, though there is more risk taking with younger diverse board membership.[17]

The War on Poverty of the 1960s and 70s led to a vast increase of purchase of service arrangements with vendors and practitioners who were by and large not public employees. Social Security amendments enacted between 1962 and 1974 for the first time authorized federal funding for social services provided by nongovernmental charitable agencies. Social services were purchased both from existing voluntary agencies and from ones newly created as a result of the new federal funding.[18] The War on Poverty program encouraged some agencies to pay more attention to the poor, sometimes paying them to do so through lucrative contracts. For the first time, some prestigious private agencies such as Family Service Association and Jewish Family Services hired low-income people from the communities they served, and the government established a human services career ladder for low-income people, subsidizing many human service programs in colleges.

Some people claim that private nonprofit agencies are more creative and innovative than government in responding to need, but it was the government during the War on Poverty that established some of the most pathbreaking programs. The Community Action Program organized poor people to fight unresponsive government bureaucracies. Largely Community Action

Programs and VISTA volunteers organized the National Welfare Rights Organization. Head Start, the government childcare program for poor families, compares favorably with high-quality private childcare programs. Users of services were brought in as equal partners in setting policy when the Economic Opportunity Act required the "maximum feasible participation" of a program's beneficiaries. That demand for democratic participation echoed the demand for participatory democracy of the 1960s New Left, and it was a radical breakthrough in social services, far beyond anything the nonprofit sector has done. It continues to live on in some programs through statutory requirements for parental involvement in Head Start programs and in planning educational programs for special needs children.

The federal government employed a social services strategy to ending poverty and increased funding of nonprofit agencies in the 1960s. Between 1967 and 1972, federal funds authorized by the 1962 Title XX amendments to the Social Security Act grew from $242 million to $1.688 billion. Congress became alarmed by the open-ended nature of funding for social services and in 1972, they put a $2.5 billion ceiling on it.[19] The federal budget for social services began to decline under the Reagan administration. The privatization of the past three decades has been associated with downsizing, cost containment, and deregulating government functions.

Conservatives believed that social programs were actually harmful, and they turned to moral regeneration as an antipoverty program. The neoliberals emphasized the moral value of work and individual initiative; neoconservatives added to that a belief in traditional values, religion, and marriage and the family. They believe in faith-based social services. The libertarian Reason Foundation advocates getting government out of the financing and delivery of services altogether. They would substitute families, churches, neighborhoods, and community groups to meet social needs.[20]

The Reagan administration turned the federal social service program (Title XX of the Social Security Act) into a block grant, which sharply reduced federal funding levels but also eliminated state matching requirements. It virtually eliminated reporting requirements and allowed even greater flexibility in the targeting of funds. The conservatives who were now in charge of social service delivery demanded more businesslike management and more business involvement. In 1986, for example, child support legislation specifically encouraged the states to contract with private companies for technical activities. By the mid-1990s, for-profit firms accounted for nearly half of all social service agencies and approximately one-third of social services employment.[21] Since the 1980s, the government has contracted for a wider variety of services, and government contracts are purchasing whole programs, rather than simply limited services.[22] Unlike the AFDC program, TANF no longer prohibited states from using personnel from private organizations to perform eligibility determination for cash assistance. However, there was a continued requirement that only public workers determine eligibility for Medicaid and Food Stamps, unless states received waivers from the Medicaid and Food Stamp Program requirements.

Corporations are eager to reap profits from food stamp programs.[23] In 1997, Indiana's Family and Social Services Administration (FSSA) implemented a 10-year contract with IBM to administer food stamps and other benefits received by 1.1 million people, in a project named Hoosier Coalition for Self Sufficiency. In response to concerns among advocates and others that the privatization of food stamp eligibility runs the risk of denying benefits to those eligible, whether through technological glitches, unfamiliarity by the vendors' employees, or other reasons, the U.S. Agriculture Department's Food and Nutrition Service tightened oversight of the program. Indiana's outsourcing was compared to one in Texas that encountered backlogs in processing benefits and other problems before that state canceled the contract. When the program began in Indiana, more than 1,500 welfare case workers and other public employees left the state's employment and went to work for IBM partner Affiliated Computer Services, Inc (ACS).[24] In their examination of the program, the U.S. Food and Nutrition Service found problems with staffing, large caseloads, and delays in processing applications for benefits and other issues.[25] They also found that IBM had broken federal food stamp rules in some cases by bypassing state employees. Some clients had been approved for food stamps without being interviewed by state employees.[26] In response to the criticism, FSSA implemented more training for its employees and the U.S. Food and Nutrition Service approved their plan.[27] However, the changes that FSSA implemented "have drawn fire from lawmakers, welfare clients and their advocates, who claim the new system loses necessary documents, leaves telephone callers on hold for long periods and creates other problems. Two lawsuits are challenging the changes, which are in place in 59 counties with about 45 percent of the state's welfare caseload."[28]

Texas attempted to privatize its entire welfare system statewide, including food stamps and Medicaid, but the federal Department of Health and Human Services (DHHS) denied the necessary waivers to the state. However, Texas continued to privatize eligibility determination and privatized other functions, such as job search and placement. Wisconsin began wide-scale privatization even before the Personal Responsibility and Work Opportunity Reconciliation Act (PRWORA) of 1996 was passed, under federal waivers that allowed the privatization of eligibility determination.[29] Arizona contracted with Maximus to administer the TANF program in one county, and Florida contracted with ACS to provide TANF services in one county. Contracting out case management, especially eligibility determination, is less prevalent than contracting out other services such as employment services, support services, and specialized social services.[30]

The two largest for-profit corporations providing welfare and related services are Maximus and ACS. ACS, a for-profit information technology provider, purchased Lockheed Martin IMS Corp. Lockheed Martin had contracted with state and local governments to provide TANF services, child support collection, electronic benefit transfers, and employment-services. In 2001, it held 26 TANF contracts worth a possible $108 million. In 2008,

Lockheed Martin won a $56.7 million contract with the U.S. DHHS to provide medical and administrative staffing to perform clinical services for the federal workforce.[31]

Maximus held TANF contracts worth a possible $56 million.[32] In 2008, they won an $8 million contract with the Los Angeles County Board of Supervisors to deliver employment and supportive services to TANF recipients in the county. They operate similar welfare-to-work programs in six other states, including Alaska, Arizona, the District of Columbia, Hawaii, and Wisconsin, as well as Australia and Israel.[33] Other for-profit corporations that provide TANF services include Curtis and Associated, Policy Studies, Inc., America Works, Association for Research and Behavior, Inc., DynCorp, Anderson Consulting, and Electronic Data Systems.[34]

Several large nonprofit organizations have won contracts to provide case management, employment services, and support services. These include Goodwill Industries, Catholic Charities, and AFL-CIO. The community services branch of AFL-CIO provides job-training services under contract with state and local governments.[35]

States have contracted out EBT (Electronic Benefit Transfer) services. By 2003, there were six primary vendors with state EBT contracts, including ACS, Citicorp Electronic Financial Services (EFS), eFunds, GM Group, Northrop Grumman, and Stored Value Systems (SVS). Citicorp (EFS) holds the majority of state EBT contracts. Some states contracted with multiple vendors, and 36 states use funds allocated for other programs such as TANF and Child Support to cover the costs of EBT. States are showing increasing interest in using EBT for programs such as Medicaid eligibility, Refugee Assistance, and State Government Assistance.[36]

Many community-based nonprofit organizations have contracted to provide TANF services as well as other services. Some partner or subcontract with for-profit organizations. In Milwaukee, the YWCA won a contract to administer TANF in one district by joining with two for-profit organizations (Kaiser Group and CNR Health) to form YW-Works.[37]

Managed care is becoming increasingly popular in several social service fields, including child welfare. For-profit businesses have entered almost every field of the social services—nursing homes, child care, foster care, vocational rehabilitation, adoption assistance, family counseling, services for the handicapped, mental health, and others.

The PRWORA of 1996 allowed state or local agencies to contract out their entire welfare program, including intake, eligibility, and services. The change to funding through block grants gave new incentives for privatization. As a result, large for-profit companies, including Ross Perot's former company, Electronic Data Systems (EDS), and IBM, entered the welfare market. The Applied Research Center in Oakland, California, referred to this phenomenon as U.S. private companies "prospecting among the poor in the welfare reform gold fields."[38] Sandy Felder, public sector coordinator of the Service Employees International Union, claimed that the 1996 welfare reforms permitted "one of the largest corporate grabs in history."[39] A Lehman Brothers analyst estimated

the potential market for welfare-related contracts at more than $20 billion a year. He noted, "It's a huge revenue target for the private sector to go after."[40]
These firms claim to save tax dollars while promoting "self-sufficiency."[41] They speak glowingly of getting people off the rolls into jobs, but they do not mention the approximately 40 percent of people who have not found jobs or the increase in homelessness, hunger, and infant mortality. Nor do they mention that most people who got jobs are still poor, earning on average between $7 and $9 an hour. Caseload reduction is the main standard specified in their contracts. Performance standards were not established for client wages, benefits, or job retention and so contractors had no incentive to work for those goals. They were, in fact, doing what the government wanted them to do when it passed the welfare law—push people into the low-wage job market as fast as possible, without regard for the consequences.

Follow-up studies of the cost savings of private contractors for social services show mixed results. A 1993 study by the Reason Foundation found that savings in the social service area were lower than in other services.[42] A 1997 survey by the Council on State Governments found that reported costs savings were modest.[43] One researcher observed that cost estimates do not include the transaction costs entailed in the contracting process.[44] "In addition, the cost comparisons between the private and public sector should control for variables, such as the proportion of clients who are 'difficult to serve' or other relevant differences."[45]

Faith-Based Grants

The PRWORA contained a "charitable choice" provision allowing religious groups to compete for grants. The Bush administration created a separate White House Office of Faith-Based and Community, which expanded "charitable choice."

> [The office] provided large grants for projects favored by the Christian right, like Charles Colson's Prison Fellowship Ministries and Teen Challenge, a drug rehabilitation program that openly pushed religious conversion (even using the phrase "completed Jews" to describe teenage converts from Judaism) as a way of overcoming addiction. John J. Dilulio Jr., the first director of Mr. Bush's faith-based office, resigned after only eight months and later complained about the politicization of the program.[46]

The "religious left" of the Democratic party did not object to faith-based grants, but complained that most of the money was going to religious and political conservatives. Barack Obama promised during his presidential campaign to expand faith-based aid but to prohibit proselytizing and discrimination in hiring. Yet he left the Bush orders in place and his new faith-based team was headed by a Pentecostal minister, Josh DuBois.[47]

Mr. Obama's compromise has drawn criticism from secularists and civil libertarians, arguing that it violates the separation of church and state by allowing discrimination in hiring. Some religious conservatives protested against any limitations on proselytizing. R. Albert Mohler Jr., president of the Southern Baptist Theological Seminary, maintained that the unlimited right to proselytize and to hire members of their own faith is essential if churches are not to compromise their mission.

Advocates of faith-based grants argue that they provide better service than secular services, but there is no objective evidence for this. A 1993 study of Mr. Colson's prison programs in Texas suggested that program participants had been rearrested at much lower rates than other released prisoners. However, the study excluded everyone who quit the program in prison—two-thirds of the starting group. "It is as if the Department of Education were to measure the success of public schools by not counting dropouts."[48]

The church-state debate has been going on since sectarian agencies began charitable activities. In the mid-1800s, Catholics have emphasized the importance of religious institutions and the moral superiority of private charity over public agencies in responding to social needs. In 1989, Joseph Doolin, the president of Catholic Social Services of Boston,

> bemoaned the fact that…75 percent of the agency's funding came from the state. In an effort to regain more independence and to reinstate an approach more consistent with a religious organization, Doolin has cut back the reliance on public funding to 50 percent: "Because it was using state funds, Catholic Charities was required to remove religious items like Bibles and crucifixes from AIDS hospices, for example, and residents were not allowed to hold prayer groups. It made no sense at all," Doolin said.[49]

QUALITY OF SERVICE

Studies of privatization focus on cost-effectiveness, but generally ignore the quality of service given. One study of the influence of privatization, a PhD dissertation, examined the effect on service providers in a program that served low-income people who have AIDS. The CARE Act of 1990, which allocated money for this program, mandates the federal government to contract with regional project directors—through state health departments—who, in turn, contract with local private nonprofit organizations to hire case managers to provide services.

> By the time the project directors and case managers provide services, their jobs have become a hodgepodge of contradictory activities and roles. Case managers struggle with mountains of paperwork and strict

eligibility rules, while trying to remain empathetic advocates for their clients...Contrary to the expectations of those supportive of privatization, social service providers engaged in incompatible, wasteful, and emotionally cumbersome problems social service providers encountered when serving as gatekeepers, strategists, and caregivers within the contract-laden, privatized welfare system.[50]

It is hard to compare privatized services with public services in foster care agencies because public agencies have a dismal record of caring for the state's children. Yet it seems that private agencies are as bad, if not worse. The Sarasota Family YMCA oversees foster care for the state of Florida in five counties. The state Department of Children & Families (DCF) found that the YMCA agency had lost track of a two-year-old foster child, whose disappearance was not reported by child protection workers for four months. DCF said that the Sarasota Family YMCA "once held up as a model of privatizing social services in Florida, must change its culture of arrogance and acknowledge its part in 'creating or perpetuating problems' or risk losing its contract next year."[51]

Public welfare agencies may be as cruel and heartless as private contractors, but public agencies are less likely to "cream" the clientele to get rid of hard to serve clients. Privatizing services is likely to put less emphasis on protecting client or employee rights than are public services, and they are likely to be less accountable. Providers "no longer must answer directly to an elected government official, and government officials exercise less direct control over services that are paid for with public funds...Privatization further decreases citizen involvement in the governance of public services because contractors typically need not be as responsible to citizen demands as public agencies must be."[52] Also, there is a legal and ethical problem with contracting out services that involve coercion, such as incarceration or decisions to sanction welfare families and remove them from the welfare roles.[53]

Public agencies, however, have problems of their own. Bureaucrats may want to minimize their work or increase their job security rather than meet the needs of citizens. Similar to nonprofit firms, they may lack any explicit incentive to minimize costs, and therefore may not use resources efficiently.[54]

An important function of the government is to insure fair and equal treatment to its citizens. When private agencies discriminate, the government should prohibit that. *New York Times* reporter Nina Bernstein in her book *The Lost Children of Wilder* documented a notorious lawsuit, which challenged the discriminatory practices of some private agencies.[55] This is discussed in the chapter on foster care.

This case points up the dangers inherent in faith-based social services. Before the charitable choice provision, agencies that were tax exempt were prohibited from mixing religion with social service provision when they received government funds. Now they can be openly religious as long as clients have a choice of a comparable nonreligious social service. Sometimes such an alternative is not easily available to a client.

The conservative morality and emphasis on faith-based charity and "self-help" has led to diminished support for public services and stigmatization of people who depend on government support. It directs the analysis of problems away from dysfunctional systems to dysfunctional individuals. The Reagan administration began the call for self-help and internal solutions to black social problems, while at the same time engaging in a massive disinvestment in black communities that increased their poverty. President Bill Clinton advocated personal responsibility among black people. The Million Man March expressed this self-help ideology, too, one that lets government off the hook while increasing people's internalized oppression and weakening their ability to fight back.

For-profit businesses often rely on performance-based and outcome-based contracts, emphasizing an efficiency that may be conservative, but is seldom compassionate. In their welfare-to-work training programs, companies focus almost exclusively on skills that will actually be used on the job, without regard to clients' emotional and cognitive needs or practical difficulties. The Ohio legislature gave Anderson consulting a million-dollar contract in 1996 to help the state restructure the welfare department based on a "tough love" approach, with strong job incentives and sanctions for failure to work.[56] Many nonprofits, on the other hand, are more likely to take a more holistic approach to the welfare-to-work process, helping clients build emotional resilience and offering them a community of supporters to help them through finding and retaining a job. A long-time community worker describes her contacts with private businesses involved in welfare reform:

> They hold these meetings to describe the proposal process for new money and we see people in the room who have never worked with poor people before...then we hear that they got big money to make people "job-ready"...pretty soon they call us up asking for help because their clients have too many problems to hold jobs.[57]

In their search for allies, welfare rights activists who oppose the current welfare reform are often disappointed by the absence of human service providers among their ranks. There are some who fight against TANF, but many are afraid to oppose the state for fear of jeopardizing their contracts. Ann Withorn studied how community-based nonprofit agencies are responding to welfare reform. She found that agencies were facing increased demands on their resources because of welfare reform, but feel intimidated about protesting. One community leader said,

> We can speak up here, with each other, but it is hard before the legislators—and not because we are afraid for our funding. A strange dynamic happens, they don't want to hear us whine; they want us "to think outside the box." So we try to speak so that we won't threaten anybody with how bad it is and our limits in dealing with it.[58]

The Commodification of Care

The United Kingdom whittled away at its National Health Service (NHS) by public funding of a massive expansion of private nursing and residential care. Long-term care for frail elderly people, the chronically ill, and the physically and mentally disabled has been almost completely eliminated from NHS and local authority provision. In 1990, the central government devolved responsibility for long-term care to local governments, giving them a block grant to carry this out. However, the grant specified that 85 percent of the money had to go to private sector providers, which effectively prevented local authorities from reverting to providing long-term care directly inhouse and making alternative provision in the community virtually impossible.[59]

But reliance on for-profit companies is tricky. If profitability drops in one sector, the company will leave the field, moving on to other, more lucrative markets. Nursing homes in the United States were at one time bringing in big returns on the stock market. However, with government cutbacks in Medicare and Medicaid reimbursements, profits are down. Sun Healthcare Group (SGH), one of the largest U.S. nursing home chains (and the holding company of the British chain Ashbourne Group, which operates 149 homes and 8,367 beds nationwide) faced reduced shares of more than 60 percent at the beginning of 1999. Companies such as SGH and Tenet are introducing cost-cutting measures such as staff cutbacks, reducing time spent with patients, and using lower-paid professionals to deliver the care. The company has already fired 7,490 employees, including 36 percent of rehabilitation workers.[60]

In 2008, Maximus sold businesses that were not profitable, including Justice Solutions, Education Systems, and Asset Solutions. They announced that they would continue with their "core offerings," ranging from Medicaid and SCHIP enrollment, welfare-to-work, program integrity, and services in special education. They bragged, "We will build on this strengthened platform to drive future growth as the leading pure-play provider for the administration of government health and human services programs."[61] Pure-play indeed, how ironic, given the Maximus record of corruption!

A 1993 World Bank report on health care "reinforced the neoliberal canon of the privatization of health care to turn it into a terrain for capital accumulation."[62] We know how that has played out with health care in the United States. Private insurance companies refuse to serve the sickest, business managers rather than doctors decide what kind of treatment people will get, care is time-limited, and more than 47 million people are uninsured. The rich still get premium care from their "boutique doctors," but as states cut back on Medicaid, the poor are denied even basic dental care.

Privatization of mental hospital care has led some hospitals to engage in financial and emotional exploitation of patients. In 1991, a Texas family told a state senator that their 14-year-old son had been apprehended, detained, and treated on an emergency basis by a private psychiatric hospital, without their consent. A Senate committee investigated, and many testified at the hearing that hospitals manipulated diagnoses to justify longer admissions and increase insurance benefits. Patients described incidents of forced and inappropriate treatment, which enabled the hospitals to collect payment from the patients' health insurance.[63] Many mentally ill people were forced out of state hospitals due to the deinstitutionalization movement that took place from the 1960s through the 1980s. Those without health insurance often received no treatment at all in the private sector. Private psychiatric hospitals prefer to treat those with money. People joke about the "60 day miracle cure" that occurs when hospitals declare people to be cured when their insurance runs out.

Conservatives want to scale back Social Security and Medicare to cover only the most vulnerable of the aged population—the poor, sick, frail, and incapacitated. This would lessen the role of government and contain expenditures. Proposals have been circulated to partially transform Old Age and Survivors Insurance (OASI) into a defined contribution plan, to issue Medicare vouchers to the old, or to impose an "affluence test" on Social Security and Medicare beneficiaries. Eligibility age for full OASI benefits rise from 65 to 67 by 2027. Raising the eligibility age for Medicare benefits was proposed during the Balanced Budget Act debates in 1997. Raising the eligibility age for services under the Older Americans Act from 60 to 65 or even 70 has also been proposed.

Proponents of these plans argue that since people are living to a longer and healthier old age, they are able to work longer and no longer need so much government assistance. They have "graduated into the private sector." Conservatives want to eliminate programs that "have the effects of bestowing entitlement and/or creating dependency."[64] They would like to turn Social Security into a means tested program without entitlements, as they have already done with TANF.

RESISTANCE

Among the opponents of privatization are unions, legal services attorneys, and welfare rights activists. Perhaps the most significant resistance to privatization in the United States is the living wage campaigns. Nationwide, 83 communities have enacted laws raising wages for thousands of low-paid workers employed by city contractors. These laws undermine the threat of privatization because contractors are less likely to bid for city services when they are required to pay higher wages, and cities are less tempted to seek to save money by privatizing services.[65]

We do not fight for public rather private programs because we assume that government programs are necessarily better. A public prison is still a prison. A government that wants welfare recipients to get into the low-wage labor market will force them there whether it pays public employees or private employees to do it. Even when their jobs are alienating, it is understandable that public employees would fight for their jobs whether they are in a prison or in a welfare department. Still, public employees are not engaged in making profits for their employer. They are less likely to be engaged in corruption because it is in the state's interest to control costs. And public employees who are unionized are more likely to fight for better wages and working conditions, which could help clients in the long run. It is in our interest to fight against privatization because companies are interested in profit, not human needs. As humanists, we are fighting not just for jobs, but also for a humane society. We want nothing less than democratic control of all of society's institutions. That begins with defending, expanding, improving and—yes—democratizing the public sector, not with capitulating to the parochial needs of property and profit making.

NOTES

1. Clinton L. Crownover and Mark Henricks, *Selling Uncle Sam.* New York: McGraw-Hill, 1993.
2. Ira W. Lieberman and Christopher D. Kirkness, eds., *Privatization and emerging equity markets.* Washington, DC: The World Bank, 1998.
3. Stephen H. Linder, "Coming to terms with the public-private partnership," *American Behavioral Scientist*, vol. 43, no. 1, September 1999, p. 38.
4. Lieberman and Kirkness, *Privatization and emerging equity markets*, pp. 3–4.
5. Eric R. Kingson and James H. Schulz, eds. *Social security in the 21st century.* New York: Oxford University Press, 1977, p. 286.
6. U.S. General Accounting Office. "Social service privatization: Expansion poses challenges in ensuring accountability for program results." Publication no. GAO/HEHS-98-6. Washington, DC: October 1997.
7. David Pace, "US awards billions without competition, analysis discloses," *Boston Globe*, April 1, 2002, p. A3.
8. Michael Rubinkam and Marycaire Dale, "Pa. youths jailed for cash?" *Boston Globe*, February 12, 2009, p. A10.
9. Mark Carl Rom, "From welfare state to opportunity, inc.: Public-private partnerships in welfare reform," in *American Behavioral Scientist*, vol. 43, no. 1, September 1999, p. 166.
10. Eliott D. Sclar, *You don't always get what you pay for: The economics of privatization.* A Century Foundation Book. Ithaca, NY: Cornell University Press, 2000, p. 132.
11. Pat Gowens, "Press conference in DC exposes Wisconsin's bloated welfare empire," press release, January 6, 2002.
12. Associated Press Financial Wire, "Medicaid contractor settles fraud claims," July 23, 2007.
13. Garrett Therolf, "Low-rated firm fights to keep rich county work," *Los Angeles Times*, October 30, 2008.
14. Ibid.

15. Stephen Rathgeb Smith and Michael Lipsky, *Nonprofits for hire: The welfare state in the age of contracting.* Cambridge, MA: Harvard University Press, 1993.
16. Gowens, "Press conference."
17. Laurence E. Lynn, Jr., "Social services and the state: The public appropriation of private charity," *Social Service Review*, vol. 76, no. 1, March 2002, p. 73.
18. Marguerite G. Rosenthal, "Public or private children' services? Privatization in retrospect," *Social Service Review*, June 2000, p. 283.
19. Ibid., pp. 63, 64.
20. John Hall and William D. Eggers. "Health and social services in the post-welfare state: Are vouchers the answer?" Policy Study no. 192. Reason Public Policy Institute, Los Angeles, 1995.
21. Lynn, "Social services and the state," p. 70.
22. Rathgeb Smith and Lipsky, *Nonprofits for hire.*
23. Food stamps are now called Supplemental Nutrition Assistance Program (SNAP).
24. Ken Kusmer, "U.S. agency tightens oversight of FSSA outsourcing," *Associated Press*, March 15, 2007.
25. Ken Kusmer, "Problems noted in privatizing welfare eligibility," *Associated Press*, June 29, 2007.
26. Ken Kusmur "AP Exclusive: Feds chide FSSA on privatized plan for food stamps," *Associated Press*, July 18, 2007.
27. Ken Kusmur, "Feds approve FSSA steps to fix privatization plan," *Associated Press*, August 15, 2007.
28. Ken Kusmur, "FSSA drops 30-day food stamp processing proposal," *Associated Press*, September 4, 2008.
29. Center for Public Policy Priorities. "The policy page: Privatization of health and human services eligibility determination." No. 56. Austin, TX: CPPP, September 1, 1997.
30. *Privatization of welfare services: A review of the literature,* http://aspe.hhs.gov/hsp/privatization02/htm
31. PR Newswire, "Lockheed Martin awarded contract to expand its federal occupational health services: Corporation to provide clinical services across the U.S.," September 17, 2008.
32. Mary Bryna Sanger, "When the private sector competes." Reform Watch brief no. 3, Center for Public Service. Washington, DC. Brookings Institutions, October 2001.
33. Business Wire, "Maximus awarded $8.1 million welfare-to-work contract by Los Angeles County," May 19, 2008.
34. *Privatization of Welfare Services,* p. 6.
35. Ibid., p. 7.
36. Food and Nutrition Service, United States Department of Agriculture, "Food Stamp Electronic Benefit Transfer Systems: A Report to Congress," October 2003.

37. Ibid.
38. Gowens, "Press conference."
39. Rom, "From welfare state to opportunity, inc.," p. 170.
40. Ibid., p. 166.
41. The term "self-sufficiency" is an ideologically loaded term, and it is widely used when talking about welfare recipients. It implies that welfare recipients have been "dependent" and unmotivated to work for a living. I prefer the term "economic stability." No one is "self-sufficient"; we all need various kinds of support from other people.
42. William D. Eggers, and Raymond Ng. "Social and health service privatization: A survey of county and state governments." Policy Study No. 168, Privatization Center. Los Angeles: Reason Foundation, October 1993.
43. Keon S. Chi, and Cindy Jasper, *Private practices: A review of privatization in state government* Lexington, KY: The Council of State Governments, 1998.
44. Sclar, *You don't always get what you pay for.*
45. Jonathan Walters, "Welfare privatization: The welfare bonanza," *Governing Magazine*, January 2000.
46. Susan Jacoby, "Keeping the faith, ignoring the history," *New York Times*, March 1, 2009, p. wk 11.
47. Ibid.
48. Ibid.
49. Alisa Valdes-Rodriguez, "State funding of nonprofits escalates: Some worry about loss of independence." *Boston Globe*, September 12, 1998.
50. Christopher Giangreco, " 'I'm just their case manager': The influence of privatization on social service providers' work." Dissertation Abstracts International, A: "The Humanities and Social Sciences, vol. 67, no. 8, February 2007.
51. The Associated Press State & Local Wire, "Florida report criticizes Sarasota foster care agency," Tallahassee, Fla., October 31, 2007.
52. Brinton H. Milward, and Keith G. Provan, "The hollow state: Private provision of public services, in *Public Policy for Democracy*, edited by Helen Ingram and Steven Rathgeb Smith. Washington, DC: Brookings Institution, 1993, pp. 222–237.
53. *Privatization of Welfare Services*, p. 22.
54. Nancy Folbre, *Economies of Care*, unpublished manuscript, 2008.
55. Nina Bernstein, *The lost children of wilder.* New York: Vintage Books, 2001.
56. Peter Frumkin and Alice Andre-Clark, "The rise of the corporate social worker," *Society*, vol. 36, no. 6, September/October 1999, p. 48.
57. Ann Withorn, "Friends or foes? Nonprofits and the puzzle of welfare reform," *The Annals of the American Academy of Political and Social Science*, September 2001, p. 112.

58. Ibid., p. 114.
59. Stewart Player and Allyson M. Pollock, "Long-term care: From public responsibility to private good," *Critical Social Policy Ltd.*, vol. 21, no. 2, Thousand Oaks, CA: Sage Publications, May 2001, p. 248.
60. Ibid., p. 249.
61. Business Wire, "Maximus completes sale of non-core businesses," September 30, 2008.
62. A. C. Laurell and O. L. Arellano, "Market commodities and poor relief: The World Bank proposal for health," *International Journal of Health Services*, vol. 26, no. 1, 1996, pp. 1–18.
63. Karen Glumm and Jennifer D. Johnson, "Creating the 'Unfit': Social darwinism or social triage?" *Journal of Applied Behavioral Science*, vol. 37, no. 2, June 2001, p. 155.
64. Robert B. Hudson, "Conflict in today's aging politics: New population encounters old ideology," *Social Service Review*, vol. 73, no. 3, September 1999, pp. 370–371.
65. Steven Greenhouse, "'Living Wage' roulette: Bigger check, or will it be a pink slip?" *New York Times*, May 19, 2002, p. 25.

CHAPTER 5

Shelters for the Homeless: A Feeble Response to Homelessness

Betty Reid Mandell

How would you like someone to say to you, "Come with me into the bathroom? I want to watch you pee into this paper cup to see if you have been taking drugs." That is what is happening in some shelters for homeless families in Massachusetts. Steve Valero, a lawyer at Greater Boston Legal Services, is indignant about this and has been telling shelters that it is an illegal practice. Some shelter directors claim they had no idea it was illegal. They thought it would be better to have all residents tested for drugs rather than singling out one person.

Valero said that he tells those directors they have it backward. It might be legal to single out a person whom you suspect of being on drugs if that person was behaving as if she is drugged—for example, if she seems completely stoned and is neglecting her kids. But to test everybody routinely is an illegal invasion of privacy.

One shelter resident said that she had to undergo drug testing every week for more than 40 weeks, with a staff member watching her pee, even though she has never taken drugs.

The war on drugs has invaded shelters for the homeless, treating homeless people as criminals. In this chapter I discuss the causes of homelessness, how the shelter system, which was presumably a temporary response to homelessness, has become institutionalized as the dominant response, and how it is used for social control. I discuss the various approaches to ending homelessness, many of them distractions from the main cause—poverty.

STRUCTURAL CAUSES OF HOMELESSNESS

Although there have always been some homeless people, their numbers increased dramatically during the Reagan administration. The federal government cut back on building houses and subsidizing housing for low-income people as well as social assistance programs. Urban renewal and gentrification forced people out of low-rent housing, and wages declined with deindustrialization and outsourcing. Cities used land use policies to help corporations and real estate interests squeeze out the poor.[1] A study by Harvard's Joint Center for Housing Studies documents that as housing costs have risen, wages have declined, increasing numbers of people cannot afford housing (including the middle class), and more jobs pay low wages. Hurricane Katrina made matters worse:

> In New Orleans, losses are estimated at over $100 billion, more than 50,000 homes have suffered severe damage, and hundreds of thousands of residents are still waiting to return…With the enormous political and logistical obstacles to rebuilding that now exist, it will be years before the Gulf region of the country works through the disruption to human lives and the destruction to the built environment.[2]

Immediately after the hurricane, the Federal Emergency Management Agency (FEMA) provided 134,000 temporary trailers and mobile homes to house people. After formaldehyde and toxics were found in the trailers, the federal government made it a priority to vacate the temporary trailers. In June 2009, FEMA and HUD (Housing and Urban Development) announced programs to help move residents from the trailers, including $50 million in housing vouchers. Four years since Hurricane Katrina, there were still nearly 3,000 mobile homes and trailers across the Gulf Coast housing victims of that disaster.[3]

Even with low wages, many poor people could afford housing if they had access to government-subsidized public housing. However, the federal government has been cutting back on building houses and providing subsidies for housing since the early 1980s. The federal government chose to subsidize private housing for poor people through Section 8 vouchers rather than build housing because it did not want to interfere with private real estate interests. Real estate interests have decimated rent control in most cities, as rents continue to rise beyond the ability of low-income people, and even middle-income people, to pay them.

The federal government has spent much more on tax benefits for homeownership than for housing the poor. The Western Regional Advocacy Project said that every year since 1981, tax benefits for homeownership have exceeded HUD's entire budget and have dwarfed direct expenditures for programs that aid low-income renters. Those benefiting the most from this tax program may actually be banks and real estate corporations that make their largest profit margins on high-end housing.[4]

The U.S. government is spending nearly 65 percent less on developing and maintaining affordable housing for poor people than it did in 1978; $83 billion was appropriated in 1978, while only $29 billion was allocated in 2005. Since 1978, annual tax expenditures for subsidies to middle-class and affluent homeowners have grown from less than $40 billion to more than $120 billion per year. From 1976 to 1982, HUD built 755,000 new public housing units, but since 1983 only 256,000.[5] In recent years, more than 200,000 private-sector rental units have been lost annually, and 1.2 million unsubsidized affordable housing units disappeared from 1993 to 2003.[6]

As the government cut funds for housing, it increased military spending. "The U.S. government plans to spend more money on *one* destroyer than it spent on *all* 2005 capital expenses for public housing; more on *ten* F-22 fighter jets than on *all* 2005 operating expenses for public housing; and *twice as much* on a *single* submarine than on *all* McKinney-Vento Act homeless assistance."[7] With the Iraq and Afghanistan wars, defense funding has continued to increase.

Homeless Shelters

Beginning in 1983, emergency public shelters for the homeless began opening in cities nationwide. Over the next couple of decades, shelters grew from being a temporary emergency response to become a permanent shelter industry. There were 62,000 homeless shelters in the United States in 2002.

Most homeless shelters for individuals allow people to stay only at night to sleep. A reason frequently given for not allowing people to stay during the day is that the homeless are expected to spend their days looking for work and housing. There are a few day shelters, such as St. Francis House in Boston, where homeless people congregate and eat their meals.

There are specialized shelters for victims of domestic violence, for teen parents, for substance abusers, and for persons with HIV/AIDS. Some shelters provide services, such as a soup kitchen, job seeking skills training and job training, job placement, support groups, information and referral services, substance abuse treatment, early intervention programs, parental skills training, training for the General Education Development (GED), playrooms for children and volunteers to staff them. Haley House in Boston, a shelter for individuals modeled after the Catholic Worker houses of hospitality, trains residents to be bakers, and they sell their products to the public. Kip Tiernan, a radical feminist who founded Rosie's Place, a shelter for homeless women in Boston, also founded a shelter for women with AIDS and a homeless women's chorus that performs at fundraisers. There are flowers on the table at the women's shelter, reflecting Kip's belief that people need beauty as well as bread ("Give us bread and give us roses.")

Many shelters do not provide storage space for people's belongings. While I was doing outreach in a welfare office, I met a woman who was crippled with severe arthritis and had stayed overnight at a shelter for individuals. The shelter had no lockers, and she was carrying her belongings in a plastic bag. There was no guarantee that she would get a bed for that night because the shelter required people to line up at 4:30 p.m., and those who were first in line got priority for shelter.

Many homeless individuals will not go to a homeless shelter because they are crowded and dangerous. If there is no place to store belongings, they often are stolen. Some of the residents have emotional problems that are exacerbated, or caused by, their homelessness. To avoid these dangerous conditions, some people sleep in the streets, in parks, in their cars, RVs, or in train or bus stations. Some live in tents in the woods or build temporary shelters in out-of-the-way spaces in the city, which are often torn down by the city. Some homeless people prefer the freedom and privacy they have in their own encampments to rigidly controlled shelters.[8] As the current recession has deepened and increasing numbers of people lose their homes and their jobs, tent cities have sprung up in many cities, reminiscent of the "Hoovervilles" of the Great Depression.

In Massachusetts, some families are lodged in hotels or motels, which cost up to $100 a night. For that money, the state could rent three apartments. The motels are located on highways where there is no easy access to grocery shopping and often not even a hot plate for cooking. Some motels have had roaches, lice, or rats. Couples on one-night stands, as well as prostitutes and pimps frequented some motels. One woman complained that there were keg parties all night and banging on the walls. Parents complained that it was an inappropriate environment for their children. Yet some parents preferred staying in the better motels rather than in a congregate shelter because they had more privacy and less intrusive inspection.

Some Massachusetts families are sheltered in private apartments, an arrangement called "scattered site shelters." Families prefer these to congregate shelters, although their freedom is restricted even in these apartments because they have strict rules, such as not allowing visitors, telling parents to keep their children quiet, imposing curfews, not allowing any alcoholic beverages, and making unannounced visits to check on housekeeping. During my outreach work at the welfare office, I met a man who lived in one of these apartments. He said, "They can inspect your apartment any time they want, without prior notice. They are very fussy about housekeeping. If you don't have the corners of your sheets tight, they can sanction you. After three sanctions, you have to leave." He was angry at the way he and his wife were treated, but he had to hold it in because there is no place else to go. He said, "They force you to save money in the shelter. When I was working I was earning $800 a month, and they tried to force me to save $500 a month, which was completely unreasonable." One woman who lived in a scattered site shelter was resentful about being constantly nagged about housekeeping. She said, "When I get my own place, I will leave it messy for a week, even though that's not my nature, just to celebrate not having anyone checking on me."

ACCESS TO SHELTERS

Most shelters for individuals operate on a first come, first served basis, although most refuse people who are drunk or abusing drugs. Family shelters have eligibility criteria that vary from agency to agency and from state to state. In Massachusetts, the eligibility criteria stipulate that a family should have no more income than 130 percent of the federal poverty line. The legislature lowered it to 100 percent a few years ago, but advocates lobbied aggressively to bring it back up to 130 percent. If a family has $1 over that amount, they are not eligible.

Undocumented immigrants are allowed access to shelters only if a child was born in the United States and is therefore a citizen. For legal immigrants to be eligible, at least one family member must be a citizen or a legally present immigrant.

A list of family shelters published by the Massachusetts Coalition for the Homeless[9] shows that some family shelters do not accept adolescent boys. The age limits they set vary from 12 to 18. Some accept women and children only. One shelter accepts women and children only, but no boys over age nine. The welfare department accepts men as part of the family only if the man is the father of the children. No boy friends are allowed.

The application process for admission to a family shelter is grueling. Workers are obsessed with documents. The goal is to keep people out, not to let them in. One worker told a mother to look through her high school yearbook and ask anyone she knows to give her a place to stay. Workers ask endless questions, some of them intimate.

One man living in a shelter had this to say about the application process: "When I was working I didn't want my boss to know I was in a shelter because he was a Bush guy, hard nosed and beer drinking. However, the worker insisted on contacting my former employer. It didn't matter at that point because I no longer had the job, but workers do what they can to humiliate you and take your dignity."

When a family has been accepted for shelter, they have to wait in the waiting room to find out what shelter they have been assigned to. This can take hours. The wait to see a worker to apply can also take hours. According to DTA regulations, families should be placed within 20 miles of their homes, but if there is no shelter available within that distance, they can be placed hundreds of miles away. If a closer shelter becomes available later, they are supposed to be moved to that shelter. A placement far from home means of course that they are removed from family and friends, from familiar or specialized medical care, from jobs, and from school. Victims of domestic violence are always moved far from home in order to escape the victimizer. Families with a compelling reason to stay close to home, such as need for specialized medical treatment, may be placed in a hotel or motel temporarily until shelter space opens up.

As part of the application process, mothers are required to be interviewed by a DSS (Department of Social Services) worker who assesses their situation in relation to the children's welfare. Mothers are terrified of this, fearing the possibility of having their children taken away and placed in foster care. I never saw a case where this interview resulted in taking the child away, but it always creates anxiety in parents, and gives them continued anxiety while in shelter about the possibility of being charged with child abuse or neglect. One mother who was applying for shelter told the DSS worker that she and the child had slept in a car last night. The worker said this constituted child abuse and could result in the child being placed in foster care. However, the mother was given shelter. (Many of the children have been placed in foster care because the family had no home.)

Life in the Shelter

The following discussion applies mostly to homeless shelters in Massachusetts. I have neither studied shelters for individuals or battered women's shelters intensively nor have I studied shelters in other states. However, Massachusetts has the reputation of being one of the better states in shelter provision. Most of my information has been obtained through six years of doing outreach in welfare offices and from interviews with shelter staff and residents; legal services lawyers, Massachusetts Coalition for the Homeless staff, welfare staff, and observations of shelters.

Shelter programs are shaped by prevailing views of the poor, who are considered to be generally inadequate and incompetent and in need of reform. In *"A Roof Over my Head,"* Jean Calterone Williams expresses this well:

> By making many aspects of their programs mandatory...shelters give the impression that homeless people will not take the initiative on their own to look for work or housing, enroll their children in school, or keep their living spaces clean. They must be forced to do so. By mandating budgeting classes, shelters suggest that people become homeless in part because they are irresponsible with their money. It is in a sense a symbiotic relationship: shelter programs influence the ways housed people think about homelessness, the views of the housed public—whether ordinary citizens or policymakers—affect the formation of shelter programs and how such programs treat homeless people.[10]

Once a family is placed in a family shelter under the DTA Emergency Assistance (EA) program, they must follow certain rules to retain shelter. A family is terminated from EA shelter after two noncompliances, and they are not eligible for shelter again for a year. These are some of the expectations placed on families after they enter shelter:

- *Develop and comply with a self-sufficiency plan.* Some of the goals included in self-sufficiency plans include housing search, work requirements, resolution of outstanding arrest warrants, and savings requirements. Parents are required to save a certain percent of their income for an apartment, ranging from 30 to 50 percent. When they are allowed to keep their food stamps, they are expected to save more toward an apartment.

If the family does not meet the goals in the self-sufficiency plan, they can lose shelter.

- *Accept any offer of safe, permanent housing.* A rejection will result in the family being cited for noncompliance, with a few exceptions.
- Follow TAFDC (Transitional Assistance for Families with Dependent Children) work requirements (These are discussed in "Appendix: Current Safety Net Programs.")
- *Comply with shelter rules.* Each shelter makes its own rules.
- *Maintain employment.* If a family has quit a job or reduced income while in shelter without "good cause," they can be terminated from shelter.

Families can appeal unfavorable decisions and sometimes win, although they lose more often.

Shelter rules vary, but all have curfews. The most lenient curfew cited in *Down and Out*[11] was 9:30 weekdays, 11 on weekends. The strictest was St. Ambrose Family Inn, which had an 8:00 p.m. curfew every night of the week. Shelters allow overnight absences only with written permission. An unauthorized absence can result in losing shelter. All shelters require sobriety on the premises; one requires a minimum of six months sobriety before being accepted for shelter.

Most shelters require residents to help with housekeeping. In some shelters, women buy and cook their own food. Some shelters allow visits by fathers, but do not allow fathers to live there. Some shelters require residents to attend church on Sunday.

The strictest shelter that I found in my study was St. Ambrose Family Inn in Boston, a shelter for 15 families run by Catholic Charities. There are 14 pages of rules in the "Family Guide"[12] given to residents. Here are a few of them:

- Personal belongings may be inspected prior to room assignment and at any time during residency at St. Ambrose.
- Residents may be required to copy their passport for St. Ambrose records.
- St. Ambrose will conduct a CORI (Criminal Offender Record Information).
- When applicable, drug-screening verification will be required.
- If a room becomes cluttered, the resident will be asked to remove any excessive items within 24 hours.
- Wall hangings are not allowed in resident rooms or bathrooms.
- Residents are not allowed to lie on or place their feet on the TV room couches or chair.
- A towel wrapped around a person is not appropriate. Robes with undergarments must be worn if a resident is walking from her bathroom to her room.

- Residents are not allowed in other residents' rooms at any time.
- Residents are required to attend all meetings with the Family Advocate or Case Managers as scheduled.
- St. Ambrose reserves the right to schedule a mandatory house meeting or training at any time.
- Staff members are required by law to report any abuse or neglect of a child to the Department of Social Services. All residents and parents should be aware of this type of report, which is called a 51-A.
- All children are required to be off the first floor by 8:30 PM and all residents in their rooms by 9:00 PM seven days a week.
- By 9:00 PM everything should be quiet in the building. Noise should be kept to a minimum after this hour. Music, radios, and TVs should not be heard outside the rooms in which they are playing.
- FOOD IS ALLOWED IN THE DINING ROOM ONLY. FOOD IS NOT ALLOWED IN THE RESIDENTS' ROOMS, TV ROOM OR HALLWAYS. ONLY WATER IS ALLOWED IN THE RESIDENT ROOMS (NO JUICE, SODA, SWEETENED MILK, etc.) (Emphasis in the original.)
- Families are required to keep their rooms clean. The rooms may be inspected daily by the St. Ambrose Shelter staff.
- It is recommended that residents not lend money to or borrow money from other residents who live at the shelter.
- Shelter staff is not allowed to lend money to or borrow money from a resident.

Any failure to the above may result in a written warning with the possibility of termination of shelter placement at St. Ambrose. *A resident is allowed three written warnings before restrictions are imposed and/or termination procedures from St. Ambrose may be put in place. A resident may be terminated at any time for Health & Safety reasons. Copies of all warnings are sent to the local DTA office for review.* (Emphasis in the original.)

In other words, anything that makes you feel at home is forbidden.

During my outreach work in the welfare office, I heard a variety of opinions about shelters from the residents and ex-residents, ranging from "It's like a prison" to "It's pretty good." Here are some of the comments, taken from my log:

- One woman told me that shelter staff threaten mothers with filing a petition of abuse against them for minor things such as letting a baby sleep in a baby swing. Her toddler had a minor fall on his bum and the staff said she had to take the child to the emergency room, even though there was not even a bruise. The doctor ridiculed her for bringing the child into the hospital when there was no evidence of injury.
- A woman is living in a Christian shelter. She has two young children. She fears that her children will catch an infection or get lead paint

poisoning. Another resident sued the shelter because her child ate lead chips, and the director of the shelter asked all the residents to sign a statement saying they won't sue them. This woman refused to do it. The shelter is very controlling, won't let anyone go out of the house unless a staff member goes with her. The woman works and says they can't control her. The only thing she likes about the place is the prayer meetings. She is here in the welfare office to request another shelter.

- A woman in the homeless unit had been kicked out of the shelter in the YMCA because she was in the hospital in a coma and had not been able to call them. She said, "I couldn't even call myself; I was in a coma."
- A woman has been kicked out of a shelter for burning some toast in a microwave. Another was kicked out of a shelter a year ago and can't get into a shelter for another several months. She had not realized that you could not get help for another year.
- A woman is in Pine Street Inn (a shelter for individuals). She has a 14-year-old son but they could not find a shelter that would take her son. She is on the waiting list for one, but has to find someone to take care of him soon because her sister cannot do it any more.
- A young woman was in a teen shelter and was sanctioned because she did not attend school daily. She could not attend daily because she had various appointments to keep, and because she was depressed. Being homeless made her more depressed. (Studies show that a large proportion of shelters residents and welfare recipients are depressed.)
- A woman said that being in a shelter is like being in prison. They keep checking up on you, criticizing your housekeeping, the children's noise, and so on. They treat you like a child. She has had to move several times, and this is not good for the children. Yesterday she was running around all day looking for furniture, getting documents, and so on, and she is exhausted. She is lucky in having a good support group, including good doctors, and relatives who help her out.
- A man with a boy about 8 or 9 wanted to talk with me privately so other people would not hear. Although he is not the father of the boy who is with him, he has custody. The child was sexually abused in a shelter and is terrified of going back to any shelter. He does not want to live with his mother because the mother has abused him and her boy friend smokes crack. He lived with his grandmother for a while but his uncle, who lived there, used heroin. Both the court and DSS are involved. The DTA worker said they want to place him in Springfield, but the boy needs to stay in the Boston area because he is disturbed and is in counseling and is also in a special school. He has attention deficit disorder. The worker also offered to place him in Stoughton, but that won't work either.
- A woman in the Homeless Unit had been kicked out of her shelter today, accused of swearing at a staff member. She was extremely upset, insisting that she had not sworn, and they admitted they would believe a staff

member rather than her. Other women waiting in the Homeless Unit sympathized with her.

Some mothers generally liked their shelter but did not like some of the staff:

- A woman likes the director Lara, thinks she is on the side of the women and really wants to help them. But she does not like David. He tells her that she cannot "just sit around doing nothing." She said that one young woman in the shelter who "was raised in the streets and has street toughs" lost it one day and told David that she was going to kill some people around here, meaning David. David told all the other residents to get in their room "just in case," but the woman pointed out to me laughingly that she didn't want to kill them, she wanted to kill David. She said that while she has learned to hold herself in, she does enjoy watching someone else express the anger that all of them feel.

The woman says this is one of the better shelters. She has her own room, comfortably furnished with a couch and a refrigerator. There is a common kitchen where the food is delivered and you can either eat there or take your food to your room. The food is not all that great, but is o.k. sometimes. The woman has been here for three months. Some people stay a year. She longs to get her own apartment, and dreams that she has one.

Some people understood the need for rules. One man said, "They have to have rules, otherwise people would be going in and out all night and they couldn't handle it." He felt it was a small enough price to pay for getting shelter, and he appreciated the help.

Conflicts often arise over the work and the housing search requirements. Housing workers are sometimes merciless in hounding women to find an apartment, even though there is little that the women can do to find affordable housing when it simply does not exist. One shelter director said they have a grievance policy, but residents are not allowed to grieve any shelter policies. (That struck me as an Alice in Wonderland sort of grievance policy.) She claimed that they promote resident participation by having weekly meetings, with rotating elected representatives.

RACE

Staffs of shelters are most often middle class and white while the residents in Massachusetts's shelters are predominantly people of color, especially in large cities. People of color make up the majority of the homeless nationwide. A survey by the U.S. Conference of Mayors in 2004 estimated the homeless population to be 49 percent African American, 35 percent white, 13 percent Hispanic, 2 percent Native American, and 1 percent Asian.[13] A black woman who worked in one of the better shelters, run by Catholic nuns, reports that the condescending attitudes of staff toward the black residents drove her nuts.

Jean Calterone Williams studied shelters in Phoenix, where the majority of shelter residents were white and found a great deal of racism toward Chicana women. One woman complained about an employee who "used to whisper in the women's ears who couldn't speak English, saying they need to go back to their own countries." (The woman was evicted from the shelter for complaining.)[14] Williams says that white workers sometimes gave preferential treatment to white residents. White homeless women often attempt to distance themselves from women of color in an attempt to appear more "deserving." This reflects the views of housed white people. Williams says that in Phoenix, where racism runs high, "white housed people perceive Latinos—in particular Chicanos—as too 'different' to be considered American, regardless of their citizenship status...These housed people claim that poor or homeless Chicanos are to blame for their own circumstances because they do not want to work to climb the social or economic ladder."[15]

Williams found that in Phoenix, which has a large Spanish-speaking community, most shelters lacked even one Spanish-speaking staff person and did not offer programs for women who are in the country illegally. Because monolingual Spanish-speaking women often could not find a battered women's shelter with a Spanish-speaking staff person, a local Chicano/a advocacy group established La Casa, a Spanish-speaking shelter for battered women. La Casa and Rose's House, another shelter for battered women, treated women more compassionately than did other shelters for the homeless, and had a more home-like atmosphere. "La Casa seems less interested in keeping residents under constant surveillance than is the case at the homeless shelters."[16] (Probably shelters that were established because of the women's movement and the civil rights struggle are more compassionate.)

Women of color who apply for shelter cannot necessarily count on getting more sympathetic treatment from a worker of their own race. Workers sometimes distance themselves from clients because of their anxiety about status, their contempt for people they view as "lower class," and their fears about their own fragile economic status.

Shelter Workers

Most of the shelter staff that I talked with had a victim-blaming attitude. One shelter director said, "They all come from dysfunctional families, but they are capable of change." One shelter in an affluent community assigns a volunteer "mentor" to each resident. These are upper-middle-class women whose goal is to help the residents change; thereby conveying the message that their mentor assumes something is wrong with them. Some of these women do have valuable things to give the residents, such as help in locating financial aid for college, giving rides to job interviews, caring for their children while the mothers rest or take care of errands, tutoring children or tutoring the mother for a GED, or teaching computer skills. But to call them "mentors" rather than "community resources" implies that they are on a superior plane.

Some shelter workers are genuinely caring. One resident said that the shelter director "is like a grandmother to me." Such workers help women find and use resources and help them with personal problems, and sometimes follow up with them after they leave the shelter. Many shelter residents are grateful for the services offered by the shelters, but they are always aware that the main goal of the shelter is to get them out of there and to get them off welfare.

Even staff members who are aware of the structural problems that the residents face nevertheless consider it their job to enforce the rules. Yet some are flexible in the way they enforce the rules and bend them as much as possible. Some, however, deny that there are major structural reasons for homelessness. When I asked a shelter worker what she thought was the cause of homelessness, she said that some women who refuse to follow rules, such as meeting regularly with the housing search worker, just prefer to be homeless. They like being taken care of in the shelter without any responsibilities, and they would rather be homeless than to follow rules.

A director of a shelter for teen parents expressed her frustration with her inability to help residents find housing and pay for it when they found it. She said, "They just go from a teen shelter to an adult shelter." Although she enjoyed her work with the residents and they liked her and liked the shelter, she felt hopeless about the job as it felt like putting Band-Aids on a gaping wound. I empathized with her and said that I often feel the same way. I told her that it helps me to get involved in some kind of social action that might help to change the situation, such as a forthcoming lobby day sponsored by the Massachusetts Coalition for the Homeless. She planned to attend and bring some of the residents with her. I put her in touch with a local organizing group, the Coalition against Poverty. (Interestingly, she is the daughter of a woman who was in my social work class when I taught at Bridgewater State College.)

Shelters may ultimately be more expensive than permanent housing. Many people believe this despite that, cities rely on shelters because building housing would compete with the real estate industry and would establish government responsibility to provide housing for people. And there is money to be made in the shelter industry. "In the mid-1980s, one-third of New York City's welfare hotel business went to two separate business partnerships that together grossed $25 million in rents."[17] New York City sold some welfare hotels that the city owned and contracted with the owners to house the homeless, "paying them $1.2 million a year to house families in a hotel that it had owned outright just four years earlier."[18]

Most family shelters are run by nonprofit agencies, and they get much of their funding from the state through the welfare department, as well as from private sources. Churches run many of them. Most are scrambling for money, and they are consequently eager to please funders. This often results in "creaming" the population, that is, accepting people who are most likely to change in desired directions. It also results in adhering to the status quo rather than trying any radical change. Vincent Lyon-Callo tells of organizing the homeless and their allies in western Massachusetts to take over buildings of an abandoned state mental hospital to create housing for the homeless. Organizing for the action took place under the auspices of a local shelter for the homeless. Several local politicians were quite upset by this event and the media coverage. They reacted by blaming the shelter staff for stirring up trouble and portrayed those involved in the takeover as "outsiders." People connected with the shelter received threats of decreased support and funding for the shelter from local business and political leaders. A few months later the staff learned that funding from the state had been decreased by almost 20 percent for the coming year, and they had to cut staff.

Most significantly, however, was the imposition of awareness among remaining staff that their assigned role was clearly limited to that of reforming homeless people and managing homelessness if they wanted to keep their job. Consequently, most staff members returned to the more familiar roles of treating deviance and surveillance of homeless people.[19]

WELFARE WORKERS

The workers in the welfare office are overworked and underpaid, although they are paid more than workers in the private sector (as in shelters) because they have a union. The leadership of the union is relatively progressive. Robert Haines, the director of AFL-CIO in Massachusetts, grew up in a family that received welfare, and he mentions this in speeches to welfare recipients and advocates.[20] He opposed the harsh welfare reform bill in Massachusetts, but the union did not exert much pressure to lobby against it, and most welfare workers do not engage in activism to change welfare policy. Yet two union leaders who were welfare workers joined in an alliance with recipients called Working Mass. The union and welfare rights activists joined in struggles where they have a common interest such as getting lower case loads and resisting the closing of welfare offices. But there are issues where their interests diverge. When clients and their advocates complain of nasty treatment by workers, welfare directors claim that, while they can talk to disrespectful workers, they are unable to fire them because the union protects workers.

Most of the workers perform like automated bureaucrats. They conduct the interview in a routine way. They enter data into the computer, often with difficulty because of the intricacies of their computer program, named Beacon, elude them and they must call a supervisor in to figure it out. They sometimes make mistakes and sometimes lose documents, but they seldom apologize. They often keep clients waiting, even when the client has an appointment. One woman said, "They act like it's their own money they're giving out."

Some workers are genuinely friendly and helpful, and the clients appreciate having one of those. One client said, "My worker is wonderful. She really helps me." A few will bend the rules as much as possible. During one interview when a client was told that she earned too much to be eligible for shelter, I suggested to the client that she lower her working hours. The worker said, "I didn't hear that."

But there are a few really nasty ones. Here are clients' comments about unsympathetic workers:

- This man had a worker who was "right out of Beavis and Butt Head. He looked just like Beavis, with a pointy head." The man gave a letter to the worker from his grandmother that said he could no longer reside with her and the worker said, "I want a letter in lay language." The man was amazed and angry because the letter was perfectly clear, but he had to get another letter from his grandmother.
- A woman was angry with her worker and said, "He has a bad attitude, and talks down like you're stupid. A lot of people complain about him. I had a worker before who was o.k. He understood my problems of having no car and no phone that made it hard to get in for appointments. I am trying to get medical disability and the doctor is filling out the form, but it takes time and this worker doesn't want to wait."

Even when workers do not agree with welfare policies, they feel that it is their job to follow them. Here is an example of such a worker:

- The client's 18-month-old child is a Family Cap baby,[21] and she has a 9-year-old daughter. The worker had her sign the form from DOR (Department of Revenue, which enforces child support) that asks about sexual intercourse with the child's father. She was deeply offended by the form, and I agreed with her. I asked the worker if she would jeopardize her benefits if she refused to sign it. He said she could write a statement saying she refused to sign it, and he would send it to the central office, and it would not jeopardize her benefits. However, the woman decided to sign it "and get it over with." The worker also did not like the form, and he did not agree with the Family Cap. He asked me who brought in that policy, and I told him that it was President Clinton who signed the bill. He was surprised, but we agreed that Clinton was more a Republican than a Democrat.

The Myth of Altruism

Michael Lipsky points out "Virtually every commentary on welfare practices draws attention to the degradation of clients."[22] Poor people receive a qualitatively different kind of treatment than middle-class people. "The ideology that street-level bureaucrats' intervention is in the interest of clients appears to be a particularly important instrument of control."[23] Lipsky calls this "the myth of altruism... This myth is usually unexamined. Social workers believe they are helping others and clients are encouraged to confide in and trust strangers and permit themselves to be manipulated and ordered about in the expectation of receiving help or fair treatment."[24] Yet social workers[25] are thrown into the most difficult work without the resources to adequately accomplish that work. To cope with the stress of being unable to individualize clients and respond to their needs, "street-level bureaucrats develop conceptions of their jobs, and of clients that reduce the strain between capabilities and goals, thereby making their jobs psychologically easier to manage."[26] Workers often begin the work as idealists, but end by getting burned out. The antidote to this is not to train the workers, but to change the conditions of work. Liberation of the client would also mean liberation of the worker.

SCRATCHING THE SURFACE

The shelter system only scratches the surface of the problem of homelessness. There are never enough shelters to house the homeless even temporarily, and practically everyone prefers to live in her or his own home rather than in a shelter. One count of the homeless in 2005 estimated that 44 percent of homeless people were unsheltered.[27] This was a rough estimate, as are all estimates of the numbers of homeless people. Counting the homeless has been described as a "high-stakes numbers game." Officials want the numbers to be low; advocates want them high, and there is continual debate about them in academic circles. It is impossible to count all of the homeless because many are not found and many are doubling up with relatives and friends. Many are homeless for only a short time. It is a revolving population. A study in 2008 by HUD found that approximately 1.6 million people used an emergency shelter between October 1, 2007 and September 30, 2008, including 516,700 people in families. Although the number of homeless individuals remained relatively stable between 2007 and 2008, the number of homeless families rose 9 percent, and in rural and suburban areas the number jumped by 56 percent. Homelessness is still concentrated in urban areas and among adult males; 20 percent of homeless people live in Los Angeles, New York, and Detroit.[28]

Women make up 81 percent of adults in homeless families. Unlike homeless men, who are usually middle-aged, homeless women tend to be younger than 25 with children younger than 5. According to Suzanne Wenzel, a social work professor at the University of Southern California School of Social Work, "The life of a homeless woman is particularly fraught with danger. These young women are at much greater risk of being victimized when they have no stable home. It can be more difficult to obtain needed services. For anyone in this situation, it is destabilizing and extremely stressful. That's why these new figures are horrifying."[29]

A growing number of children are homeless. The National Center on Family Homelessness estimates that as many as 1 in 50 U.S. children (1.5 million) are homeless or "precariously housed" in temporary quarters such as motels and shelters. As home foreclosures and job layoffs continue, the number of at-risk children will likely rise.[30]

Homelessness exposes children to a constellation of risks and hardships during crucial early stages in their development. "Without decisive action, millions of children will carry the burden of homelessness for their entire lives," says Ellen L. Bassuk, president of the National Center on Family Homelessness and professor of psychiatry at Harvard Medical School.[31]

School districts across the nation are scrambling to educate an increasing number of homeless children. "The instability can be ruinous to schooling, educators say, adding multiple moves and lost class time to the inherent distress of homelessness."[32] Since 2001, federal law has required every district to appoint a liaison to the homeless. The law requires immediate school placement without proof of residence and a right to stay in the same school as the student's home school. School districts are required to provide transportation from the shelter, motel, doubled-up houses, trailer parks, and RV campgrounds to help children stay in the familiar schools as the families move about. While the law's goals are widely praised, school superintendents complain that Congress has provided little money, adding to the fiscal woes of districts.[33]

A December 2008 annual survey of 25 major cities by the U.S. Conference of Mayors found that cities reported a 12 percent increase in homelessness from 2007 to 2008, with 16 cities citing an increase in the number of homeless families.[34]

Many veterans have become homeless. Although they are only 11 percent of the population, they make up one in four homeless people in the United States.[35] Although women's share of veterans who end up homeless is still relatively small at an estimated 6,500, their numbers have doubled over the last decade, according to the Department of Veterans Affairs. And unlike their male counterparts, many have the added burden of being a single parent. They often face unique homelessness risk factors, including sexual assault while in the military and diminished earning potential in civilian life.[36]

There has been a dramatic rise in homelessness since the foreclosure crisis began in 2007, according to a study by the National Coalition for the Homeless. Those facing homelessness include the working poor, who were among those hardest hit by the collapse in subprime mortgages, and by the foreclosures of rental properties. But others are middle-class families who never expected to find themselves unable to afford their homes or pay the rent. Michael Stoops of the National Coalition for the Homeless said, "People first try to downsize, then wind up living with family and friends or in vehicles. At the shelters, there's almost no room at the inn. It's first come, first served."[37] The public image of the homeless has been that of a man or woman living on the street and panhandling for loose change. But with the foreclosure crisis, stagnant economy, and rising unemployment, advocates for the homeless say they are seeing more two-parent families seeking shelter.[38] The National Alliance to End Homelessness warns that 1.5 million Americans could be thrown into homelessness over the next 2 years.[39]

According to a 2009 study by the Community Partnership for the Prevention of Homelessness, 24 percent of single homeless people are employed. Their meager incomes, however do not pay enough for them to afford an apartment in Washington DC, where the average rent for a 1-bedroom apartment was $1,400.[40]

Many people who had no health insurance, or had inadequate converge, are homeless because of medical expenses. Approximately 70 percent of homeless people are uninsured, with only 25 percent eligible for Medicaid, according to Michael Stoops, director of the National Coalition for Homelessness.[41]

The Obama administration said that extending publicly funded programs such as Medicaid and Medicare was essential to combating homelessness. Shaun Donovan, secretary of HUD, said there was "no question" that successful health-care reform would limit the growing number of homeless families. He also said that tackling homelessness would drive down overall medical costs, citing a study that showed that homeless people who were given supportive housing visited hospitals 42 percent less often than those who live on the street.

BLAMING THE VICTIM

I am bemused by announcements that come over the radio from time to time by foundations or institutes saying they are studying the causes of homelessness and seeking cures. In fact, the causes are quite simple and have been studied quite enough. Homelessness is caused by poverty, insufficient affordable housing and insufficient money to pay for housing, and a weak or nonexistent safety net of income maintenance and support services. It is true that many of the homeless are alcoholics or drug addicts, but they need a home while they are coping with their problem, and they need treatment programs, and both are in short supply. It is also true that many of the homeless have emotional problems. Who would not have emotional problems if they were homeless? A large percentage of homeless women have been abused.[42] Although they may need a temporary refuge to escape the abuser and counseling to help them heal, they also need permanent housing, childcare, a job that pays a living wage, and social supports.

The focus on individual problems shifts attention away from structural problems and obscures the real causes of homelessness. It leads to stereotyping of homeless people as deviant and degenerate, drunk or drugged, or crazy. When these stereotypes are embedded in people's minds, they view every beggar as a scammer. Stereotyping gives implicit permission to delinquent thugs to beat them up. One man made a series of documentaries in which homeless men fight each other, while being plied with liquor. Reality show producers took the homeless on shopping trips as a subject of amusement. On the Boston radio station WBCN-FM, Djs Opie and Anthony ran an event called the Homeless Shopping Spree, taking street people to a high-end shopping center, giving them liquor and money to shop, and ridiculing their purchases for the amusement of their listeners. Boston's Mayor Menino publicly expressed his outrage at the show.

Stereotyping the homeless leads people to view them as criminals. As the homeless population increases, cities are criminalizing homelessness by passing laws to ban panhandling and to clear city streets. They are also forcibly removing encampments of the homeless. David Metz, the Deputy Mayor of St. Petersburg said the town altered its laws because of an increase in complaints by businesses and residents about public drunkenness and public nuisances. The county's homeless population has increased 20 percent in the past 2 years. Although Metz acknowledged that there are not enough beds in shelters to accommodate all those who want them (the city says it has 2,200 people living in the streets), he said there is no reason for them to move onto a sidewalk. He said, "We are blessed to have 34 public parks in downtown St. Pete, and there's nothing to prevent any individuals from using those facilities."[43]

Six homeless people filed a lawsuit against the city. Joseph Patner, a city attorney representing St. Petersburg, said, "If you're living on a sidewalk, whether you're homeless or a millionaire, you're in violation of the ordinance."[44] Tulin Ozdeger, civil rights director for the National Law Center on Homelessness and Poverty, said, "Many people are being forced to live out on the streets. Penalizing them violates the U.S. Constitution and is inhumane."[45] Catholic Charities wanted to set up a tent city for the homeless of St. Petersburg in hardsided tents on property that the church owned. But residents protested, fearing that it would decrease property values and increase crime. At a crowded town meeting set up to discuss the proposal, city residents showed up wearing T-shirts that read "Stop Tent City."[46]

A report entitled "Homes not Handcuffs," issued in July 2009 by the National Law Center on Homelessness and Poverty and the National Coalition for the Homeless, rated Los Angeles as the meanest city in criminalizing the homeless. St. Petersburg ranked second. The report analyzed how cities target homeless people, such as laws against sleeping, eating, or sitting in public spaces. The full report is available at http://nlchp.org/content/pubs/2009HomesNotHandcuffs1.pdf

The homeless internalize the public stereotype and try to distance themselves from the "undeserving Other," however they visualize the "Other." I met many people in the welfare office who told me that they were "not like those others" who are lazy and do not want to work. I told one woman that what might look like laziness is actually depression, and she admitted that she was depressed.

Homeless men resist being categorized as "homeless" because that conjures up the image of a drunken bum. Homeless women resist being categorized as "homeless" because that conjures up the image of a crazy disheveled "bag lady." Battered women resist being described as "battered," preferring to see themselves as "survivors."

There is a hierarchy of deserving versus undeserving in the public's mind. Battered women are seen as deserving because they are victims. Parents and children are more deserving than single men because children are innocent victims. Homeless men are the least deserving, because they should be working. These "social imaginary significations," as Castoriades calls them,[47] help to shape the way shelters treat their residents and the way the residents view themselves.

Even though many women who have been victims of domestic violence are not in battered women's shelters, the women in battered women's shelters often see themselves as superior to homeless women in family shelters. Battered women's shelters usually get more funding, have less strict surveillance, have more amenities, and are more likely to be in residential areas. In her comparison of battered women's shelters with homeless shelters, Jean Calterone Williams says that the battered women's shelters require residents to engage in several hours of counseling and attendance at support groups, but give little support to working or looking for housing, in contrast to homeless shelters that require housing search. One battered women's shelter had an outdated resource list that was more frustrating than helpful. Some women appreciated the counseling and said it helped them to stabilize their lives. Others would have preferred to spend more time in working or looking for housing.[48] Arlene Avakian discusses how battered women's shelters changed as they became professionalized:

> Like many other grass roots movements, the battered women's movement changed drastically when it stopped relying on volunteers and raised funds to hire professionals who no longer aimed to empower women to overthrow patriarchy but helped them adapt to a bad situation. While the battered women's movement has helped thousands of women get out of abusive situations as well as raised the general awareness about domestic abuse, it has also changed from a movement for social change to a social service agency with all the pitfalls accompanying the distance between the worker and the client.[49]

FEDERAL HOUSING PROGRAMS

In 1987, Congress passed the Stewart B. McKinney Homeless Assistance Act, the first and only major federal legislation devoted solely to addressing homelessness. "A small portion supported some transitional housing and mobile health care programs, (but) Federal funding of HUD's low-income affordable housing programs...continued to be cut."[50]

During the Bush administration in the 1990s, the federal government funded "supported housing" programs, called "Housing First," which focused on "chronic homelessness" of severely disabled people, including alcoholics, substance abusers, and the mentally ill. The program did not require people to quit drinking or using drugs, although it encouraged them to get treatment. Several big cities implemented the program. In Washington DC, people were placed in apartments across the city.[51] People in New York City were housed in a renovated hotel that had previously been the city's largest welfare hotel and was transformed into permanent residences of the homeless and low-income tenants.[52] In Seattle, 75 formerly homeless alcoholics were housed in a new building. The residents were free to continue drinking in their apartments. This was controversial in the community, but a study showed that it saved Seattle more than $2 million a year. A follow-up study showed that residents were jailed less than they had been before being housed, spent fewer days in a sobering center, and required less medical treatment.[53]

The "chronically homeless" are the most visible homeless, which was part of the reason they were given priority by cities. Businesses complained about people sleeping on the sidewalk in the downtown area, which shoppers and tourists found annoying.

Commenting on the concern of cities about homeless people on the streets, Genny Nelson of the Western Regional Advocacy Project says,

> For years now, local efforts across the country to deal with growing homeless populations often start with innocuous-sounding language about the "quality of life" of the housed and business sectors of the community. Or perhaps they are billed as an effort to ensure that communities don't become a "magnet for the homeless" or, as in Portland, that there is "street access for everyone."[54]

Dennis Culhane, a professor at the University of Pennsylvania, said that housing chronically homeless single people should be a priority because they are the homeless who are most susceptible to injury and death. They are also the most tangible indicators of a city's homeless. "Their visibility tends to give people a sense that the problem is intractable," Mr. Culhane said, "So demonstrating success with the most visible population is important for sustaining the political will to address the rest of the problem."[55] But it seems to me that removing homeless people from the streets is just as likely to make people think that the problem has been solved, since homeless families are less visible.

Philip Mangano, director of the Interagency Council on Homeless during the Bush administration, claimed that the program contributed to "the largest documented decrease in homelessness in our nation's history."[56] Chronic homeless dropped 30 percent from 2005 to 2007. However, the figures were based on 2007 and did not reflect the full impact of the foreclosure crisis. Homelessness increased after that, especially family homelessness. Critics of the program said that it neglected homeless families. In 2009, some of the Housing First money was used to alleviate family homelessness. Michael Stoops, director of the National Coalition for the Homeless, faulted the Bush administration for playing what he called "a shell game" by cutting resources from affordable-housing programs in general while increasing funds for supportive housing for the chronically homeless. He said, "We need a greater investment in low-income housing in this country."[57]

The federal government created a program in 1993 named HOPE VI. This involved destroying much existing public housing and replacing it with housing that encouraged middle-class people to live there, on the theory that contact with middle-class people would be good for poor people. Although the program created some housing for poor people that was arguably more attractive than large housing projects, it also created more affordable housing for middle-income people. When one of these developments was built in Boston, I read in the *Boston Globe* that two women who lived there said it would be good for their poor neighbors to see them go to work in the morning. The program was named "community building," which aimed to "weave positive ties among public housing residents, neighborhood associations and community institutions."[58] In addition to housing, some sites included social services such as childcare, after school programs, computer labs, employment services, training, recreation, and health care. One of the goals of HOPE VI was to get residents off welfare and into work. Here is the government's official version of the goals of the program:

> HOPE VI occurred in the context of welfare reform. The Personal Responsibility and Work Opportunity Reconciliation Act changed the old welfare system. Operating in this new environment, a central focus of HOPE VI projects is to help residents overcome obstacles to work, and placing residents in employment.[59]

Much of the public housing that was destroyed for the HOPE VI program was not actually "severely distressed." A 1992 commission report found that only 6 percent of the total public housing stock was severely distressed. The HOPE VI program often did more harm than good. "It resulted in the forced displacement of tens of thousands of families and the permanent loss of large amounts of guaranteed affordable housing."[60]

In 2007, the federal government invited local communities to apply for McKinney funds to draw up 5-year "Continuum of Care" plans and 10-year planning bodies to "end chronic homelessness."

> These planning and granting procedures have led to intense competition among local service providers across the nation, pitting communities against each other in the constant scramble for pieces of a federal funding stream that is only a tiny fraction of what used to be spent on affordable housing production and subsidies before the cuts of the 1980s...[These local communities] are competing for the same small pool of McKinney homeless assistance funding. They are told that the small pittance the federal government currently allocates to address homelessness is ample if used in "efficient and innovative" ways.[61]

It is a cruel hoax. These people who are fighting for a piece of a very small pie are being fooled into the belief that they can end homelessness, while they are being denied the resources to make real progress toward that goal. It is similar to officials forcing welfare recipients to get a job and housing, while not providing affordable housing or jobs that pay a living wage.

One of the most important federal programs to deal with homelessness subsidizes rent for low-income people by Section 8 vouchers. When Congress passed the Housing and Community Development Act in 1974, the law included a goal of closing the gap between the rising cost of housing and the slower rate of increase in wages. The bill established that a family should pay no more than 15–20 percent of their income in federally assisted housing, and that a Section 8 voucher would cover the difference. After compromise with the Senate, the cap was set at 25 percent.

Over the years, this program has been whittled away by special interest groups.

In 1983, the percentage of a family's income that could go toward rent was increased to 30 percent. However, many families that get Section 8 are paying upward of 40 percent and 50 percent of their income because they cannot find an apartment that meets the established rent cap.

The federal Department of Housing and Urban Development estimates that 3 million families would receive aid under Section 8 in 2009. The number of individuals in need is far greater. The New York City Housing Authority reports that there are 127,825 New York families on the wait list. Their hopes for affordable housing are dependent on the chance that their number is picked out of a hat.

The Federal Housing Administration advocates that a family should spend no more than 30 percent of their income on housing. In 2006, according to the U.S. Census Bureau, more than half of renters exceeded this guideline, with almost 25 percent of renters spending more than 50 percent. The situation is particularly dire in New York, where nearly one in three New Yorkers use half of their income on rent.

While the anti-foreclosure bill signed by President Obama is of assistance to homeowners affected by the current financial meltdown, the bill and its $13.6 billion of housing recovery money have ignored the nearly one-third of American households who rent, including more than 2 million households in New York City.[62]

Rent subsidies were increased in August 2009, when the Obama administration announced its intention to give $4.25 billion of economic stimulus money to create tens of thousands of federally subsidized rental units in American cities. The $4.25 billion will come from $14 billion that HUD has received from the federal economic stimulus package. Another $4 billion of the money will be used to fix up the nation's existing public housing stock of 1.2 million units.[63]

The Bush administration touted the "ownership society," as a way to create national wealth and provide upward mobility for low- and working-class families, especially minorities. The federal government, through Fannie Mae and Freddie Mac, offered mortgage assistance to low-income people. These subprime loans, manipulated by greedy banks, real estate agents, and financiers, along with the bursting of the housing bubble, contributed to the current financial crisis.

Some people blame the current housing crisis on Freddie Mae and Fannie Mac, because they subsidized mortgages for people who were unable to pay them. Although the facts are more complex than this, there is a grain of truth in their claim. Rather than build housing or subsidize housing, the federal government encouraged poor people to own their own homes, in line with the conservative desire to privatize everything and the conservative belief in an "ownership society." The Conservative Prime Minister Margaret Thatcher shared this belief in the "ownership society" and sold public council housing to individual owners, thus doing away with public housing. A *New York Times* article documents President Bush's involvement in the housing crisis:

> He pushed hard to expand homeownership, especially among minorities, an initiative that dovetailed with his ambition to expand the Republican tent—and with the business interests of some of his biggest donors. But his housing policies and hands-off approach to regulation encouraged lax lending standards.[64]

The rental assistance program of the Obama administration is not only an ideological shift; it is also a practical response to skyrocketing foreclosure rates, tight credit, and the economic crisis. Carol Galante, HUD's assistant secretary for multifamily housing, said HUD would still help people to buy homes, using existing lending subsidies. The difference from the Bush administration, she said, is "we're trying to have a balanced policy. We're not trying to say homeownership isn't important, because it is. But we have to be sure we're helping people get into homes that are sustainable for them."[65] In addition to the stimulus money, Obama's budget also seeks $1.8 billion for the construction of rental housing, the same amount that Congress approved in the last year.[66]

In 2009, HUD allocated $1.5 billion over the next three years to combat homelessness nationwide, with funding particularly targeted at families and individuals in danger of becoming homeless for the first time.[67] The money, available through the stimulus bill, doubles the federal funds available to fight homelessness. It is being allocated to cities and states to help families pay rent and utility bills, as well as increasing "case-management units" to help people find jobs and get rehoused. Cities and states receiving the money have been urged to spend it quickly.[68] Although it will help some families to avoid eviction, it is not likely to make a large dent in homelessness because of the shortage of affordable rental apartments and a shortage of jobs. Some people complain that because the money is for prevention only, it cannot be used for maintaining existing services for those who are already homeless. Larry Meredith, director of the Department of Health and Human Services in Marin County, California says that a shelter that provides beds for about 60 people in Marin will probably soon close because of lack of funding.[69]

RESISTANCE

It is difficult to organize shelter residents. Shelter directors are reluctant to grant outsiders access to residents. It is very hard for women in a shelter to develop the solidarity necessary for collective resistance because of the close surveillance they are subjected to and because they are kept constantly busy at required activities.

Despite their resentment of onerous rules and staff attitudes, mothers depend on shelters to meet their basic needs. When women do resist by defiant acts, that behavior is defined as "deviant," and it is generally met with repression. Yet shelter residents do engage in covert collective resistance. Jean Calderone Williams tells of an incident where residents were resentful of one particularly nasty staff member. "Residents held an ongoing contest to see who could spend the least amount of time in his office for their weekly appointments (supposed to last an hour). The record was three minutes."[70]

Since the 1980s, organizers have made a few courageous forays into grassroots organizing that involves setting up tent cities or resisting arrests for camping in public spaces. One of the most highly publicized occurred in August 1988 in New York City when the police attempted to clear the Tompkins Square Park of homeless people and a riot erupted, which was labeled a "police riot." At least one case went to trial, but no police officers were punished.[71]

Since the Tompkins Square protests, there have been periodic militant protests by homeless people in Seattle,[72] Northampton, Massachusetts,[73] Springfield, Massachusetts (organized by ARISE for Social Justice), San Jose, Chicago, and Philadelphia (organized by the Kensington Welfare Rights Organization). In his book *Checkerboard Square*,[74] David Wagner describes the organizing done by homeless people in Portland, Maine. They put up a tent city and used it, as well as a drop-in center, as a base for organizing. Wagner shows that poor people "are not just acted upon or just passive victims of society (but) develop their own self-consciousness, culture, and alternative community."[75] He raises the possibility that street communities can develop into loosely organized social movements that can develop "collective approaches to poverty that build on existing social networks to assist poor people in obtaining housing and other benefits *collectively*."[76] Wagner said that homeless people are challenging society's norms of family, work, and institutions.

Talmadge Wright, analyzing tent city protests in San Jose and Chicago, says that squatters who choose encampments (i.e., tents and huts) as opposed to shelters in their organizing "speak to the desire for community, autonomy, and privacy."[77] Talmadge says that whenever homeless groups actively organized with political organizations, the response was swift and repressive, but "for a brief moment...the San Jose encampments offered utopic spaces for reimagining a different social identity for the homeless and very poor."[78]

A majority of the participants in the protests described by Wagner and Talmadge were single men. They were joined by college professors (Wagner and Talmadge), college students, and church members. Women are less likely to join street protests. They are more vulnerable to violence and rape, and mothers fear that their children might be taken away if they join street protests. However, women make up the majority of welfare rights activists because the majority of welfare recipients are mothers.

There are many advocacy groups in the nation trying to solve the problem of homelessness. Most do not actively involve many homeless people. They lobby for increased money to prevent homelessness, that is, to prevent eviction or to pay up-front expenses for renting an apartment, for more vouchers to subsidize rent, and for more affordable housing.

Lawyers across the nation have documented violations of the rights of homeless people and sued institutions, states, and cities for those violations.[79] The National Law Center on Homelessness and Poverty has said that homelessness is a violation of the international Covenant on Civil and Political Rights and submitted a "shadow report" that documented these violations to the Human Rights Committee on May 31, 2006.[80] It is a radical statement to say, as the Universal Declaration of Human Rights does, that every human has a right to housing. If housing becomes a universal right, then poor people who need housing will not be stigmatized.

States and nonprofit organizations have worked to provided affordable housing and subsidized rent vouchers. Community Development agencies and other nonprofit agencies have built affordable housing.

In tracing the history of poor people's movements, Frances Fox Piven and Richard Cloward conclude that the only power that poor people have is the power of disruption. Therefore, they argue, the role of organizers is not to try to form permanent membership organizations but to mobilize the poor for disruptive action when the time is ripe. Membership organizations, they argue, always end up by losing their base in their struggles to get funding and to hold on to leadership roles.

> Organizations endure…by abandoning their oppositional politics…Organizers tended to work against disruption because, in their search for resources to maintain their organizations, they were driven inexorably to elites, and to the tangible and symbolic supports that elites could provide. Elites conferred these resources because they understood that it was organization building, not disruption, that organizers were about.[81]

During the Great Depression, there were rent riots when small bands of people prevented marshals from putting furniture on the street. People also stormed the relief offices demanding relief.

> As the unemployed became more disruptive, even cherished procedures of investigation and surveillance of recipients were relinquished…As

indignation mounted...some people not only defied the prohibition against going on the dole, but some even began to defy the apparatus of ritualized humiliation that had made that prohibition so effective.[82]

People began to shake free of what William Blake described in his poem *London* as "mind-forged manacles," which had locked them into submission and into internalizing their oppressor's view of them as not deserving of respect and equal rights. The general population also began to shake those mind-forged manacles when they understood that structural reasons created poverty, not people's individual failings.

The playwright Jean Racine expressed it well in his play *Brittanicus*. Narcissus says to Brittanicus,

> As long as you are seen as a mere suppliant,
> Uttering complaints but not inspiring fear;
> While your resentments spend themselves in talk,
> No doubt of it, you will complain forever.[83]

Piven and Cloward conclude that

> One can never predict with certainty when the "heavings and rumblings of the social foundations" will force up large-scale defiance, although changes of great magnitude were at work. Who, after all, could have predicted the extraordinary mobilization of black people beginning in 1955? Nor can one calculate with certainty the responses of elites to mass disruption. There are no blueprints to guide movements of the poor. But if organizers and leaders want to help those movements emerge, they must always proceed as if protest were possible. They may fail. The time may not be right. But then, they may sometimes succeed.[84]

In *The Fiddler on the Roof* (based on Sholem Alaichem's *Teyve's Daughters*), Pertschik, a university student who is the husband of Teyve's daughter Hodel, is a young firebrand revolutionary who wants to turn the world upside down. Teyve tells him that he would do better to fix the leaking roof on the women's bathhouse and leave the revolution to the future. Until the heavings and rumblings of the social foundations force up large-scale defiance, we will continue to patch the roof. But we know that another world is possible. Finland does not believe that families should be in shelters, and they provide them with apartments.

France endorsed housing as a legal right in January 2007 after an organizing group calling itself "The Children of Don Quixote" (*les Enfants de Don Quichotte*) set up 100 red tents on the Canal Saint-Martin in Paris and moved into a vacant office block to draw attention to the homeless sleeping outside. "The issue has dominated the news and forced politicians from all main parties to promise more help for those without a roof over their heads."[85] By the end of 2008, the right to housing will apply to homeless people, impoverished workers, and single mothers. The new legislation is designed to put housing in the same legal category as education and health in French law.

Maybe the "heavings and rumblings" are beginning.

NOTES

1. Talmadge Wright, *Out of place*. New York: State University of New York Press, 1997. Wright has an excellent discussion of how cities have helped corporations and real estate interests squeeze out the poor.

2. Joint Center for housing Studies of Harvard University, "The State of the Nation's Housing 2006," Cambridge, MA: Harvard University Press, June 13, 2006, p. 28.

3. "Thousands remain in FEMA trailers," *USA Today*, June 29, 2009.

4. Ibid., p. 3.

5. Genny Nelson, Western Regional Advocacy Project blog, http://www.wraphome.org/index.php/blog/archives/271#more-271. Accessed January 31, 2010.

6. Western Regional Advocacy Project, *Without housing: Decades of federal housing cutbacks, massive homelessness, and policy failures.* San Francisco, CA, 2006, p. i.

7. Ibid., p. 24. Emphasis in the original.

8. Three excellent studies of encampments built by the homeless themselves are as follows: Wright, *Out of place*; David Wagner, *Checkerboard square*. Boulder, CO: Westview Press, 1993; Gwendolyn A. Dordick, *Something left to lose*. Philadelphia, PA: Temple University Press, 1997.

9. *Down and Out*, Massachusetts Coalition for the Homeless, Boston, MA, 2005, pp. 195–204.

10. Jean Calterone Williams, *A roof over my head*. Boulder, CO: University Press of Colorado, 2003.

11. *Down and Out*.

12. *Family Guide*, St. Ambrose Family Inn, 25 Leonard St., Dorchester, MA 02122, April 2005.

13. U.S. Conference of Mayors, *Hunger and homelessness 2004*. Washington, DC, December 2004.

14. Williams, *A roof over my head*, p. 90.

15. Ibid.

16. Williams, *A roof over my head*, p. 88.

17. Joel Blau, *The visible poor: Homelessness in the United States*. New York: Oxford University Press, 1992, p. 159.

18. Ibid., pp. 159–160.

19. Vincent Lyon-Callo, "Constraining responses to homelessness: An ethnographic exploration of the impact of funding concerns on resistance," *Human Organization*, vol. 57, no. 1, 1998, pp. 1–7.
20. It is important for people who hold high positions to talk about having received welfare, as it helps to reduce the stigma of welfare. The recently elected governor of Massachusetts, Deval Patrick, said that his family received welfare when he was a child.
21. The Family Cap policy states that a child born while a mother is on TAFDC is ineligible for cash benefits. This results in the family grant being reduced by $90 a month. The federal government does not mandate states to enforce it, but encourages them to do so.
22. Michael Lipsky, *Street level bureaucracy*. New York: Russell Sage Foundation, 1980.
23. Ibid., p. 119.
24. Ibid., p. 71.
25. Although Michael Lipsky uses the term "social workers," the people who work in welfare offices are generally not professional social workers and are not accepted by the social work profession as such. (It probably would not make much difference if they were professional social workers, as they would still be forced to take the same repressive measures, although perhaps with more finesse.) Workers now are not expected to provide services, but only to investigate and administer financial assistance. Before 1974, workers provided both services and investigation, but those functions were separated in that year because welfare rights activists saw the services as attempts to "reform" them with the goal of getting them off welfare, and demanded that services be separated from eligibility investigation. They did not want reform; they wanted cash. This separation of services from investigation actually resulted in officials cutting out the few services that were previously offered—yet another example of the unintended consequences of reform.
26. Ibid., p. 141.
27. National Alliance to End Homelessness, "Homelessness counts," Washington, DC, 2005.
28. Alexi Mostrous, "More families are becoming homeless; Largest increases in 2008 came in rural and suburban areas, study finds," *Washington Post*, July 12, 2009, p. A04.
29. Ibid.
30. "Child homelessness on the rise," *The Futurist*, July–August 2009, p. 7.
31. Ibid.
32. Erik Eckholm, "Surge in homeless children strains school districts," *New York Times*, September 6, 2009, p. A01.
33. Ibid.
34. Jim Wallis, "What should America do about its homeless families?" *Washington Times*, May 17, 2009, p. M10.

35. James Key, "Homeless vets reveal a hidden cost of war," *USA Today*, January 18, 2008, p. 11A.
36. Bryan Bender, "More female veterans are winding up homeless; VA resources strained; many are single parents," *Boston Globe*, July 6, 2009, p. 1.
37. Stephanie Armour, "New faces join ranks of nation's homeless; Renters, middle class hit hard by rising foreclosures," *USA Today*, June 26, 2008, p. 1B.
38. Chris L. Jenkins, "Homelesness: The family portrait; Across region, economy pulls rug from under more and more 2-Parent households," *Washington Post*, February 16, 2009, p. A01.
39. Ben Ehrenreich, "Tales of Tent City," *Nation*, June 22, 2009, p. 18.
40. Joseph Young, "Employed, but still no home: Minimal pay of part-time or entry-level jobs not enough," *Washington Times*, June 3, 2009, p. A17.
41. Alexi Mostrous, "HUD chief: Health reform will help homeless," *Washington Post*, July 31, 2009, p. A10.
42. Kathleen McCourt and Gwendolyn Nyden, *Promises made, promises broken... the crisis and challenge: Homeless families in Chicago*. Chicago Institute on Urban Poverty and Travelers & Immigrants Aid, 1990. This Chicago study of 258 women who entered the shelter system showed that 46 percent had left their housing because of abuse and 24 percent had left because of harassment by an ex-partner.
43. *USA Today*, "Cities crack down on panhandling," June 10, 2009, p. 03a.
44. Ibid.
45. Ibid.
46. Chandra Broadwater, "Not here, residents say to tent city," *St. Petersburg Times*, May 20, 2009, p. 1B.
47. Cornelius Castoriades, *The imaginary institution of society*. Cambridge, MA: MIT Press, 1987.
48. Williams, *A roof over my head*, studied both family shelters and battered women's shelters and gives an interesting comparison of the two.
49. Personal communication.
50. Ibid.
51. Derek Kravitz, "Homelessness official wins praise with focus on permanent housing: Detractors cite Mangano's frequent travel, including trips abroad," *Washington Post*, December 30, 2008, p. A13.
52. John Eligon, "A rejuvenated tenant in a renovated hotel," *New York Times*, September 1, 2007, p. 2.
53. Laura Venderkam, "Give them homes; Seattle hatched an innovative, if obvious, plan to tackle its growing homeless population: House homeless alcoholics. The kicker: The city saved money in what could provide a model for solving a national problem," *USA Today*, April 29, 2008, p. 9A.

54. Nelson, Western Regional Advocacy Project blog.
55. Eligon, "A rejuvenated tenant in a renovated hotel."
56. Alexandra Marks, "Strides in fighting homelessness," *Christian Science Monitor*, August 8, 2008, p. 2.
57. Ibid.
58. Housing and Urban Development, "Hope VI: Community building makes a difference," www. huduser. org/publications/pubasst/hope2, p. 1. Accessed January 17, 2007.
59. Ibid., p. 2.
60. National Housing Law Project et al. *False HOPE: A critical assessment of the Hope VI Public Housing Redevelopment Program*. Supra note 54, 2002. www.nhlp.org/html/pubhsg/FalseHOPE. pdf. Accessed January 31, 2010.
61. Western Regional Advocacy Project, *Without housing*, p. ii.
62. Edward I. Koch and Robert S. Weiner, "Renters across America need more help from Congress," *New York Daily News*, July 5, 2009.
63. Joseph Williams, "President shifts focus to renting, not owning," *Boston Globe*, August 16, 2009, p. A1.
64. Jo Becker, Sheryl Gay Stolberg, and Stephen Labaton, "White House philosophy stoked mortgage bonfire." *New York Times*, December 31, 2008, p. 1.
65. Ibid., p. A16.
66. Ibid.
67. Ibid.
68. *The Economist*, "Shelter from the storm: Homelessness," March 26, 2009.
69. Ibid.
70. Jean Calterone Williams, *A roof over my head*, pp. 91–92.
71. Wikipedia, "Tompkins Square Park," http://en.wikipedia.org/wiki/Tompkins_Square_Park. Accessed January 21, 2007.
72. Jonathan Martin, *The Seattle Times*, November 2, 2005, Accessed at Lexis-Nexis January 2, 2007.
73. Lyon-Callo, "Constraining responses to homelessness."
74. Wagner, *Checkerboard square*.
75. Ibid., p. 18.
76. Ibid., p. 19.
77. Wright, *Out of place*, p. 249.
78. Ibid., p. 300.
79. The National Coalition for the Homeless and The National Law Center n Homelessness and Poverty, *A Dream denied: The criminalization of homelessness in U.S. Cities*, January 2006. report.pdf.
80. National Law Center on Homelessness & Poverty, "Homelessness and United States compliance with the international covenant on civil and political rights," Washington DC, May 31, 2006.
81. Frances Fox Piven and Richard A. Cloward, *Poor people's movements: Why they succeed, how they fail*. New York: Random House, 1979.

82. Ibid., p. 58.
83. Jean Racine, *Brittanicus; Phaedra; Athaliah.* New York: Oxford University Press, 1987.
84. Ibid., pp. 358–359.
85. Kerstin Gehmlich, "France endorses housing as a legal right," *Boston Globe*, January 4, 2007, p. A14.

CHAPTER 6

Foster Care

Betty Reid Mandell

Victorian philanthropists did not mince words when they talked about poor kids—those kids were dangerous or perishing—that is, in danger of becoming criminals or already sunk in crime. The philanthropists formed charity schools, "Ragged Schools," and Sunday Schools to teach these children some morals and a little reading—not enough to give them big ideas about their station in life, but enough to get them to work a little more efficiently and obediently. Boys got a little math; girls did not because they were headed for domestic work. The Sunday Schools, held on the only day when the children did not work, had a further purpose—to keep the "city Arabs" off the streets so that the respectable citizens could have a quiet Sabbath.

In the streets of New York City, poor children were as much of a threat to the bourgeoisie as the London kids were. Charles Loring Brace, a Yale-educated Protestant minister who hated Catholics, founded the New York City Children's Aid Society. He preached that immigrants were genetically inferior and that the only hope for their children was immediate removal from their parents' "evil influence."[1] He conceived the idea of shipping "the children of the dangerous classes"—mostly children of poor immigrants—to farms in the West, Midwest, and South. The farmers needed farm hands and their wives needed domestic help. Thus foster care began in the United States (called "placing out" in those days), and between 1854 and 1929 the Children's Aid Society shipped approximately 100,000 children out of New York City. Society members combed the streets looking for children. Poor parents were often terrified that they would snatch their children. "To many of the poor, the child savers were actually child stealers."[2] Most of the children were not orphans but had parents who were too poor to care for them. Most of the parents were single mothers.

Some people called the program "the wolf of indentured labor in the sheep's clothing of Christian charity." Most of the children were Catholic, and most of the foster homes were Protestant. "Expressing a quintessentially new-world romance about rural life,"[3] Brace believed that the poorest rural home was better than the best institution. In fact, many of the children were overworked and some were sexually assaulted.

Westward expansion ended; the Catholic Church protested placements of Catholic children in Protestant homes; child labor was no longer as profitable; and the "free" foster home changed into the agency-supervised foster home. Since its beginning, state- and agency-sponsored foster care has been mainly a program for the children of the poor.

The root meaning of "proletariat" is "people who have no other wealth but their children." Since the beginnings of foster care, most poor parents have been afraid of the power of the state to take away their children, their last remaining wealth. The nineteenth-century Massachusetts Society for the Prevention of Cruelty to Children was called "the Cruelty" by its clients. "Poor children said to their immigrant parents, mothers-in-law said to mothers, feuding neighbors said to each other, 'Don't cross me or I'll report you to the Cruelty.' "[4] Malcolm X, describing in his autobiography how the state put his mother in a mental hospital and placed him in a foster home, called foster care legalized slavery:

> We were "state children," court wards: (The judge) had the full say over us. A white man in charge of a black man's children! Nothing but legal, modern slavery—however kindly intentioned...I truly believe that if ever a state social agency destroyed a family, it destroyed ours. We wanted and tried to stay together. Our home didn't have to be destroyed. But the Welfare, the courts, and their doctor, gave us the one-to-three punch.[5]

In a 1966 survey of 624 children in foster care in New York City, some Puerto Rican and black parents expressed the same feeling that Malcolm X had; they felt that their children had been "taken by the Whites." Approximately 15 percent of the parents studied—those on the lowest socioeconomic level—thought agencies were usurpers and believed that "agencies act like parents have no rights at all—they think they own the children."[6]

Defining the Problem

The goal of child welfare agencies is to protect children from abuse and neglect. But how do they define abuse and neglect? Definitions are shaped by economic and political conditions and by attitudes toward race, religion, gender, social class, the family, and children. Legal definitions of neglect and abuse are ambiguous, giving rise to many law suits against child protection agencies.

The white Protestants of the nineteenth century viewed immigrants as the dangerous Other who needed to be brought under control and disciplined. They did not like the smell of garlic in Italian homes and thought it was an aphrodisiac. They did not like the smell of cabbage in Irish homes. They did not like Catholics, and most of the immigrants were Catholic. They did not like children on the street. In the countries they came from, the immigrants expected their children to help make a living. If they had a job in the United States, their wages were low and there was no safety net. They sent their children into the streets to beg, collect junk to sell, or sing or play instruments. The child savers suspected that entertaining on the streets led to sexual delinquency, particularly for girls.

In tracing the history of child protection, Linda Gordon said, "More conservative times bring psychological explanations to the foreground, while social explanations dominate when progressive attitudes and social reform movements are stronger."[7] In the 1950s, a period of social conservatism, women-blaming escalated. Social workers tended to support marriage, even at great cost, but also looked suspiciously on active extended-family networks. Child protection workers coined a new diagnostic category of "emotional neglect," which became primarily a description of an inadequate mother-child relationship. "Child neglect discussion has particularly vividly revealed anxieties about women's 'desertion' of domesticity."[8] Mother blaming has continued to the present. A child welfare worker in Massachusetts says that in her office all case records are under the name of the mother, even when the abuser was the father or boy friend. The majority of the parents who have been charged with neglect or abuse are single mothers.

"Alarms about the 'decline of the family' have been periodic in U.S. history since the 1840s, and they have been mainly backlashes against the increasing autonomy of women and children."[9]

NEGLECT

Accusations of neglect are usually connected in some way to poverty—lack of adequate nutrition, homelessness, dirty homes, and poor supervision. A study of how 214 mothers on welfare provided for their families showed that most of them supplemented their meager welfare grants with help from families, boy friends, agencies, or under-the-table work. The only mother who was able to meet her expenses with her welfare grant (by doing without entertainment, school supplies, transportation, laundry, clothing, Christmas or birthday gifts) had been reported by several neighbors to child protective services for neglect. Her child frequently went hungry, had only one change of clothes, and often missed school because he lacked adequate winter clothing.[10]

The welfare reform bill (Personal Responsibility and Work Opportunity Reconciliation Act of 1996) put more parents at risk for being charged with neglect and having their children taken away. If a mother is unable to find or to do a job, she is at risk of becoming homeless and of being unable to buy food and clothing for her child. If she gets a job and cannot find day care or cannot afford it, she may leave her child unsupervised. Those families who have reached their five-year lifetime time limit for assistance are at the greatest risk. A study of mothers of young children who receive welfare found that relatively less generous AFDC benefits were associated with higher rates of children living apart from their mothers.[11] Welfare reform ended the guarantee of basic economic support for families, but mandated efforts to protect children from maltreatment. Some states use Temporary Assistance to Needy Families (TANF) money to pay for foster care. This is well spent when it goes to kinship care programs to help extended family members care for their children, but much of the money is being spent on foster care with strangers rather than for services that would prevent placement.

The White House Conference on Children of 1909 proclaimed that children should not be removed from their homes for poverty alone, but, as Linda Gordon says, "Poverty is never alone; rather it comes packaged with depression and anger, poor nutrition and housekeeping, lack of education and medical care, leaving children alone, exposing children to improper influences."[12]

ABUSE

There has been a steady enlarging of the definition of abuse in the past thirty years. It has expanded beyond physical harm to emotional harm, even to "educational harm." There has been increasing concern for "failure to thrive" infants. Physicians explore "sudden infant death syndrome" to detect cases in which the child was suffocated. Physicians are also detecting more cases in which violent shaking has resulted in injury or death.[13]

Definitions become hotly contested arenas. Following is a discussion of some differing definitions of child abuse.

Cultural Practices

Different cultural practices pose a problem for child welfare workers and for the general public. At the extreme, there is general agreement in the United States that clitorectomy of girls constitutes child abuse, but there are many gray areas in between. Randy Cohen responded to one of these in "The Ethicist" column of the *New York Times* magazine. The questioner asked about a coworker who is taking a week off to be with her six-year-old daughter while the little girl fasts for 6 days—not a total fast, but a diet of fruit, nuts and water, part of a tradition observed in her native India. The questioner asks if this should be reported as child abuse. Cohen responded, "You keep quiet not because you defer to tradition but because you've no knowledge of actual abuse. A few days on a vegetarian diet, even an austere diet like this one, does not meet that standard."[14] Cohen goes on to say that while some professions have a legal duty to report suspected child abuse, we all have a duty to thwart imminent serious harm to a particular person, whether the harm arises from religious conviction, local custom, or ordinary boneheadedness. He concludes, "I'd feel no better about your burning me at the stake out of deep spiritual yearning than I would because you were just having a bad day."[15]

Spanking

There is no general agreement in the United States about whether spanking constitutes abuse. This country is not yet ready to pass a law prohibiting spanking, as Sweden, Finland, and Norway have done. Yet there was a tentative step in that direction by the City Council of Oakland California, which introduced a resolution in 1999 to make Oakland the nation's first official No Spanking Zone. They planned to place stop signs with that message in libraries and other public buildings. "We want people to know it's not a good idea to hit kids. And when the government takes a stand against it, it helps them realize they're not supposed to do it," said Dr. Irwin Hyman, a psychologist who runs the National Center for the Study of Corporal Punishment and Alternatives at Philadelphia's Temple University. Opponents of the purely symbolic resolution argued that local government has no business telling parents how to discipline their children, and that laws already exist to protect youngsters from child abuse. (The resolution did not pass.)[16]

In one episode of his animated cartoon "Boondocks," Aaron McGruder shows a little boy having a destructive temper tantrum in a supermarket while his mother looks on, feeling powerless to stop it. The grandfather loans his belt to her. She whips the child while several onlookers look on in approval, and she herself finds that she enjoys it. The grandfather tells the mother, "I believe no child should go unwhipped."

In May 1992, approximately 200 aggrieved people held a rally in the parking lot of the Division for Children and Youth Services (DCYS) in Concord, New Hampshire. They were supporting Stephen and Joan DeCosta, both born-again Christians whose four children were placed in foster care during a highly publicized dispute with the division in 1989. The DeCostas were accused of child abuse when the children's grandmother reported that one of the DeCosta children had been spanked until he bled. The DeCostas are one of a group of parents who claim they have a right to decide how to discipline their children, while DCYS maintains it has an obligation to draw the line. A district court judge found the DeCostas guilty of abuse, but the case was resolved by a consent decree between the family and the division. The family was reunited, which the division insists is always its ultimate goal.[17]

Sexual Abuse

The definition of sexual abuse changed through history. In the years between 1880 and 1910, the Massachusetts Society for the Prevention of Children recognized incest but thought it was exclusively a vice of the poor, whom they considered to be animalistic and lacking in standards of family life. "Its agents did not see themselves in incestuous fathers, or their own daughters in the incest victims they met."[18] Although they saw incest as a brutal male crime, they did not view its victims as innocent. They drew a connection between the incest and a girl's subsequent sexual misbehavior.

In the years between 1910 and 1960, child protection agencies were alarmed about sexual attacks on young girls, but assumed strangers perpetrated these attacks. They paid less attention to incest and more attention to the sexual delinquency of girls. There was heightened concern about the girls' sexual delinquency during the war, as there was panic about venereal disease. "With VD as the emphasis, soldiers and sailors became the victims, and their female sexual partners the disease-spreading sources."[19]

"Incest was brought out into the open only when a women's rights movement challenged assumptions that conventional family life was inherently superior."[20] Before that, social workers and psychiatrists had been skeptical toward claims of young girls who said their fathers had seduced them. A Boston psychiatrist said in 1954, "We must ask ourselves whether our tendency to disbelief is not in part at least based on denial. The incest barrier is perhaps the strongest support of our cultural family structure, and we may well shrink from the thought of its being threatened."[21]

The women's movement created widespread public consciousness about sexual abuse. That consciousness sometimes turned into hysteria, as in the accusations about sexual abuse in day care centers such as Fells Acre in Massachusetts in 1984 where the staff were accused of highly unlikely acts of sexual molestation of children. The staff were jailed, but this triggered a study of false memories of children, showing that children could be coached by social workers and psychologists to "remember" things that never actually happened. This happened in a period when more women were entering the paid labor market, and there was much anxiety and guilt about working mothers who placed their children in day care, which buttressed the resistance of conservatives toward expanding day care for working mothers.

Hysteria about sexual abuse sometimes leads to a kind of Puritanism that is detrimental to children. A male day care teacher in the 1980s told me that he was not allowed to hug little girls because of the fear of accusations of sexual abuse.

A single mother on welfare was caught in this hysteria. In September 1986 a social worker with the Massachusetts DSS informed Brenda Frank that an anonymous complaint of sexual abuse and neglect of her two young daughters had been filed against her. Frank said, "I was frozen. Shocked. It was beyond my comprehension... The allegations included the fact that my 4-year-old, Emily, was still being breast-fed occasionally and that both girls (Emily and Rebecca, then 6) slept in my bed with me."[22] Frank belonged to the La Leche League, a group advocating breast-feeding until a child naturally weans herself. Frank had read dozens of books on nutrition, childbirth, and parenting during her two pregnancies and said, "I felt sure that all I had to do was explain the La Leche philosophy of child-led weaning and give her some of their literature. I thought I would show her their literature and the stuff I've been reading about the concept of mother and child sharing a bed. I had a book by Tine Thevenin called The *Family Bed: An Age-Old concept in Child Rearing.* I told the worker that I didn't agree with the fact that in our country children are expected to sleep alone at night in their own rooms behind closed doors. I told her my girls slept with me because I wanted them to feel safe at night."[23]

The social worker was not impressed by Frank's progressive ideas. She sent a letter to Frank telling her that the allegations against her had been substantiated. Frank got a lawyer who appealed to the commissioner of DSS for a review of her case. The allegations were dropped, but it would be two years before her name was finally taken off DSS's central list as an alleged perpetrator. Frank became an advocate for other parents. She helped to start Families United, a support group for families having problems with DSS. At the time of the Frank case, there was no mechanism by which a person could appeal a complaint of abuse or neglect. Frank helped to change that. Now there is an automatic review process in place in Massachusetts.

Frank believed that the person who anonymously reported her to DSS worked at her complex and might have been angered by Frank's advocacy against the use of pesticides on the grounds and for the ability of elderly residents to have pets.

Sexual hysteria is not confined to the United States. A highly publicized case involving sexual abuse in France led to a reexamination of the entire French penal system. In February 2000, the social services office of Boulogne-sur-Mer reported suspicions of sexual abuse of children by their parents in the working-class neighborhood of Tour-du-Renard, in Outreau, and placed the children of the couple in foster care. The examining magistrate in charge of the Outreau case seemed to have been convinced he was confronted with a vast pedophilic network. The accused couple implicated other people, and the magistrate imprisoned them. Some were imprisoned for three years. One committed suicide after a year of detention. The media described the accused as modern-day "monsters." Eventually 17 people were indicted. All of the 24 children of the accused were placed in foster homes.

In May 2003, after three years of denial, the man of the original couple confessed that he raped his daughters and exculpated all the other defendants except his wife and two neighbors. Four years after the Outreau affair ended, an official commission of inquiry was appointed to "examine the malfunction of justice" and make proposals for reforming the French penal system. The affair provoked outrage among all French citizens. The commission's meetings were broadcast in their entirety by several TV stations. The meetings of the parliamentary commission broke all records for viewership.[24] Some of the innocent defendants were still not able to recover custody of their children.

In 2006 Warren Jeffs, the leader of a Mormon sect that believed in polygamy, was placed on the FBI's Ten Most Wanted List for unlawful flight to avoid prosecution in Utah for charges related to his alleged arrangement of extralegal marriages between his adult male followers and underage girls. He was arrested in August 2006 in Nevada and on November 20, 2007 he was sentenced to prison for 10 years to life. He has been serving his sentence at the Utah State Prison.[25] This case received a great deal of national publicity and focused attention on a Mormon cult at a Texas ranch called Yearning for Zion. On April 3, 2008, the Texas Department of Family and Protective Services removed 468 girls and boys from the ranch on the grounds of physical and sexual abuse. The families from which the children were removed included 168 mothers and 69 fathers. Lawyers at Texas Rio Grande Legal Aid appealed the state decision on behalf of the mothers, and the case was brought to court. Rather than dealing with each case individually, the department treated all the children as one undifferentiated mass. Even as court hearings began, the state had not matched more than 100 of the children with mothers. It appeared that two dozen of the children might actually be adults. State authorities conceded that two women who gave birth since the raid were actually aged 18 and 22. A spokesperson for the Department of Family and Protective Services said the state was using a template for the plans but said the cases would eventually be individualized.

In a sample provided to the Associated Press, the plan does not outline a specific allegation of abuse involving a particular child and only repeats broad accusations made previously of the entire sect.

The template calls for parents to do things like "establish safe living arrangements" and "follow the recommendations of professionals who will be working with you to develop the skills necessary to work with your child."

The template plan does not require them to renounce polygamy or to offer guarantees that their children will not be pushed into underage of polygamous marriages or teen pregnancies.[26]

Richard Wexler, executive director of the National Coalition for Child Protection Reform, wrote an article about the event entitled "Polygamists' kids in their own private Gitmo."[27] He said that the children, with their mothers, were jammed into a building dating to the 1800s, with no air conditioning and no indoor plumbing. Chicken pox quickly spread; many children came down with diarrhea, some of them were hospitalized. At night, hostile overseers kept the women awake with their loud conversations and sometimes shined lights in their eyes.

The physical conditions ultimately improved, "but the emotional conditions deteriorated, as the children, even toddlers, were separated from their mothers."[28] Wexler said that it may have been necessary to take some of the children from the ranch, but none needed to be taken from their mothers. And the lack of any legal safeguards from the arbitrary actions of the state were, according to Wexler, typical of the entire foster care system, including "indefinite detention without meaningful hearings, inadequate defense counsel, standards of proof that range from low to nonexistent and, in most states, secret tribunals."[29]

On May 22, 2008, the Texas Supreme Court ruled that state authorities and a lower court judge abused their authority by seizing the children and placing them in foster care. It ruled that the state failed to show that any more than five of the teenage girls were being sexually abused and had offered no evidence of sexual or physical abuse against the other children. Under Texas law, children can be taken from their parents if there is a danger to their physical safety, an urgent need for protection, and if officials made a reasonable effort to keep the children in their homes. The court ruled that the seizures fell short of that standard and said that child welfare officials could take numerous actions to protect children short of separating them from their parents and placing them in foster care.[30]

Homosexuality

Some people think that living with homosexual parents is a form of child abuse. This issue became a political football in Massachusetts in the 1980s. The state child welfare department DSS placed two brothers, age 22 months and 2 1/2 years, with two gay men, Donald Babets and David Jean, in May 1985. When some neighbors complained, the *Boston Globe* published an article about the placement.[31] Two weeks after the placement, DSS removed the children and placed them in another foster home. They later returned the children to their mother, who had originally requested the placement and had approved of their being placed with the gay men.

After the article appeared, a firestorm of controversy ensued and the case gained national publicity. The men had been highly recommended to DSS by a Unitarian pastor and a Catholic priest. The pastor said, "We're dealing with a very stable family in the community," but a neighbor who complained said, "I see it ultimately as a breakdown of the society and its values and morals."[32]

On May 24 the state secretary of human services Philip W. Johnston (later the chair of the Democratic party in Massachusetts), serving with Michael Dukakis as Governor, announced that "this administration believes that foster children are served best when placed in traditional family settings—that is, with relatives, or in families with married couples," except in exceptional circumstances.[33] Columnist Ellen Goodman supported the right of Babets and Jean to be foster parents, but saw it as a second-best choice, saying, "In the best of all possible worlds, each child would have its own caring mother and father."[34]

As a result of the publicity, New Hampshire banned placing children with gays. The director of the Bureau of Children sent a directive to workers "to make it 'crystal clear' that New Hampshire does not want gays as foster parents."[35]

Babets and Jean challenged the DSS decision and threatened to organize to defeat Dukakis in the 1986 gubernatorial campaign, saying, "The man does not have one fiber of intellectual or moral integrity in his bones."[36] Gay rights activists picketed the governor, testified at hearings, and sat in at the governor's office. They were supported by the Massachusetts chapter of National Association of Social Workers, the Massachusetts Psychiatric Society, the Massachusetts Psychological Association, and Simmons College School of Social Work. The Massachusetts Civil Liberties Union sued the state along with Gay and Lesbian Advocates, asking the state to nullify the rule that requires the foster parent application to ask about sexual preference.

In November 1989, the Massachusetts legislature passed a bill adding "sexual orientation" to a state law that bans discrimination on the basis of race, color, creed, sex, ancestry, and religion.[37] In April 1990, the Dukakis administration changed its policy on gay foster parenting. The new state policy made parenting experience—not sexual orientation or marital status— the key factor in assigning children for foster care in Massachusetts.

In 2003, the Massachusetts Supreme Judicial Court declared same-sex marriage to be legal, making Massachusetts the first state to allow same-sex marriage.

Dukakis lost the support of Boston's Gay/Lesbian Political Alliance in his bid for the president. They unanimously endorsed the candidacy of Rev. Jesse Jackson in the Democratic primary.[38] Most of the homosexual vote in California's primary was expected to go to Jackson, who was the only candidate to address gay and lesbian issues during the presidential campaign.[39]

WITNESSING DOMESTIC VIOLENCE

Children of battered mothers have been removed from their homes and placed in foster care solely because the children saw their mothers being beaten by husbands or boyfriends. Judge Jack Weinstein of the U.S. District court, Eastern District of New York, ruled this practice to be unconstitutional and ordered it stopped. An expert witness in the case, Jeffrey L. Edelson, who surveyed the existing research on how children respond to witnessing domestic violence, observed that

> some child protection agencies in the United States appear to be defining exposure to domestic violence as a form of child maltreatment...Defining witnessing as maltreatment is a mistake. Doing so ignores the fact that large numbers of children in these studies showed no negative development problems and some showed evidence of strong coping abilities. Automatically defining witnessing as maltreatment may also ignore battered mothers' efforts to develop safe environments for their children and themselves.[40]

The 1999 Minnesota legislature amended the definition of child neglect to include a child's exposure to family violence. Referrals to county child protection agencies expanded rapidly in the months following the law change, and no new state funding was provided to implement the legislation. A coalition of child welfare administrators and battered women's advocates successfully lobbied for the repeal of this change in definition. Many were dissatisfied with both the impact of the legislation and the fact that exposed children and their families were left without badly needed services.[41]

Advocates for battered women feared that child protective services would blame more mothers for their male partners' violent behavior and blame them for "failure to protect." In fact, one county began to ask shelters to identify women entering local shelters with children and then referred these mothers to the local child protection agency for fuller screening and investigation. This began to create fear among women that going to a shelter would result in removal of their children from custody.

In contrast to the Minnesota legislation, Alaska passed legislation that requires a showing of substantial risk before finding maltreatment. It promotes keeping the child with the nonabusive parent and mandates safety services not just for children but also for adult victims. It made it clear that if a family member is removed from the home, it should be the perpetrator of violence. It also exempted battered women's advocates and sexual assault crisis workers from being required to report to child protection when children and their mothers were involved in services such as shelter or advocacy.[42]

SUBSTANCE ABUSE

The "war on drugs" not only resulted in a dramatic increase in the prison population: it also led to a dramatic increase in the foster care population. A woman in Illinois was put on trial in 1988 before a grand jury for manslaughter in the death of her addicted newborn. A Florida woman was convicted in 1989 of delivering drugs to the recipient (the fetus) in her womb. A judge sent a woman in Washington to jail for the last few months of her pregnancy after a drug test revealed cocaine use.[43]

Some people believe that jailing drug-addicted mothers serves as a warning to other woman, but Dr. Ira Chasnoff, a pediatrician who heads a Chicago perinatal association, says, "If you jail one woman, the only lesson you teach women is to stay out of the prenatal health care system." The lesson he wants to deliver to these mothers is "Come in for health care. **Now.** If we jail women until delivery in a mythical drug-free prison, do we then send them and their babies back to the same streets? Or do we take the children away from their mothers and put them into the beleaguered foster care system? And will we jail those children again when they are 16, pregnant and strung out?" The columnist Ellen Goodman comments, " How ironic to spend money jailing mothers while others who seek help are being turned away, because there is no room at the treatment center."[44]

In a University of Florida study of children born with cocaine in their systems, one group was placed in foster care and another group with birth mothers able to care for them. After one year, the babies were tested using all the usual measures of infant development: rolling over, sitting up, and reaching out. Consistently, the children placed with their birth mothers did better. For the foster children, the separation from their mothers was more toxic than the cocaine.[45]

A System in Crisis

More than 500,000 children in America are in foster care at any given time; relatives are caring for approximately one-fourth of them. Each year, nearly 130,000 children in foster care are waiting to be adopted, and 44 percent of them entered foster care before age six. More than 26,000 older youths leave foster care each year—most at 18—without being returned home or adopted. Compared to children and youths who have not been in foster care, young people in care are more likely to become homeless, unemployed, or to be incarcerated. They are more likely to have physical, developmental, and mental health challenges.[46]

A director of the Child Welfare League of America in 1969 said that foster care is "a mess."[47] It is still a mess. Many of the children have been bounced from home to home, and sometimes to residential institutions, and become more emotionally damaged than they were when they went into the system. Most children who remain in foster care for more than a few weeks experience multiple placements. Lamont Wilder, a child described by Nina Bernstein in *The Lost Children of Wilder*, had experienced four different placements and said that the only emotion he really knew how to feel was anger. This was the way the system had damaged him, he thought. It had made him really good at feeling angry, and confused by any other emotion.[48]

There are never enough foster parents because they are not paid enough to attract more people, and they are often given little training. Because of the shortage of foster homes, children are often placed with unqualified people or foster homes are overloaded. Workers are generally overloaded and often inexperienced. It is a difficult and often dangerous job, and there is high turnover. While most have college degrees, the degrees are not necessarily related to their work. They spend a large portion of their time investigating false allegations of abuse or neglect and do not have enough time to get deeply involved with their clients.

Foster care does not necessarily protect children from abuse. According to data compiled by the Department of Health and Human Services in 1999, the rate of child maltreatment was more than 75 percent higher—and the rate of fatal maltreatment almost 350 percent higher in foster care than in the general population.[49]

Children who "age out" of foster care, at the age of 18 (or in some states 21), are at greater risk of mental illness, poverty, and homelessness, than are adults who had not been in foster care. A 2005 study, based on a random sample of 659 case records and interviews with 479 foster-care survivors, showed that when compared to adults of the same age and ethnic background who had not been in foster care:

- Only 20 percent could be said to be "doing well."
- They had double the rate of mental illness. Their rate of posttraumatic stress disorder was double the rate for Iraq war veterans.

• They were three times more likely to be living in poverty—and fifteen times less likely to have finished college.[50]

A 2009 Massachusetts study of 96 former foster children who came out of the system at the age of 18 in 2005 showed that

• Nearly half had become pregnant or had impregnated someone,
• More than one-third had experienced homelessness, and
• Nearly one-third had been threatened or injured with a weapon since going out on their own.[51]

Nationwide, approximately 60 percent of reports of child abuse and neglect received by child welfare agencies are found on investigation to be "unfounded."[52] Disgruntled spouses make complaints about their spouses; boyfriends and girlfriends make complaints about each other; relatives report each other; neighbors report neighbors; workers report their coworkers. People are allowed to remain anonymous when they complain, without fear of reprisal. A Canadian study found that intentionally false reports of neglect or abuse were relatively infrequent (4 percent of all reported cases), but in cases where a custody or access dispute occurred, the rate of intentionally fabricated allegations was higher (12 percent). Anonymous reporters and noncustodial parents (usually fathers) most often make intentionally false reports, while custodial parents (usually mothers) and children were least likely to fabricate reports of abuse or neglect. Neglect is the most common form of intentionally fabricated maltreatment.[53]

There are few due process rights for parents who have been accused. Workers have the power to remove a child on the spot in 20 states. (There is no equivalent of a "Miranda warning.") In all but four of the rest, they need merely to call the police to do it for them. Often these removals occur at night. Parents must then go to court to try to get their children back. In most states, there is supposed to be a hearing in a matter of days, but often it takes longer to get their day in court. Such hearings tend to be five-minute assembly line procedures with a Child Protection Services lawyer who does this for a living on one side, and a bewildered, impoverished parent who just met her lawyer five minutes before—if she has a lawyer at all—on the other. Children are almost never returned at these hearings. If the children are lucky, they get to go home after the next hearing in 30 or 90 days. Or maybe they will never go home at all.[54]

Children are often removed from their homes or schools without warning, subjected to intrusive interrogations, medical examinations, and/or strip searches, and placed in foster homes or group residences while the legal system sorts out their future. This can be a terrifying experience for children and families. The number of emergency removals has increased in the past two decades. This has led to a dramatic increase in the foster care population, which grew from 262,000 in 1982 to nearly 550,000 in 2001. More than one in three were later found not to have been maltreated at all.[55]

HISTORY OF CHILD PROTECTION

Child protection grew out of eighteenth-century child-saving activities, devoted to placing poor and abandoned children in asylums and apprenticeships. Child-saving drew heavily on women's reform and philanthropic work, springing not only from condescension toward the "lower classes" but also from their search for an arena in which to feel powerful. They were motivated by religious convictions.

The nineteenth-century child-savers were influenced by the women's movement and by the temperance movement. Their critique of the patriarchy led them to define cruelty to children as primarily a male problem, "usually presumed to be an ignorant, 'depraved immigrant man.'"[56] They blamed drinking for virtually all family irregularities.

During the Progressive Era, middle-class "experts" replaced the upper-class charity ladies in child-saving. They emphasized child neglect more than abuse and regarded poverty, unemployment, and illness as contributing causes, in addition to alcohol. They were alarmed by the numbers of single mothers involved in neglect cases, which they believed indicated a weakening of the family. This attitude toward single mothers has persisted to the present time. The Progressives assumed the ideal family norm to be a father working and earning "family wages" and a wife staying home to care for the children. Poor mothers could never live up to this norm because they had to work to support their family. As more middle-class mothers entered the wage labor market, the norm was increasingly outdated for all families.

The Progressive Era child protection work helped build the new profession of social work, which dominated the child protection field until the 1960s, when doctors medicalized child abuse by defining "the battered child syndrome." Since then pediatricians have been the final arbiters of child abuse, although social workers are still primarily the arbiters of child neglect.

The development of social work contained two divergent streams—casework on the one hand, and group work and community organizing on the other. Casework focuses on individuals and their problems, while group work focuses on people giving each other support in solving problems, and community organization mobilizes people to solve problems through social action.

Charity Organization Society (COS) workers began casework in the 1880s, who were politically conservative. They believed that charitable giving eroded personal responsibility and their main goal was to prevent the undeserving from receiving relief. Social work schools were begun by COS workers, which emphasized casework and drew on psychological theory. Settlement house workers were contemptuous of the COS approach. They lived and worked *with* the people in their neighborhoods, building on their strengths and valuing their heritage. Jane Addams helped immigrants develop their native crafts and helped their children to be proud of their parents' achievements.

Some caseworkers have always worked for progressive reforms, but their reliance on casework meant that few social workers formed support groups of parents, foster parents, and children, and fewer still mobilized their clients to change the system. When I worked in a child welfare department in Greeley, Colorado in the late 1950s, I organized a foster parent support group, and the foster parents in turn organized a support group of the adolescents in their care. At the time there was a policy that prohibited foster children from getting a driver's license. These adolescents protested that policy, and persuaded the director of child welfare to rescind it.

In the late 1960s at a child welfare agency in Hartford, Connecticut, I helped to organize a foster parents' group.[57] The agency encouraged them to be partners with the social workers in decision making. The foster parents worked closely with the parents of the children in their care to strengthen the ties between the children and their parents. One foster parent even invited the child's mother to live at the foster parent's house for a week to help the parent gain a better understanding of the child, in preparation for the child's return to his mother. After the child returned, the mother and child continued contact with the foster parent.

Like all caring professions dominated by women, foster care is both undervalued and underpaid. Most social work staff are female, except for the executives, who are mostly male. Many foster parents are married couples, but the foster mother does most of the day-to-day care of the children. Social workers are often unionized, especially in public agencies, but as far as I know there has been no attempt to unionize foster parents, although there is a national organization of foster parents, with state chapters. The money that foster parents receive from agencies is usually called "board payments" rather than "wages." This carries the message that foster parents are not considered to be professionals, but are doing the work out of their love of children. Foster parents often complain that they spend more on the children than they receive and studies bear this out.

Paying foster parents a living wage would prevent many of the moves that children undergo in the system. For example, Lamont Wilder had to leave a loving foster home where he was thriving because the foster mother separated from her husband and had no marketable skills because she had stayed home to care for her own child and the foster child. She had to get training and find a job and could not afford to keep the foster child. The child was then placed in several foster homes and treatment institutions and suffered serious emotional damage as a result. If the foster mother had been paid a living wage, she would probably have kept the child. "Lamont's 21 years in foster care had cost the public $531,021."[58] That amount of money could have been used to pay the first foster mother a salary of $25,286 for 21 years. When Lamont "aged out" of foster at the age of 21, he could not afford the price of a bed.

RACE AND RELIGION

Charles Loring Brace viewed the children whom he put on the "orphan trains" as racially inferior. While the Irish, Italians, and Poles were not black, they were seen as something other than white. Catholics believed that the purpose of the orphan trains was to destroy the Catholic faith by stealing and converting its children.[59] In response, the Catholic charity establishment expanded its own child saving operation and organized their own "orphan trains." The children they sent west were predominantly Irish.

The clash between religion and race surfaced again in New York City in the 1970s. A liberal children's court judge, Justine Wise Polier, a founder of the Children's Defense Fund, teamed up with a New York Civil Liberties Union lawyer Marcia Lowry to challenge New York City's private Jewish and Catholic agencies for their practice of denying services to black Protestant children, and for their violation of the First Amendment's separation of church and state. The plaintiff in the case, Shirley Wilder, was 13 years old when the case was filed and had been committed to the state training school at Hudson, New York, a harsh reformatory for delinquents. In the foster care system that had evolved for over a century in New York City, 90 percent of all foster beds were controlled by private agencies. "State law let the leading Catholic and Jewish charities select their own kind, leaving behind a growing pool of black, Protestant children like Shirley."[60]

Although 85–95 percent of their funding came from the government, the private agencies resisted government oversight of their practices. In fact, there had been very little government oversight of their practices. "The stunted public sector, long forbidden by statute to compete with the institutional offerings of the religious agencies, provided only temporary shelters—the 'black holes' of the system, Polier called them—and reformatories for delinquents."[61]

The administrators of the private agencies and their elite board members dug in their heels and fought fiercely. The case dragged on for years. Some people compared it to Jarndyce versus Jarndyce, the legal battle described in Charles Dickens' *Bleak House*. A settlement stipulated that children should be placed on a first come, first served basis in the best available placement consistent with the wish for an in-religion preference. An Orthodox Jewish agency was exempted from the religious requirement.

By the time of the final decree in 1987, city officials argued that the decree was obsolete because the city's demographics of poverty, drugs, and AIDS had nearly tripled the total number of children in the system, even as they had reduced the percentage of white children to the vanishing point. "Agencies that wanted to stay in business had little choice but to fill their foster homes and beds with black Protestant children."[62]

In 1990 Robert L. Little, the youngest brother to Malcolm X, became the director of the New York City Child Welfare Administration. He saw the entire foster care system as dominated by whites. He favored kinship care for children, that is, placement in homes where relatives were paid as foster parents. He saw this as similar to the foster home in which he and his sister Yvonne had grown up. They had been the only ones of the Little children placed by their mother's arrangement with friends of hers from the West Indies, in a foster home that would continue to be a gathering place for the Little siblings even after Robert aged out of foster care at 19. Little created new black-run social service agencies. He redirected money toward a program of family preservation, and he championed sibling reunification at all costs for children already divided among different foster homes. By March 1993, 43 percent of all children placed by the city went to kinship homes. The basic foster care rate was more than triple the AFDC grant. As new minority-run agencies sprang up, Little transferred kinship-care cases to those that he found deserving of support. Critics complained that foster care was now being used as a form of economic development for the black community, "a back-door method of income redistribution."[63]

A highly publicized death of a child brought a surge in removals that swept many children into an already chaotic and overwhelmed system. Whenever this happens, an overwhelmed system typically sees a rise, rather than a reduction, in the number of children known to the child protection agency who die of abuse. A former child abuse investigator for the New York City Administration for Children's Services (ACS) describes the agency climate after a highly publicized case of child abuse:

> At moments of uncertainty, the mantra was "Cover your ass"—a phrase heard often around the office…The obsessive concern with liability at the field offices quickly overshadows the reasonable criteria (workers) have been taught for identifying abuse and neglect. Most quickly learn to abandon their training and to do what it takes to survive…Caseworkers are also quiet about unnecessary removals because doing a removal and then transferring a case to foster care takes them a lot less time than keeping it and trying to work with a family.[64]

The mayor appointed a new director, Nick Scoppetta, to restructure and reform the Child Welfare Administration. Although he made neighborhood-based foster care central to reform and stressed the need for more drug-treatment options for parents and more preventive programs to make the removal of children unnecessary, he also emphasized the necessity of removing children from their homes to protect them. Preventive programs were severely hurt by Giuliani budget cuts. In an era of welfare reform, poverty became criminalized and parents who could not provide for their children were suspect.

Poor mothers were led away in handcuffs because they had left a child unattended while trying to buy milk at the grocery store, or because a child had wandered away during a family eviction. One severely depressed mother in Brooklyn was actually criminally charged with endangering the welfare of a child after she notified the authorities that she had taken an overdose of sleeping pills in a suicide attempt; had she died, prosecutors said, her three-year-old would have been left alone in the apartment.[65]

Marcia Lowry said she could not fix poverty, but surely she could fix foster care. Both she and Nick Scoppetta believed in the fiction that the two realms could be separated.

The mother of Lamont Wilder's child, Lakisha Reynolds, was in and out of low-wage jobs, college, welfare, and a homeless shelter. When she applied for food stamps for herself and her child in 1999, she was turned down. The Legal Aid Society recruited her for a class action suit, *Lakisha Reynolds v. Guiliani* which charged that the city's Human Resources Administration had endangered needy children because city workers turned away people who had a right to food stamps and Medicaid.

Shirley Wilder became a crack addict and died of AIDS in 1998 at the age of 38 in a hospice. When he aged out of foster care at the age of 21, Lamont Wilder was homeless.

From Exclusion to Overinclusion

Black children were originally virtually excluded from the child protection system and even when they were included, as in almshouses in the 1700s, they were treated more harshly. When the women of the Society of Friends established the Philadelphia Association for the Care of Colored Children in 1822 for 12 children, "the shelter so angered whites that a mob destroyed it in 1837."[66] During Reconstruction, the Freedmen's Bureau helped to develop orphanages for black children, but blacks were treated separately from white children and in an inferior manner.[67] White-run charity organizations, mutual aid societies, and the settlement house movement of the mid-1800s and early 1900s excluded blacks. Black children continued to be excluded from the formal child welfare system through the Progressive Era reform movement.

But from the 1950s to the present, black children have been disproportionately represented in out-of-home care nationally. Although blacks comprise 12.3 percent of the U.S. population, in September 2008 31 percent of foster children were black, 20 percent were Hispanic, and 40 percent were white.[68] As laws requiring uniform reporting in child welfare were passed, black children were at greater risk for being reported as abused or neglected. Black children were less likely to be placed in adoptive homes and were likely to remain two-and-one-half times longer than white children who also waited for permanent homes.

A study done at the Children's Hospital of Philadelphia found that when doctors examined children, "toddlers with accidental injuries were over five times more likely to be evaluated for child abuse, and over three times more likely to be reported to child protection services if they were African American or Latino."[69] A study of decisions to "substantiate" allegations of maltreatment after they are reported found that caseworkers were more likely to substantiate allegations of neglect by black and Latino families—and the only variable that could explain the discrepancy is race.[70] A study of women whose newborns tested positive for cocaine found that the child was more than 72 percent more likely to be taken away if the mother was black.[71] In one study, caseworkers were given hypothetical situations and asked to evaluate the risk to the child. The scenarios were identical—except for the race of the family. Consistently, if the family was black, then the workers said the child was at greater risk.[72]

A blatant example of racism occurred in 1992 when a 10-year-old black girl was living with warm stable, black foster parents who wanted to adopt her. The girl's relatives lived close by and frequently visited her. Even though the girl wanted to stay, the child welfare agency tried to place her for adoption with strangers, a white couple from an affluent suburb. The relatives feared they would lose contact with her because none owned a car. They felt this move was motivated by the social agency's elitism—"money equals a more loving family." The aunt said, "A child belongs to people who love it, even if they are not rich."[73]

Latino children may be taken from Spanish-speaking parents and thrown into foster homes where only English is spoken. In a notorious case in Texas, a judge threatened to take a young Latino child from her mother and place the girl with her father unless the mother agreed to speak only English in her own home.[74]

The stereotype of the "drug-addicted welfare mother" often propagated by the "family values" Christian right has contributed to a dramatic increase in incarcerated mothers, who are disproportionately women of color. The female state and federal female prisons populations increased 275 percent between 1980 and 1992, while violent offenses increased only 1.3 percent. Many of them are mothers whose children are placed in foster care, and all of them are poor.[75]

Some people argue that the greater poverty of black people explains the higher incidence of child abuse. However, national incidence studies of child maltreatment find that all races experience child maltreatment at roughly the same rates. Further, the poorest of the poor—rural African American and American Indians—actually show lower rates of maltreatment than less impoverished populations do. Clearly, poverty is not the explanation.[76]

Substance abuse rates among American Indians are the highest in the nation for any cultural population, while rates of child abuse are lower and neglect is only somewhat higher. Although substance abuse is highly correlated with child maltreatment, It does not appear that the differences between cultures with regard to substance use and abuse are sufficient to understand the problem of disproportionality. What is different is the response of the helping professions. For example, African American and white women are equally as likely to test positive for drugs in their systems at birth, but African American women are 10 times more likely to be reported to child protective services as a result.[77]

Terry Cross, the Executive Director of the National Indian Child Welfare Association, says that

The real culprit appears to be our own desire to do good and to protect children from perceived threats and our unwillingness to come to terms with our own fears, deeply ingrained prejudices, and dangerous ignorance of those who are different from us. These factors cumulatively add up to an unintended race or culture bias that pervades the field and exponentially compounds the problem of disproportionality at every decision point in the system. For example, of 100 white children that come to the attention of Child Protective Services (CPS) intake, 25 will be substantiated and 8 will be eventually placed in substitute care. Of 100 American Indian children coming to the attention of non–American Indian CPS agencies, 50 will be substantiated and 25 will be placed. Here is the heart of the problem—100 children from each group have about the same likelihood of being maltreated. Why are twice as many American Indian families substantiated? And then why are three times as many placed of those substantiated? There is no explanation other than racial bias. But how is it that racial bias can function among professionals of good will that get into a field to help people, most of whom would define themselves as against racism and discrimination?[78]

Cross has been doing cross-cultural training and advocacy for 30 years. In his workshops with child welfare workers, he has found that fear has been a constant theme among participants. The majority of workers are female, and many workers admit they are afraid of going to African American, Latino, or even low-income neighborhoods or onto American Indian reservations. Some workers find it safer to place a child in "good" foster care rather than provide preventive and restorative services are often unaware of the bias in their decisions and behavior. "Some are less innocent. I have been asked by participants in my workshop why they would want to leave American Indian children on reservations or with extended family when 'everyone' is dysfunctional. These workers use their stereotypes and prejudices to justify their 'rescue' of children from environments judged unwholesome. Still others simply lack the cultural competence to engage effectively across language and or cultural barriers."[79]

The problem, according to Cross, is that "In general, our field tends to blame parents and label them as the problem rather than to engage them as a resource for positive change. Our passion about child safety is admirable, but the resulting tendency to rescue children makes us vulnerable to becoming excessively negative toward families. This phenomenon is magnified when families are of a culture that can also be perceived as a risk to the child. Our belief is that child welfare offers something superior—a better life or a more hopeful future. History would indicate that we cannot be so sure."[80]

PERMANENCY PLANNING AND FAMILY PRESERVATION

Until the 1970s, the focus of the child welfare field was child saving and adoption. There were few resources and minimal federal oversight, public attention, or press. It was hard for families to gain access to services and hard for children to be discharged from out-of-home care.

Although child welfare ideology has changed since then, much of the practice remains the same. The three principles governing child welfare today are as follows: (1) reasonable efforts to prevent placement, (2) permanency planning for children in out-of-home care, and (3) placement in the least detrimental alternative. The Adoption Assistance and Child Welfare Act of 1980 required "reasonable efforts" to be made to reunify families and children. However, "reasonable" is an ambiguous term, and compliance was often perfunctory. Judges were likely simply to rubber stamp the recommendations of social workers to remove the child rather than investigating whether reasonable efforts had been made to find an alternative.

A reasonable effort to prevent placement should include providing needed services such as day care or housing, but that was seldom done. A study of "lack of supervision" cases in New York City by the Child Welfare League of America found that in 52 percent of the cases studied, the service needed most was day care or babysitting. But the "service" offered most often was foster care.[81] Courts in New York City and Illinois have found that families are repeatedly kept apart solely because they lacked decent housing.[82] In Washington DC, where the foster care system has been taken over by the federal courts, the first receiver named by the court to run the agency found that between one-third and one-half of DC's foster children could be returned to their parents right now—if they just had a decent place to live.[83]

Part of the reason for not providing those services is that those services simply do not exist. There is not enough housing or day care, and there is not enough financial assistance for impoverished families. There is not enough treatment for substance abuse. But there are other reasons as well. One is the financial aid received by states from the federal government. The National Commission on Children found that children often are removed from their families "prematurely or unnecessarily" because federal aid formulas give states "a strong financial incentive" to do so rather than provide services to keep families together.[84] There is also a bureaucratic incentive to keep children in foster care. "No worker or administrator will ever be penalized for wrongly placing a child in foster care—even if the child is abused there. But if a child is left at home and something goes wrong, workers may be fired, judges transferred, and all face the wrath of the media."[85] Finally, there is the attitude of the social worker whose first instinct is to "rescue" a child whom she/he sees living in poverty on the assumption that the child will be "better off" in care. She/he fails to assess the dangers of foster care, both physical and emotional, and the emotional damage done to the child when separated from his/her parents.

Child welfare ideology has established a hierarchy of alternatives for children. The preferred alternative is the biological home, followed by adoption, foster care in the home of a relative, long-term foster care in the home of a stranger, and care in an institution. These principles are vague and have given rise to numerous lawsuits that charge states with noncompliance with "reasonable alternative" requirements.

KINSHIP CARE

The expansion of kinship care has been a major component of the explosion in foster care. It has been used extensively with black families, who have a long tradition of kinship care. Approximately 25 percent of children in foster care in 2000 were placed with relatives, two-thirds of them with grandparents. Approximately two-thirds of relative placements were wards of the state; the rest were in private arrangements. A U.S. Supreme Court decision in 1979 ruled that children living in relatives' homes were entitled to the same level of foster care payments as children living with non-kin. However, many states, in order to save money, place children with relatives in private arrangement and do not pay them or give them services. Many relatives get welfare assistance rather than foster care payments. In most jurisdictions, foster home payments greatly exceed assistance payments (sometimes three times as much). Kinship homes often receive inferior services to other foster homes. In the face of high caseloads, workers may ignore kinship placements.

Kinship care is more stable for children than foster care provided by unrelated families. They generally have higher levels of parental involvement, and often result in children returning to their parents. However, children are likely to remain in kinship care longer than in other kinds of out-of-home care. There has been some public resentment about kinship foster care payments, assuming that "bad" parents are boarding their children simply to obtain extra money from the state. Yet, children placed with relatives fare better than children placed in foster care. A study in New York City compared a group of 55 children who were placed in foster care with another group of 52 who were placed in a kinship foster home. Significantly more of mothers of the kinship foster care children and youth were homeless or substance abusing, yet visited their children more often than the family foster care youth. The kinship-placed children and youth had significantly more robust self-concept, performance, and personal attribute scores.[86]

The Fostering Connections to Success and Increasing Adoptions Act (Fostering Connections Act), passed by Congress in 2008, promotes family connections by helping children being raised by grandparents and other relative caregivers link up with the supports they need. It also helps children who have lived with relatives in foster care to remain permanently with them outside of foster care when returning home or adoption are not options. The new law requires that siblings live together in foster care whenever possible and offers greater federal support to states to increase adoptions of older youths and children with disabilities or other special needs from foster care.

FAMILY PRESERVATION

All states have implemented some form of "family preservation," intended to prevent placement in out-of-home care. The most commonly used model was called Homebuilders. This was derived from crisis intervention theory that held that intensive therapeutic intervention in a family crisis could resolve their problems. Caseworkers carried from 2 to 4 cases and were available 24 hours a day 7 days a week for 4–6 weeks. They used psychodynamic and behavioral approaches and used behavioral checklists. They sometimes gave concrete services.

A large-scale study of the Homebuilders model in Illinois, conducted by two University of Chicago professors and a Bryn Mawr professor, found that Homebuilders was ineffective in preventing out-of-home placement.[87] They concluded that crisis intervention was an inappropriate methodology as it was originally developed as a way to respond to disasters. Poverty is not that kind of crisis but is a chronic condition. Furthermore, it was coercive. While some parents received services they would not have received otherwise and some parents benefited from the counseling, coercive therapy is often resisted. Most of the treatment relied on casework, and several studies have shown that casework is ineffective in solving large-scale social problems.

The families in the Illinois program that the researchers studied were most often poor, female-headed, and single-parent households. Between one-half and three-fourths said they had emotional, financial, and housing problems. Clients wanted concrete services. Workers found it frustrating when clients did not want to work on other problems that workers viewed as important. The researchers' conclusion about family preservation programs is that "the approaches that have been tried tend to focus on the parent or the family and often ignore conditions in the community or larger social environment that may contribute to child maltreatment."[88]

BACKLASH

In the 1990s there was a backlash against the "family preservation" approach to child welfare. Richard Herrnstein and Charles Murray suggested in 1994 in *The Bell Curve* that we should encourage single women to give up their children for adoption at birth. "And even within the child welfare professional community, the mantra of 'child safety' was beginning to replace, or at least overshadow, that of 'family preservation.' "[89]

In 1993 there was a substantial backlash against family preservation in Illinois. The deaths of several children precipitated outrage among state legislators, the media, a congressman, and the Cook County public guardian. Critics claimed that family preservation has been allowed to supersede the best interests of the child, and that family preservation programs "reward" parents for the abuse of their children. Laws were passed to include "the best interests of the minor."[90]

The backlash against family preservation also occurred in other states, and in 1997 Congress passed The Adoption and Safe Families Act (ASFA), which requires states to file a termination petition in cases in which children have been in care for 15 of the past 22 months, regardless of the child's age or special needs. We discuss this act in the chapter on adoption.

"Child safety" and "family preservation" are not incompatible, but many people equate "child safety" with removing the child from the home. Leroy

Pelton, a professor at the University of Nevada School of Social Work, says that Richard Gelles, in his book *The Book of David*, seemed to view child safety as incompatible with family preservation. Gelles said that the policy of family reunification and family preservation fails because it assumes that *all* biological parents can become fit and acceptable parents if only appropriate and sufficient support is provided. But Pelton points out that family preservation policy has implicitly assumed, and the promoters of this policy have often explicitly stated that families should be preserved only if it is at all possible to maintain the child safely within the family. The policy states a preference for family preservation, not a blind dictate.[91]

REFORM

After two decades as head of the American Civil Liberties Union (ACLU) Children's Rights Project, Marcia Lowry struck out on her own in 1995 and set up Children's Rights, Inc., an independent, national nonprofit advocacy organization. The organization has filed numerous class action suits around the country.[92] One of these suits is against the state of Mississippi, where child welfare caseloads are as high as 130 per worker. (National standards call for a maximum of 12 to 17 cases per worker.) An official in the Mississippi Department of Human Services said the state would "not necessarily investigate" whether sexual abuse had occurred if a "little girl" contracted a sexually transmitted disease. Governor Haley Barbour acknowledged that the state's Department of Human Services had "collapsed for lack of management and a lack of leadership."[93]

The National Center for Child Protection Reform (NCCPR) was set up with funds from the Annie E. Casey Foundation and the Open Society Institute, a part of the Soros Foundation Network. They seek to influence public opinion and provide assistance to lawyers bringing suit to try to change the system. They have helped New York City's ACS introduce a system of accountability for the private agencies that the city contracts with to place children. They report that "child welfare reform in New York City is succeeding. The dramatic reduction in foster care placements since 1988 has been accomplished *without compromising safety* and children who come to the attention of ACS are far better off now than they were a decade ago."[94]

New York City's ACS has instituted a neighborhood-based system of foster care, the "Community Partnership to Strengthen Families" project. The goal is to place children in their own neighborhoods where they can "stay in their schools, maintain contact with their friends, and keep appropriate contact with family members and community supports. Visits with parents and siblings can occur with greater ease and frequency in neighborhood settings."[95] This plan draws on community agencies to give supports to families. They report that "for the first time, more children are receiving preventive services (more than 33,000 children) than foster care services in New York City.[96]

One of the proposals made by the NCCPR is to reverse financial incentives that encourage foster care and discourage programs to keep children out of foster care. Richard Wexler, director of the NCCPR, explains this:

> Right now the federal government pays part of the cost of foster care for every eligible foster child. If the child's birth parents are poor enough, the federal government will pay anywhere from 50 cents to 83 cents on the dollar for foster care. There is no comparable funding for programs to keep children out of foster care. So even though alternatives cost less in total dollars, sometimes foster care actually can cost less for a state or local child welfare agency. It's the ultimate perverse incentive, promoting foster care and discouraging alternatives.[97]

In fiscal year 2002, for every dollar spent to prevent foster care or speed reunification the federal government spent at least nine dollars on foster care and three more dollars on adoption.[98] Wexler believes that a large part of the problem is what he calls the "Foster Care-Industrial Complex," the network of providers that lives off a steady supply of foster children, and their trade association, the Child Welfare League of America. He says that they resist any effort to reduce funding for foster care.[99]

Other recommendations of NCCPR are as follows:

- Require daily visits, in most cases, between children and parents, when children are removed on a worker's own authority, until a full-scale trial is held. This will force workers to use more care when exercising their authority to remove children, and will help ease the trauma of removal for children.
- Prohibit searches of homes and strip-searches of children without either the informed consent of the parents or a warrant based on "probable cause" to believe maltreatment has occurred.
- Establish a rational system for screening calls to child protective hotlines.[100]

I would add the following recommendations:

- Pay foster parents a living wage and give them good training. Hire foster parents who are able to work closely with the child's parents, whenever possible to work for reunification with the family.
- Work with parents and children as partners in making decisions about their lives.
- Work with foster parents as co-professionals in decision making.

David Gil, a professor at Brandeis University and a socialist, believes that there will always be child abuse in a competitive society and that the only way to eliminate child abuse is to have an egalitarian society. He says that there was no child abuse in the cooperative participatory democracy of Israeli kibbutzim.[101]

The novelist Kurt Vonnegut believes that the extended family would prevent child abuse. He says,

I have just read about a teenage father who shook his baby to death because it couldn't control its anal sphincter yet and wouldn't stop crying. In an extended family, there would have been other people around, who would have rescued and comforted the baby, and the father, too. If the father had been raised in an extended family, he might not have been such an awful father, or maybe not a father at all yet, because he was still too young to be a good one, or because he was too crazy to *ever* be a good one.[102]

Leroy Pelton is aware that child abuse and neglect are strongly related to poverty but he does not believe that poverty is the driving force behind the rise in out-of-home placements. Rather, he believes that stereotyping of poor parents drives it. Even when the rate of poverty declined, as in the 1960s, the foster care population expanded. The coercive system of child "rescue" has a life of its own, coated with a helping façade. Funding for investigation, child removal, and foster care has increased while funding for preventive services has declined. Pelton says, "Child removal is a way to serve 'innocent' children without 'rewarding' their 'undeserving parents.'"[103]

As a result, we now have a well-entrenched child abuse industry whose power resides in its ability to manufacture, by sleight of definition and encouragement, of overzealous accusation, a continuous stream of statistics designed to horrify the public.[104]

As a solution to this system, Pelton proposes to restructure the public child-welfare system. He would limit definitions of child abuse and neglect to "severe harm or endangerment resulting from clearly deliberate acts of gross abdication (deliberate or not) of parental responsibility. Reports would be received directly by law-enforcement agencies, to be investigated by the police." The public child-welfare agency, "stripped of its investigative and foster care functions, would then be transformed into a family-preservation agency, devoted solely to the provision of preventive supports and services, largely to impoverished families, on a voluntary-acceptance basis."[105]

A study by Joseph J. Doyle, Jr., funded by the National Science Foundation, gives scientific support to Pelton's proposal. It showed that foster care placements are detrimental to children who are near the margin of needing to be placed out of home. These children, especially when they are older, seem to fare better with their birth parents. The children are less likely to become juvenile delinquents or teen mothers and more likely to hold jobs as young adults. Doyle said, "The size of the effects surprised me because all the children come from tough families."[106]

Pelton's proposal to separate services from investigation has theoretical appeal, but it risks the danger of further criminalizing child abuse and neglect, particularly in the present "lock-em-up-and-throw-away-the-key" climate. On the other hand, police may do a better job of investigating abuse than social workers do. In a highly publicized case in Massachusetts, a child by the name of Haleigh Poutre was beaten into a coma by her adoptive parents. The investigating social worker believed the parents when they said that the child was abusing herself. Further investigation proved that the parents were lying. The case was further complicated when the DSS, the agency responsible for the child, sought to remove life support, winning a ruling by the state's highest court, only to back off a day later after she started showing signs of improvement. The legislature appointed a commission to study DSS, which recommended that police and prosecutors replace social workers in investigating violence against foster children. The proposal would also limit DSS powers in making end-of-life decisions for grievously injured and comatose children. And the proposal would place the social service agency's 500-plus private contractors under greater scrutiny.[107]

There is no doubt that parents should be offered voluntary community-based services to prevent placement in foster care. Finland has such a program. They do not believe that families should live in shelters and provide homes for homeless families. They guarantee childcare to all families, and they have generous family leave provisions. Taking the child into care is seen as a last resort intervention. Care in the family as well as social, financial, and psychological support are priorities. Public day care has been much used for child protection/welfare purposes.[108]

Some parents are incapable of caring for their children for whatever reason. Their children need to be put in a stable home, either long-term foster care, adoption, or guardianship. Most parents, however, love their children and want to take good care of them. Although they may seem to be poor parents at first glance, they could be helped to be good parents with adequate support. Some of them need day care. Some need a home. Some need treatment for emotional problems or substance abuse. Some need respite care to give them a rest from the stress of parenting. All need money, whether from a job that pays a living wage or from adequate financial assistance. Given these supports, the risk of child maltreatment would be dramatically reduced. There is no other way.

NOTES

1. Charles Loring Brace, *The dangerous classes o f New York and twenty years' work among them*. London: Wynkoop and Hallenbeck, 1872, pp. 26–31.
2. Linda Gordon, *The Great Arizona Orphan Abduction*. Cambridge, MA: Harvard University Press, 1999, p. 11.
3. Ibid.
4. Linda Gordon, *Heroes of their own lives: The politics and history of family violence*. New York: Viking Penguin, 1988, p. 28.
5. *The Autobiography of Malcolm X*, New York: Grove Press, 1965, pp. 20–21.

6. Shirley Jenkins and Elaine Norman, "Families in foster care," *Children*, vol. 16, no. 4 (July–August 1969).
7. Gordon, *Heroes of their own lives.* p. 5.
8. Ibid., p. 165.
9. Ibid., p. 73.
10. Kathryn Edin and Laura Lein, *Making ends meet.* New York: Russell Sage Foundation, 1997, p. 42.
11. Peter D. Brandon, "Did the AFDC program succeed in keeping mothers and young children living together?" *Social Service Review*, June 2000, p. 214.
12. Gordon, *The Great Arizona Orphan Abduction*, p. 309.
13. John R. Schuerman, Tina L. Rzepnicki, and Julia H. Littell, *Putting families first.* New York: Aldine De Gruyter, 1994.
14. Randy Cohen, "The ethicist." *New York Times Magazine*, January 1, 2006, p. 17.
15. Ibid.
16. L. Gorov, "Oakland council mulls spanking ban," *Boston Globe*, January 22, 1999.
17. P. Doten, "Falsely accused, a mother fights back," *Boston Globe*, April 20, 1992, p. 31.
18. Gordon, *Heroes of their own lives*, p. 217.
19. Ibid., p. 220.
20. Ibid., p. 208
21. Ibid.
22. Doten, "Falsely accused, a mother fights back."
23. Ibid.
24. Mathieu Laine, "The Outreau case: Horror of a miscarriage of justice," translated by Charlotte Mandell, n.p.n.d.
25. Wikipedia, http://en.wikipedia.org/wiki/WarrenJeffs, accessed July 30, 2009.
26. Michelle Roberts, "Hearings to begin in polygamist sect cases," *Boston Globe*, May 19, 2008, p. 1.
27. Richard Wexler, *The Nation*, May 28, 2008.
28. Ibid.
29. Ibid.
30. Michelle Roberts, "Polygamous sect reaches deal for children's return," *Boston Globe*, May 31, 2008, p. A2.
31. Kenneth J. Cooper, "Some oppose foster placement with gay couple," *Boston Globe*, May 8, 1985, p. 21.
32. Ibid.
33. Kenneth J. Cooper, "New Policy On Foster Care Parenting by Gays All But Ruled Out," *Boston Globe*, May 25, 1985, p. 24.
34. Ellen Goodman, "Who lost in foster care case?" *Boston Globe*, May 30, 1985, p. 23.
35. Kenneth J. Cooper, "New Hampshire bars gays as foster parents," *Boston Globe*, June 22, 1985.

36. Kenneth J. Cooper and Donna Bryson, "Gay rights activists vow to step up campaign against foster-care policy." *Boston Globe*, June 22, 1985.
37. Kay Longcope, "Gay rights bill a victory of endurance," *Boston Globe*, November 19, 1989.
38. Joanne Ball, "Boston's gay, lesbian alliance unanimously endorses Jackson," *Boston Globe*, February 24, 1988.
39. Andrew Blake, "LA gays challenge Dukakis' foster care policy other stands garner an endorsement," *Boston Globe*, May 15, 1988.
40. National Coalition for Child Protection Reform, "When children witness domestic violence: Expert opinion," http://nccpr.info/when-children-witness-domestic-violence-expert-opinion/ Accessed February 1, 2010.
41. Jeffrey L. Edleson, "Defining child exposure to domestic violence as neglect: Minnesota's difficult experience," *Social Work*, vol. 51, no. 2, April 2006, pp. 167–174.
42. Ibid., p. 173.
43. Ellen Goodman, "The fallout of pregnant drug abusers," *Boston Globe*, August 17, 1989, p. 23.
44. Ibid.
45. Kathleen Wobie, Marylou Behnke, Fonda Davis Tyler, and Cynthia Willson Garvan, *To have and to hold: A descriptive study of custody status following prenatal exposure to cocaine*, paper presented at joint annual meeting of the American Pediatric Society and the Society for Pediatric Research, May 3, 1998.
46. Children's Defense Fund, 2009. http://cdf.childrensdefense.org/site/MessageViewer?em_id=15661.Odlv_id=16182
47. Joseph H. Reid, "Pattern of Partnership" mimeographed, NY: Child Welfare League of America, 1969, p. 11.
48. Nina Bernstein, *The lost children of wilder*, New York: Pantheon, 2001, p. 187.
49. Children's Bureau, U.S. Department of Health and Human Services, Child Maltreatment 1999, Reports from the states to the National Child Abuse and neglect Data System (1999), Tables 3.2, 4.1, available at 40_PDF.pdf Accessed February 1, 2010.
50. Peter Pecora, Ronald C. Kessler, Jason Williams, Kirk O'Brien, A. Curtis Downs, Diana English, James White, Eva Hiripi, Catherine Roller White, Tamera Wiggins, and Kate Holmes, *Improving family foster care: Findings from the northwest foster care alumni study*. Seattle: Casey Family Programs, 2005.
51. David Abel, "Report grim on teens after foster care, *Boston Globe*, June 5, 2008, p. B3.
52. Schuerman, Rzepnicki, and Littell, *Putting families first*, p. 4.
53. Nico Trocmé and Nicholas Bala, "False allegations of abuse and neglect when parents separate," *Child Abuse and Neglect*, vol. 29, no. 12, 2005, pp. 1333–1345.

54. National Coalition for Child Protection Reform, http://nccpr.info/ other-issue-papers/ Accessed February 1, 2010.

55. Paul Chill, "Burden of Proof Begone: The Pernicious Effect of Emergency Removal in Child Protective Proceedings, " University of Connecticut School of Law rticles and Working Papers. Paper 55, July 2004." http://lsr.nellco.org/uconn_wps/55 Accessed 2/1/31.

56. Gordon, *Heroes of their own lives*, p. 20

57. For a full description of this project, see my book *Where are the children? A class analysis of foster care and adoption.* Lexington, MA: D. C. Heath and Company, 1973.

58. Bernstein, *The lost children of wilder*, p. 419.

59. Gordon, *The Great Arizona Orphan Abduction*, p. 11.

60. Bernstein, p. 4.

61. Ibid., p. 54.

62. Ibid., p. 372.

63. Ibid., p. 376.

64. Richard Wexler, *Don't turn back*. Alexandria, VA: National Coalition for Child Protection Reform, January 18, 2006, p. 7.

65. Ibid., p. 438.

66. L. Ashby, *Endangered children*. New York: Twayne Publishers, 1977.

67. W. I. Trattner, *From poor law to welfare state* (6th ed.), 1999, pp. 84–85.

68. U.S. Department of Health and Human Services, Children's Bureau, *The AFCARS Report 2008*. Available online at http://www.acf.hhs. programs/cb/stats_research/afcars/tar/report16.htm.

69. The Children's Hospital of Philadelphia, Press Release, *Minority children more likely to be evaluated for physical abuse; Abuse in white children may be overlooked*, PR Newswire, October 1, 2002.

70. J. Eckenrode, J. Doris, J. Munsch, and N. Bolger, "Substantiation of Child Abuse and Neglect Reports," *Journal of Consulting and Clinical Psychology* vol. 56 No. 1 (1988): 9–16.

71. Daniel R. Neupiel and Terry Martin Zingman, "Custody of cocaine-exposed newborns: Determinants of discharge decisions," *American Journal of Public Health* vol. 83 (1993): 1726.

72. Thomas D. Morton, "The increasing colorization of America's child welfare system," *Policy and Practice*, December 1999. Cited in Dorothy Roberts, *Shattered bonds: The color of child welfare*. New York: Basic *Civitas* Books, 2002, p. 48.

73. L. Matchan, "Once homeless, now in tug of war. *Boston Globe*, January 8, 1992, p. 1

74. Sam Howe Verhovek, "Mother scolded by judge for speaking in Spanish," *New York Times*, August 30, 1995.

75. Tom Montgomery-Fate, "The cost of prisons," *Sojourners Magazine*, February 2006, pp. 45–47.

76. Terry L. Cross, "Disproportionality in child welfare," *Child Welfare*, vol. 87, no. 2, March/April 2008.
77. Ibid.
78. Ibid.
79. Ibid.
80. Ibid.
81. Mary Ann Jones, *Parental lack of supervision: Nature and consequences of a major child neglect problem*. Washington: Child Welfare League of America, 1987.
82. New York: Decision of Justice Elliott Wilk, Cosentino v. Perales 43236–85, New York State Supreme Court, New York County, April 27, 1988. Illinois: Rob Karwath, "DCFS Hit on Family Separation," *Chicago Tribune*, January 19, 1990, sec. 2, p. 2. See also: Janita Poe and Peter Kendall, "Cases of neglect may be only poverty in disguise," *Chicago Tribune*, December 24, 1995, p. 6.
83. Tamar Lewin, "Child welfare is slow to improve despite court order," *New York Times*, December 30, 1995, p. 6.
84. National Commission on Children, *Beyond Rhetoric: A new American agenda for children and families*. Washington, DC, May 1991, p. 290.
85. National Coalition for Child Protection Reform, "The unreasonable assault on 'Reasonable Efforts,'" http://nccpr.info/issue-papers Accessed February 1, 2010.
86. Jed Metzger, "Resiliency in children and youth in kinship care and family foster care," *Child Welfare*, vol. 87, no. 6, 2008, pp. 115–140.
87. Schuerman, Rzepnicki, and Littell, *Putting Families First*.
88. Ibid., p. 48.
89. Leroy H. Pelton, "Informing child welfare: The promise and limits of empirical research," in Child *Welfare Research*, edited by Duncan Lindsey and Aron Shlonsky, New York: Oxford University, 2007, pp. 25–48.
90. Ibid., p. 225.
91. Pelton, "Informing child welfare."
92. Bernstein, p. 436.
93. Bob Herbert, "Gross Neglect," *New York Times*, March 13, 2006, p. A23.
94. Wexler, *Don't Turn Back*.
95. Zeinab Chahine, Justine van Straaten, and Anne Williams-Isom, "The New York City neighborhood-bases services strategy," *Child Welfare*, vol. LXXXIV, no. 2, March/April 2005, p. 142.
96. Ibid., p. 151.
97. Richard Wexler, personal communication.
98. Cynthia Andrews Scarcella, Roseanna Bess, Erica H. Zielewski, Lindsay Warner, and Rob Geen, *The cost of protecting vulnerable children*. Washington DC, The Urban Institute, December 20, 2004.

99. Wexler, personal communication.
100. National Coalition for Child Protection Reform, http://http:nccpr. info/issue-papers. Accessed February 1, 2010.
101. David Gil, "The political and economic context of child abuse," in *Unhappy families: Clinical and research perspectives on family violence*, edited by Eli H. Newberger and Richard Bourne. Littleton, MA: PSG Publishing, 1985, p. 9.
102. Kurt Vonnegut, *Timequake*. New York: Berkley Books, 1997, p. 200. Original emphasis.
103. Leroy H. Pelton, "Child welfare policy and practice: The myth of family preservation," *American Journal of Orthopsychiatry*, vol. 67, no. 4, October 1997.
104. Ibid., p. 550.
105. Ibid.
106. Wendy Koch, "Troubled homes better than foster care," *USA Today*, July 3, 2007.
107. Raja Mishra, "Lawmakers to unveil DSS overhaul plan," *Boston Globe*, April 1, 2006, p. B1.
108. Jerr Hearn, Tarja Pösö, Carole Smith, Sue White, and Johanna Korpinen, "What is child protection? Historical and methodological issues in comparative research on *lastensuojelu*/child protection," *Journal of International Social Welfare*, 2004: 13, 28–41.

CHAPTER 7

Adoption

Betty Reid Mandell

A country's economic system and its cultural practices shape its adoption practices. For example, in Western societies adoption practices are very different from the preliterate subsistence economies of Eastern Oceania. In Western societies, the patriarchal nuclear family is the norm; illegitimacy and sexual permissiveness have until fairly recently been stigmatized; property is owned privately and the accumulation of property is highly valued; most people are engaged in wage labor; children are regarded as private property; adoption is atypical and, until relatively recently in some countries, tied very closely to inheritance laws. Some countries, such as France, Greece, Spain, and most Latin American countries, still do not allow adoption when it would interfere with the inheritance rights of biological heirs. The rigidly patriarchal countries of ancient Rome, Ancient Greece, India, Japan, and pre-revolutionary China, allowed adoption only for the securing of heirs for a propertied childless family. In those countries illegitimacy was strongly stigmatized and women were devalued—so much so in pre-revolutionary China and in ancient Rome that female infanticide was practiced. After the Russian Revolution the Bolsheviks—perceiving the relationship between adoption and inheritance—not only abolished inheritance, but also abolished adoption in1918. They legalized it again in 1926, apparently because of the need for homes for the many homeless children after the civil war. The Islamic religion prohibits adoption, as does the Jewish religious code.[1] No national adoption law was proposed in Israel until 1958.[2]

Frederick Engels' theory on the family provides some rewarding leads for understanding the prohibition of adoption in patriarchal societies.[3] He postulated that the patriarchal monogamous family had served the function of stratifying society by assuring inheritance of surplus goods through the male lineage. For the inheritance system to work, said Engels, a man had to be sure who his heirs were. In a society where sexual promiscuity was condoned and a woman could have children by many men, a man could not be sure he was the father of a child. Therefore, according to Engels, monogamous marriage was instituted, along with patrilineage. From this came the requirement of premarital chastity for women, prohibition of extramarital affairs for women, and the double standard of sexuality. Since men were allowed free sexual expression, prostitution arose to serve the men's sexual needs.

INHERITANCE RIGHTS

In countries concerned with inheritance rights, the inheritance rights of "blood relatives" are protected in a variety of ways.[4] The original reason for a probationary period before the legalization of adoption was for the protection of heirs, as in France.[5]

Adoption legislation that gives the adopted child the same inheritance rights as a biological child is more oriented to what is generally considered a "child welfare" concept of adoption. Massachusetts' first adoption statute was in 1851, some 75 years before England's first general adoption statute in 1926. It "was drawn with the avowed object of securing to adopted children a proper share in the estate of adopting parents who should die intestate."[6] By 1929 all states had enacted some form of adoption legislation.[7] A shift to a child welfare philosophy loosens or abolishes inheritance ties to natural parents.

In the status-conscious circles of nineteenth- and early twentieth-century France, the child welfare function of adoption was déclassé. Marcel Proust, writing at the beginning of the twentieth century in *Remembrance of Things Past*, gives an example of the sewing-maid, an orphan girl, who had been cared for as a child by strangers. In the eyes of Francoise, the servant of the narrator's family, such an arrangement was beneath her status:

> (The orphan's) situation aroused pity, and also her benevolent contempt. She who had a family, a little house that had come to her from her parents, with a field in which her brother kept a few cows could not regard so uprooted a creature as her equal. And since this girl hoped, on Assumption Day, to be allowed to pay her benefactors a visit, Francoise kept on repeating: "She does make me laugh! She says, 'I hope to be going home for the Assumption.' Home, says she! It isn't just that it's not her own place, it's people as took her in from nowhere, and the creature says 'home' just as if it really was her home. Poor thing! What a misery it must be, not to know what it is to have a home."[8]

Adoption in the United States now is seldom done for inheritance purposes, although some gay and lesbian couples use it as a way to secure an inheritance, as well as some others who want to provide for a stepchild, a loyal employee, or a distant relative. Almost half the states prohibit adult adoption and laws, which vary by state, can be restrictive.[9]

As countries, and sections of countries, move toward a child welfare orientation where the children do not inherit from their natural parents, the biological parents become excluded.

EASTERN OCEANIA

In sharp contrast to patrilineal societies, in many preliterate subsistence economies of Eastern Oceania, kinship is matrilineal, the clan is the most important socioeconomic unit of society, the sibling group is more important than the marital unit; children are regarded as communal, rather than private, property; clan property is owned communally; illegitimacy and sexual permissiveness are not stigmatized. Adoption among consanguinal kin is a common practice, and children retain ties with the natal clan and parents as well as with their adoptive parents.[10] Tahitians attach no social stigma to illegitimacy. A Tahitian woman often has one or two children before beginning an approved conjugal relationship. Hopper says, "It is an ethically neutral act for a woman to give such children to her parents or to other close relatives for adoption. The woman is thus freed to continue... 'the business of adolescence' if she should wish to do so."[11]

In Ponape, where missionaries were established in 1850 by colonial governments, the custom of adoption was of interest to both missionaries and administrators. Neither the Protestant church nor the Catholic Church gave ritual acceptance to adoption; in fact they discouraged it when the biological parents were alive and in good health. Fischer says, "Some missionaries have seen a connection, correctly, I think, between the frequency of adoption and the emphasis on sibling ties as opposed to marital ties, and they regard adoption as a renunciation of the responsibility and importance of marriage."[12]

In her study of Samoa, Margaret Mead said, "few children live continuously in one household, but are always testing out other possible residences."[13] This is done under the guise of visits, with no suggestion of truancy. She says, "No Samoan child, except the taupo (like a princess), or the thoroughly delinquent, ever has to deal with a feeling of being trapped. There are always relatives to whom one can flee."[14] All boys and girls call each other brother and sister regardless of the kinship relationship. Perhaps Mead had this society in mind when she suggested that America build communities where many "relatives" will help each other out—even if they are not biological relatives. Mead says that World War II marked a dividing line in the structure of the family in the United States. The nuclear family (husband, wife, and young children living by themselves in their own house) was a postwar development against which many young people are rebelling. Mead does not advocate eliminating the family, but advocates giving the family more protection and more support. She believes that you cannot have a viable community without three generations.

What we want to do is surround the family, each young couple with children, with enough people to help them, with many pairs of hands, with aunts and uncles—not necessarily biological ones but people who will play the roles of aunts and uncles and grandparents and older brothers and sisters—with a whole group of people such as we had in the small neighborhoods and small towns in this country 75 and 100 years ago.[15]

A CHILD WELFARE FOCUS

The child welfare profession developed with the rise of the middle class. Adoptions carried out by middle-class professionals have until relatively recently completely severed the ties between children and their biological parents. Childless middle-class parents want children to adopt, and middle-class professionals help them to do it through adoption agencies. Adoptive parents have always had more political clout than birth parents and their children, and have more influence in shaping policy.

In the more advanced industrialized countries, the concern about adoption shifts from anxiety about disinheriting biological heirs to a desire for exclusive possession of children, unencumbered by claims of biological parents. I believe that one of the functions of adoption agencies has been to pose an institutional and almost impenetrable barrier between natural parents and the adopted child. In Hawaii, for example, where kinship ties have traditionally been strong and most adoptions have occurred between relatives because of greater trust between relatives, those kinship ties are beginning to weaken, and adoption through agencies is becoming more popular because of fear of the stranger. Similarly, in urbanized, industrialized societies, high mobility has weakened family and community ties. To obtain children, the middle and upper classes are more likely than the working and lower classes to turn to adoption agencies rather than to relatives or informal community contacts. The adopted children come not only from strangers, but most often from poor strangers and from unmarried mothers, who until fairly recently had a stigmatized social status. In a polarized class society, the middle and upper classes in general do not want contact with poor or "deviant" people, and they do not want contact with the poor or the stigmatized parents of their adopted children. In fact, many do not want to discuss the background of the biological parents with their adopted children, and some of them do not even want to tell the children that they are adopted, although as I shall discuss in the following text, this is changing.

The Stigma of Adoption

The sociologist H. David Kirk described the adoptive mother as "role handicapped" because women are biologically structured to bear children and are socialized to believe it is their destiny to have children.[16] Kirk was writing in 1964, and things are better now. Women's Liberation has helped to open up many more options for women. More women are in the work force, and many women voluntarily choose to remain childless. Yet many women still feel that they have not fulfilled their destiny if they remain childless. They consider adoption as a second best solution to having their own biological children. Many go through the expensive, lengthy, and often unsuccessful, process of in vitro fertilization rather than adopt. Others pay a lot of money to a surrogate mother, so that the child will at least have the husband's genetic heritage. Some adopt embryos left over from the in vitro fertilization process.

The general public meanwhile has become much more accepting of adoption:

> After generations when it was shrouded in shame and protected by lies, it has come into vogue. Politicians across the ideological landscape embrace adoption as a solution for the foster care crisis and as an alternative to abortion. Rosie O'Donnell and Steven Speilberg proudly announce the arrival of their nonbiological children. Infertile couples, once embarrassed about their inability to produce offspring, gleefully tell anyone who will listen about their trips to Minneapolis or Moscow, Baltimore or Beijing, wherever they traveled to pick up their babies.[17]

Nobody knows exactly how many adoptions have been done because the process was so private in the past, but as adoption has become more open, experts are concluding that it is far more prevalent than they had thought. The Census Bureau did not ask about adoption until 2000, when they found that 2,058,915 adopted children are in U.S. households. However, the numbers of adoptees that are heads of household were not counted.

The idea that one's biological children are preferable to adopted children still hangs on. Elizabeth Barthelet, a Harvard law professor and an ardent advocate of adoption, says that adoption is constructed as a last-resort parenting choice, vastly inferior to biologic parenting. She says, "This reinforces for the infertile the message that 'true women' get pregnant and give birth. A more positive construction of adoption would help free the infertile from the obsession to restore their sense of personhood by obtaining a medical fix."[18] Barthelet calls for deregulating adoption, as the current regulatory system makes adoption costly and unpleasant, "and simultaneously degrades and demeans this form of family."[19] She believes that state and federal tax systems should be revised to provide credits for the costs of all adoptions, and she believes that insurance plans and employee benefit plans should be revised so that those who parent through adoption receive at least the same benefits as those who parent through procreation. She would like to see certain practices discouraged altogether, such as egg and embryo sale and commercial surrogacy.

Unmarried Mothers

During the first half of the twentieth century, states passed laws requiring the sealing of adoption records to insure secrecy and anonymity, a policy urged by social workers in child-placing agencies with the goal of removing the stigma of illegitimacy from children born out of wedlock. These practices "were not designed to preserve anonymity between biological parents and adopters, but to shield the adoption proceedings from public scrutiny. These statutes barred all persons from inspecting the files and records on adoption except for the parties to the adoption and their attorneys."[20] These laws required the identities of the birthparents and the adoptive parents to remain secret, even from each other. The original birth certificate would be sealed and an amended one would be issued at the time of legal finalization of the adoption. Minnesota passed the first of these in 1917, and from then and until well into the 1940s; all other states passed similar laws.[21] This practice of sealing adoption records is still in place but has come under increasing attack since the 1950s.

The stigma of adoption is partly due to the fact that, until relatively recently, unmarried mothers supplied most of the children for adoptive couples. The number of their children available for adoption is decreasing because both contraceptive devices and abortions are easier to get, and because there is less stigma attached to keeping out-of-wedlock children. Current attitudes toward unmarried mothers are much more accepting than were attitudes in the late nineteenth and early twentieth centuries, when legislators resisted adoption because it would make it easy for an unmarried mother to get rid of the "fruits of her sin." The legislators feared that providing such a social outlet for giving up babies would encourage more "sinning" and ultimately undermine the structure of the family and of society itself.

Unmarried mothers were shunned by society and put in maternity homes until relatively recently. The period around World War II and before Roe v. Wade in 1973 was called by some the "baby scoop era."[22] In most cases, adoption was presented to the mothers as the only option and little or no effort was made to help the mothers keep and raise the children.

Karen Wilson Buterbaugh was one of those mothers in 1966 when she was 17 years old. She was forced to go to a maternity home by her family, shocked and ashamed by her pregnancy. This was how she experienced the event:

> On the 10th day after giving birth, she took her baby to a church down the street to be baptized. A few hours later, she was taken into a room at the home that was empty except for a rocking chair. Soon after, a nurse entered the room and gave Buterbaugh her baby and an hour to say goodbye.
>
> "I didn't know what was coming," recalled Buterbaugh. "I sat and rocked her for an hour and talked to her." Then the baby, whom Buterbaugh named Michelle Renee, was gone, whisked away first to foster care and then to an adoptive home. Buterbaugh was left alone, shell-shocked into silence.
>
> While the pain lasted, the silence didn't.[23]

Buterbaugh has since become an outspoken opponent of adoption and one of the leaders of the adoption-rights movement, sometimes called the "search movement." She is a cofounder of Origins USA. She says that those in the movement do not think of themselves as antiadoption but as "natural family preservationists." She thinks of adoption as " 'legalized kidnapping,' " fraught with coercion, fraud, and class discrimination. She considers adoption "an amputation of a family," saying, "I've lost my daughter and my grandson, and then my great-grandchildren. It goes on to infinity."[24]

Not everyone in the movement is entirely against adoption. Some see a need for adoption, but campaign for more openness in adoption where information is shared between biological and adoptive parents, or biological mothers know the adoptive parents and can sometimes maintain contact with the child. Many of them search for their biological mother.

But the most zealous are against adoption under any circumstances, believing it dooms parents and children to a lifetime of misery. They believe the first option should always be to help the mother and father keep their child. If that is impossible, a family member or other caring adult should assume the role of legal guardian. But the child's identity should never be changed, the child should be made aware of family relationships, and all birth records should remain open. No money should change hands.[25]

In the second half of the twentieth century, adults who had been adopted developed an urgent need to know their origins, often precipitated by marriage and the prospect of bearing children of their own. They formed advocacy groups to gain access to their birth records and other background information, to which they believed they were constitutionally entitled. Jean Paton founded the first of these groups in 1954.[26] Since then, several advocacy groups have been formed. The largest group of adult adoptees is the Adoptees Liberty Movement Association (ALMA) founded by Florence Fisher in 1971. Birth parents also began to demand greater involvement in the adoption process, including the right to know the progress of the children they had relinquished. They formed Concerned United Birthparents (CUB).[27] Some people joined the movement after the Hyde Amendment was passed in 1973, which prohibited the use of federal funds for abortions. Joseph Califano, secretary of the U.S. Department of Health and Human Services, proposed to pay indigent women to bear children to be surrendered for adoption as an alternative to Medicaid abortion. One birth mother said, in response to Califano's statement, "I'm not saying that having an abortion doesn't have psychological or emotional aftereffects, but at least there can be some kind of mourning period or some kind of resolution. With adoption, the mourning period never ends because you never know."[28]

These groups focus not only on the emotional distress they have suffered, but also on "a billion dollar industry that focuses more on money than youngsters' welfare."[29] The research firm Marketdata Enterprises Inc.

estimated in a 2000 national report that adoption services are a $1.4 billion business.[30] The cost of adopting an infant—domestically or abroad, using a private attorney or an agency—averages $15,000 to $30,000 and sometimes far more.[31]

Adoption supporters disagree with these activists. Thomas Atwood, president and CEO of the National Council for Adoption, says, "Parenting is vastly more than conceiving and giving birth. It takes the full-time, selfless commitment of a mature person. If a woman is not ready to parent, her most loving and responsible decision may be to make an adoption plan."[32] But psychologist Joe Soll, himself an adoptee and longtime antiadoption activist, takes issue with the practice of sealing adoption records. "There will always be babies who need new homes, but why must names be changed, records sealed, why must children lose contact with their family?"[33]

Although the stigma of unwed parenthood has lessened, there is still stigma attached to women who give up their babies to be adopted. Judith Green, an adoption worker at the Spence-Chapin adoption agency in New York, said "If a young woman in difficult circumstances chooses to keep her baby, people think she's brave and wonderful; if she goes instead for an abortion, they think, that's a...personal decision and she can get on with her life. But if that woman says she's giving up her child for adoption, people are uncomfortable...They don't know what to think of her or what to say. They have an uneasy feeling that she's doing something wrong.[34] A secretary in St. Louis said the attitudes she encountered when she considered giving up her baby contributed to her decision to keep her daughter. She said, "Vilification isn't too strong a word. It wasn't everyone...but once I tuned into the message between the lines of the attitudes around me...it was that I must be a low-class slut or stupid or something[35] to let myself get into this predicament, so I might as well give my baby to some decent people."

Professionals say that the majority of mothers who surrendered their children are not reckless teens, but women in their early 20s to mid-30s, usually single, who have anguished over their decisions. Most of them have graduated from high school; many have attended college. Invariably, their primary motivation is not to jettison a personal problem, but to give their babies a better life. And while they often bear emotional scars and want to know about their children for the rest of their lives, they rarely attempt to interfere in the adoptive families or consider trying to get their children back.[36]

Some married women surrender their children to adoption because they already have all the children they can care for. In one such case described in the *New York Times*, the birth mother lived with the adoptive mother before delivering the baby. The birth mother did this because, as she said to the adoptive mother, "I want you to feel that this is your baby, your family."[37] Some birth mothers look for adoptive couples themselves. Adoption agencies and lawyers frequently advise clients to advertise for birth mothers. "Typically, the ads are placed by white couples who earn a minimum of $50,000 a year, at least one of whom is in their late 30s or older; have repeatedly been unable to produce biological children, and have exhausted their insurance coverage and/or spent tens of thousands of dollars on failed *in vitro* fertilization and other fertility treatments. And they badly want a white infant."[38]

Being able to choose the adoptive parents helps birth mothers live more comfortably with their decision and relieves their worry about the baby's welfare. Many birth mothers are offered counseling by adoption agencies to help them deal with their decision, which is a far cry from the days when agencies gave mothers no choice but to give up their babies. Barthelet discusses how the search movement has contributed to anti-adoption sentiment. She says,

The current emphasis on the importance of genetic heritage has revived certain classic fears about the viability of adoption—fears rooted in an assumption that parent-child relationships are likely to work only to the degree that parent and child are significantly alike. In the ongoing nature-nurture debate, the voices of genetics theorists have prevailed lately.[39]

Barthelet points out that the choice of giving a child up for adoption adds to the mother's choices and can be liberating. It also adds to the choices of infertile couples to choose to adopt, rather than obsessing over the need to have their own biological children. This is true, yet Barthelet downplays the importance of birth mothers' desire to know how their children are faring, their resentment at having been coerced in their decision, and the emotional turmoil they go through. She says that people who oppose adoption because it is the ultimate form of exploitation of the poor by the rich ignore the fact that "adoption functions to improve the economic situation of birth mother and child."[40] Surely this reduces the issue to the cash nexus.

Biological Fathers

Biological fathers get far less attention than mothers because few are involved in the decision to adopt. By law and common practice, it has always been the mother's decision to give a child up for adoption. Biological fathers often do not even know about the pregnancy, sometimes leave if they do know, or show little or no interest. There are, however, occasional exceptions. In the early 1990s there was a two-year fight over baby Jessica and a four-year battle over Baby Richard, whose fathers gained custody over babies who had been adopted years earlier. These cases raised a public outcry and resulted in the establishment of "putative father" registries in 30 states.

To claim his rights to a child, a father must put his name on a registry. In some states fathers must actually claim paternity; in others, just the possibility of paternity. Deadlines vary, but must be done any time before an adoption petition is filed. However, registries are generally not publicized and fathers do not know about them. One exception is Indiana, where men are notified of the registry when a birth mother names them as a father. Because registries vary from state to state, if a mother moves to another state or if the baby was surrendered for adoption in another state to avoid a challenge, the registry would not apply.

Carol Sanger, a professor at Columbia Law School, said registries reflect a deep societal belief that unmarried fathers are irresponsible. She says, "If we want registries to mean anything, we'd have to teach them in every sex education curriculum in every school, and publicize them everywhere."[41] If a man does not know that registry exists, he will not be able to protest a prospective adoption. One father, Clayton Jones, lost his rights to custody because he had not known about the need to register in Florida. He discovered that his former fiancée was pregnant just three weeks before the baby was due, when an adoption agency lawyer called and asked if he would consent to have his baby adopted. He said, "Absolutely not. It was an awkward moment, hearing for the first time that I would be a father, and then right away being told, 'We want to take your kid away.' But I knew that if I was having a baby, I wanted that baby."[42] He appealed the termination of his rights, arguing that the Florida law is an unconstitutional intrusion on men's fundamental rights. However, it is unusual for men to contest adoption and rare for them to succeed. They lose because courts give precedence to the mother's wishes and because most states require birth fathers to show significant personal and financial interest to retain their rights.

The registries were probably put in place more to protect adoptive parents from custody challenges than to help the father.

When parents are not married, judges routinely order that a legal notice searching for a possible father to advise him of his rights be put in the newspaper. Many mothers resist this requirement, because personal information about them must be included in the ad, and they find that publishing the most private details of their lives is often debasing. Some do not want to do it because they are afraid of the father and do not want to be involved with him.[43]

Few birth fathers come forward to claim their children, despite the ads that mothers are required to put in the newspaper. Herbert Friedman, an adoption attorney who placed such ads for almost 20 years, said, "I've never had a birth father respond to one."[44]

Kidnapped Children

The root meaning of the word "proletarian" is "people who have no other wealth but their children." That is the ultimate form of exploitation of the poor. Unmarried mothers in the "baby scoop" era were manipulated and coerced, but for those who were able, there was still the possibility of resistance, and some did resist. But there have been several occasions in history when children were kidnapped, and there was no possibility of resistance.

Linda Gordon describes one such case where Irish-American children were sent by train (as part of the "orphan train" movement) in 1904 to an Arizona copper mining town, where the Catholic priest had arranged for them to be adopted by Mexican mine workers. When one of the orphan trains arrived at a town, townspeople would flock to the station to look them over and selected the child they preferred. However, the Catholics, through the New York Foundling Hospital run by the Sisters of Charity, arranged foster home placements in advance through the local priest. One of these placements involved 41 children aged two to six who were shipped with seven staff members to two Arizona copper towns, Clifton and Morenci in 1904. Almost all the practicing Catholics in the towns were Mexicans, whose men worked in the copper mines. The priest had arranged to place the children in these Mexican homes. While the Irish children had been seen as something other than white in New York City, the train ride "transformed them from Irish to white"[45] in the eyes of the white Anglos who met the children at the station. They were shocked that white children should be given to Mexicans. They wanted the children for themselves. The women persuaded their husbands and the sheriff to form a posse, which went into the homes of the Mexicans with guns and forcibly removed the children. The nuns took 21 children back to New York and 19 remained with Anglo parents. At the court trial in Phoenix, no Mexicans were present or heard from. "It was an Anglo courtroom in its personnel and equally in its definition of non-Anglo people."[46] The court ruled that it was "in the best interests of the children" to leave them in the Anglo homes. The country's leading progressive social work periodical, *Charities*, approved of the Arizona court decision and declared the Mexican homes "degraded and unfit."[47]

The Swiss government kidnapped Romany children.[48]

Thousands of Native American children in the United States were stolen from their families over the years and put on the black market for adoption. Efforts to find these so-called lost birds have intensified recently by Navajo and other tribes. The Lost Bird Society has a Web site that received many more inquiries after a nationally publicized case about a Native American woman who had been adopted by whites and found her biological family on a Navajo reservation in Arizona. A 1978 federal bill requires that Indian children removed from their home be placed with relatives or other Native families. In 1996, tribes fought against a bill in Congress that would make the adoption of Indian children by whites easier.[49]

Canada also enforced policies for decades that took native children from their families. In 1998 the Canadian government apologized to Indian and Inuit communities for past acts of oppression, including setting up boarding schools aimed at severing youths from their culture. They allocated $245 million to fund counseling and treatment programs for victims of abuse at the schools.

Canada's apology prompted the only Aborigine ever elected to Australia's parliament to ask their government to apologize to the Aborigines. From the 1910s to the early 1970s, approximately 100,000 part-Aboriginal children and babies were placed in government or church care in the belief that the Aborigines would die out. After hearing testimony that many of the children were sexually and physically abused and faced widespread discrimination, a human rights commission concluded that the policies amounted to attempted genocide.[50]

At that time, the Australian government refused to apologize, but later the government did apologize and declared May 26 to be "National Sorry Day," to express regret at the "gross violation of human rights" of the "stolen generation."[51]

In Israel, authorities took hundreds of Yemeni infants who were in hospitals between 1948 and 1950 and gave them to Jewish adoptive families of European origin. Their parents were told that the children had died. The Yemeni families had immigrated to Israel as part of the Jewish state's clandestine "Operation Magic Carpet," in which more than 50,000 Jews were spirited out of Yemen and airlifted to Israel, where they were settled in crowded shantytowns.[52]

In Argentina, during the reign of a brutal military dictatorship between 1976 and 1983, approximately 300 babies and children of disappeared dissidents were abducted by the military and given to childless families linked to the security forces. Women whose children and grandchildren had disappeared organized themselves, as Grandmothers of Plaza de Mayo to search for their missing loved ones. Through the use of genetic identification and mental health professionals, approximately 50 children have been located, identified, and restituted.[53]

In Peru there have been charges of an illegal industry soliciting babies from poor mothers, bribing officials in isolated jungle towns to issue false birth certificates, and selling them at a high price to adoptive couples. In the late 1980 and early 1990s, Peru was famous for its relatively quick, easy adoptions. Thousands of foreign couples flocked to the country, and Americans alone adopted more than 720 Peruvian babies in 1991. That changed after a series of scandals in which children were allegedly kidnapped from poor families, and lawyers and judges were bribed to fake paperwork.[54]

In China, thousands of children have been stolen from the industrial section of China's Pearl River Delta and in rural areas of South China, and they have never been recovered by their parents or by the police. The children are stolen by human traffickers and sold to families. Families desperate purchase most of the boys domestically for a male heir.

> Su Quingcai, a tea farmer from the mountainous coast of Fujian Province, explained why he spent $3,500 last year on a five-year-old boy. "A girl is just not as good as a son," said Su, 38, who has a 14-year-old daughter but whose biological son died at 3 months. "It doesn't matter how much money you have. If you don't have a son, you are not as good as other people who have one."[55]

The centuries-old tradition of cherishing boys is reinforced by the absence of a real social safety net in China. Many parents fear they will be left to fend for themselves in old age.

The "Ideal" Family

Before World War I, relatives and friends often raised the child of someone they knew and the biological parents were in touch with the child. But adoption gradually became institutionalized by doctors, lawyers, and social workers, "most of whom sought a match of physical traits that would allow parents and children to pass as a 'real family.' "[56]

In the 1950s, motherhood was glorified. For those unable to conceive on their own, adoption was a blessing, one often kept secret to mimic the wished-for idyll. In addition, social workers seized on a postwar embrace of psychoanalytic theories—which tended to view unmarried mothers as disturbed, adoptees seeking information about their roots as neurotic, and infertile people as unstable—as a rationale for keeping adoptive families and biological families apart.[57]

Adoption agencies in the 1950s sought to replicate their vision of the ideal nuclear family by their adoption practices. A study of adoption practices in nine regions of the country in the 1950s found that the adoptive parents chosen by social workers in all the communities were "shockingly similar."[58] The typical man and wife were white and Protestant, had strong inner controls and little personal flexibility, placed a heavy emphasis on education and ambition, were rational and task-oriented, lived in a single family dwelling, and earned much more than the average income in their communities. Parents who adopted children other than white infants, however, were more accepting of imperfections, were less anxious about achievement, and placed a high value on loving a child.[59]

A decade after this study, another study said essentially the same thing about adoption workers:

Adoption agencies (are) a product of our middle class culture, responding to pressures within the community in order to gain its support, and also incorporating some aspects of the value system of that environment, which includes values that are not wholly accepting of the deviant child.[60]

As Gunter Grass said in *The Tin Drum*, "The trend is toward the bourgeois-smug."

Many adoption agencies do not view gays and lesbians as acceptable adoptive parents, and many states forbid them to adopt. Arkansas, Utah, Michigan, Mississippi, and Florida ban adoption by same-sex couples. Massachusetts passed a law banning adoption by same-sex couples, but the law was struck down as a result of a strong campaign against it.

Kathryn Kutil and Cheryl Hess, a lesbian couple in West Virginia, were foster parents for a total of 18 kids between the ages of 1 and 16, and were viewed as excellent foster parents by the Department of Health and Human Resources. However, when they applied in 2007 to adopt a baby who was placed with them, the court appointed lawyer was upset by their homosexuality and recommended that the child be removed from their home. While stating that the child seemed to be doing well and the household was comfortable and physically safe for the infant, he stated that children reared by homosexuals were more likely to be sexually or other abused and to become homosexuals themselves. Kutil and Hess were stunned and wondered, "Was it somehow O.K. for a lesbian couple to care for older kids no one else would take in but not for a newborn whom another set of more 'deserving' parents might want?"[61] They retained a lawyer to fight the decision, and finally won the right to adopt the child when on June 5, 2009, the West Virginia Supreme Court voted unanimously to overturn the decision of the judge who had ruled that the child should be removed from their home.[62]

Open Adoption

Open adoption can range anywhere from simply opening adoptees' records for inspection when they are 18 or 21, to a full sharing of parenting between the birth mother and the adoptive parents. Sometimes there is occasional correspondence between the two. Sometimes it simply involves the birth mother knowing where the child is, without having any contact. Open adoption is a *fait accompli* with older children who know their parents. Occasionally the open adoption is made legal.

Not everyone agrees that open adoption is a good idea. Many adoptive parents do not want any contact with the birth mother. Many birth mothers do not want their children to contact them, sometimes fearing that their husband and children will find out. People on the religious right oppose it because they fear that it will lead to more abortions. The "adoption, not abortion" mantra of the pro-life movement may simply be political rhetoric as they have done little or nothing to help women adopt, yet it could also be part of the conservative push to get women to give up their children for adoption, as is happening in foster care.

Women who come from cultures where illegitimacy is highly stigmatized often prefer a closed adoption. Both adoptive parents and birth parents were promised confidentiality when the adoption occurred. Some states set up a registry for people to state whether they are willing to be contacted, or they let the birth mother file a consent form in court. Some agencies let adoptees ask intermediaries to sound out the birth parent's feelings and arrange a reunion with them, if they are amenable. Most children who search simply want to know where they came from and are sensitive to the birth parents' desires.

Yet the search movement has changed the experience of adoption even for those with more traditional views. Most people who adopt know something about their children's backgrounds. They often have medical histories, photographs of biological relatives, and letters and gifts for the children from the birth mothers. Campaigns of the search movement have helped to change public attitudes and adoption practice. A study of more than 1,000 birth parents and adoptees who had been involved in searching found that "participants agreed resoundingly that reunion services should be available to anyone who seeks that option. Over 90 percent of all searchers and search subjects reported that reunion was a positive experience."[63]

Most adoption agencies initially resisted opening birth records and searching for adoptive parents, fearing that birth parents would disrupt the adoption, but some agencies have begun to reassess their policies. It has become more common for the birth mother to choose the adoptive parents. Birth mothers tend to choose higher income parents, assuming that this will insure their children better life chances, which fuels a trend toward higher income adoptive parents. Although direct payments to birth mother are prohibited as illegal baby selling, some unscrupulous lawyers and other adoption facilitators do agree to such under-the-table arrangements. There is also more "shopping" by birth mothers for an agency or lawyer who will offer better health coverage, nicer apartments during their pregnancies, or other indirect benefits permitted in some states. One lawyer commented, "I'm not saying it's baby-selling, but the empowerment of birth mother is making it much more of a sellers' market."[64] Some lawyers recruit birth parents aggressively through Web sites and outreach at hospitals, abortion clinics, teen pregnancy programs, high schools, and colleges.

Britain made open adoption legal in 1975, but only four states have made it legal in the United States—Alaska, Kansas, Tennessee, and Oregon. Adoptee-rights organizations are making a long march through the states to try to make it legal everywhere. The Internet has made the search for a biological family much easier and increased the number of searchers. There are also professional searchers who charge for their services and act as intermediaries between the birth mother and her biological family. Some of them charge thousands of dollars, but one of them, Joe Collins, charges $900, nothing up front, and nothing if the search is unsuccessful. He has found that the vast majority of searches are instigated by female adoptees looking for birth mothers rather than fathers. And he says he has never run into anyone exploring her past because she is unhappy with her adoptive family. He says, "I sense that a lot of adoptees are just curious, others have this compulsive need to know...and some subconsciously believe they were given away because they did something wrong. They want to hear the reasons to ease their minds, and they want to hear it from the source."[65]

Race and Class

Most adoptive families are white and middle class or rich, except for relative adoptions. Most of the children adopted come from poor or working-class families. This has led some progressives to oppose adoption or to regard it skeptically on the grounds that it exploits poor people and people of color. During the 1960s, adoption agencies were relatively open to adoption of black children by white families, but in 1972 the National Association of Black Social Workers opposed these adoptions, saying that black children should only be placed with black families to maintain their cultural heritage and psychological well-being. White social workers generally concurred, whether out of liberal guilt or because of their own feelings about such adoptions. There have been some efforts to increase the supply of black adoptive families through recruitment and subsidies, but the supply has never matched the numbers of black children in the foster care system who are freed for adoption.

Congress passed the Multiethnic Placement Act in 1994 after several white couples said they had not been provided the opportunity to adopt minority children. The law prohibits delaying or denying a child's foster care or adoptive placement on the basis of race or nationality. It prohibited the use of race to delay, deny, or otherwise discriminate in adoptive placements. The National Association of Black Social Workers, the NAACP, and the North American Council on Adoptable Children opposed transracial placement under any circumstances, and the bill was amended to allow race matching, prohibit only "undue" delay, and permit social workers to choose "long-term foster care" in preference to adoption. "Dozens of law professors across the country and across the political spectrum signed a letter to Congress urging rejection of this legislation as "unwise, intolerable, and unconstitutional."[66] In response to a *New York Times* editorial that said, "Clearly, matching adoptive parents with children of the same race is a good idea," Charles Freid, a Harvard law professor, said,

> Why is this so clear? Lurking behind this unproven assumption is the same logic that held that "clearly" blacks and whites should serve in segregated military units. Or, "clearly" it is preferable not to award custody of a child to a parent who after divorced entered in interracial marriage—a judgment the Supreme Court many years ago ruled unconstitutional...Mandating, or even explicitly authorizing preference based on race...is to place in the hands of a militant hostile social-worker bureaucracy a device that will easily be used to perpetuate the very situation you deplore.[67]

Many agencies were slow to comply with the law, and some states assessed stiff penalties on social workers that violated the law. In 2003, social workers in Ohio were accused of discriminating against a white couple by requiring them to prepare a plan to address the child's cultural needs and to evaluate the racial demographics of their neighborhood. The state paid $1.8 million in fines. In 2005, a social service agency in South Carolina was fined $107,000 after workers used a database to match children to prospective adoptive parents, which the federal government said overemphasized race.[68] However, even though the law required that agencies "engage in diligent recruitment" to find foster and adoptive parents who reflect the racial and ethnic diversity of the children needing placement, states are not penalized for failing to do so.

These lawsuits had a chilling effect on social workers' efforts to consider race in adoption. Jan Ran Kim, a social worker in Minnesota and a transracial adoptee herself, said social service agencies felt damned if they do and damned if they do not. If you talk to parents about racial and cultural issues they are likely to face, Ms. Kim said that workers risks violating the law, and if they try to recruit families through minority organizations, even that can look like they are using race. The law needs to reflect the fact that race is an issue in our society, and prospective white parents need to realize that this goes beyond whether you can love your child or even whether you live in a diverse neighborhood. Rather, it is about what is in the best interest of the child, not the parent.

In 2008, an examination of the law's impact over a decade said that minority children adopted into white households face special challenges and that white parents need preparation and training for what might lie ahead. The report was issued by the Evan B. Donaldson Adoption Institute and was endorsed by several child welfare organizations—including the National Association of Black Social Workers. Adam Pertman, executive director of the Adoption Institute, said, "The idea of being color-blind is great, and we'd all like to get there, but the reality is that we live in a very race-conscious society, and that needs to be addressed. We can't simply pretend that the problem doesn't exist and leave it up to the child to cope."[69]

Federal and state legislation designed to limit the consideration of race as a major factor in the selection of adoptive families has made it harder for agencies that do special recruitment of black families to get funding. The authors of an article on recruiting black families end their article with an observation, probably made with tongue in cheek: "It will be interesting to observe whether in the future the new legislation will be interpreted to facilitate transracial placement of Caucasian children as well as of minority children."[70]

An Urban League study found that of 800 African American families who applied to adopt, only 2 were approved. White social workers generally think that affluent families would provide more advantages to children, and African American families are disproportionately poor. In fact, studies show that working-class and low-income families are often better parents for children because they do not have the same high educational and achievement expectations, as do middle-class parents.[71]

Some prospective adoptive parents are rejected by white-dominated agencies because they are members of Alcoholics Anonymous. Some are rejected because of a CORI (Criminal Offender Record Information) record for a minor offense. A CORI is a record of past crime or crimes that a person has committed. Often the "crime" is no more serious than a minor drug violation. A CORI check by officials can prevent people from getting jobs or public housing or from becoming foster or adoptive parents.

Black adoptive parents are often discouraged from adopting because of high agency fees and inflexible standards, as well as systemic racism and lack of minority staff members. Some agencies staffed by African Americans have had a high success rate of finding African American adoptive parents. They have established offices in black neighborhoods, kept flexible working hours, recruited through black churches and other black organizations, lowered fees or not charged at all, educated rather than investigated, done more personal outreach to families, and cut through bureaucratic procedures. Families are allowed to change social workers if they do not like the one they were assigned.[72]

The welfare reform act (Personal Responsibility and Work Opportunity Reconciliation Act of 1996) led to a rise in the numbers of children being placed in foster care, and some single mothers who do not have money to care for their children have given up their babies to adoptive couples. I know a lesbian couple who were told that they could get a quicker adoption if they applied in a state that had low welfare grants and few social supports. They adopted two girls of mixed Mexican and Native American heritage from Arizona.

Adoption and Safe Families Act

Amid great fanfare and in the company of a family with approximately 10 adopted children looking over his shoulder, President Clinton signed into law the Adoption and Safe Families Act (ASFA) of 1997. He challenged states to double their adoptions within five years. The act requires states to file a termination petition in cases in which children have been in foster care for 15 of the past 22 months, regardless of the child's age or special needs. This means that parents who cannot resolve the problems that led to placement in foster care within 15 months are at risk of having their parental rights terminated. This will be especially hard on parents who are substance abusers and require at least 18 months treatment, as well as on women who are imprisoned.

More than half of all prisoners have left minor children behind. When a man goes to prison, his children are cared for by their biological mother, but when a mother goes to prison her children are more likely to be cared for by a grandparent, another nonparent relative, or have no one to care for them. An incarcerated mother's children are five times more likely to enter the foster care system, thus increasing her chances of losing legal custody.[73] Many prisons are far from the prisoner's home, and it is very difficult to arrange visits from children. Even when the facility is relatively near, the lack of transportation prevents many caretakers—especially those with meager resources—from bringing children to visit. One of the exceptions to ASFA's stringent guidelines is that a foster care agency may delay filing for termination of parental rights if there is a strong parent-child bond—as demonstrated during visits and by other contact,[74] but when children are unable to visit, many mothers lose custody.

Congress viewed adoption as the panacea for the problems of foster care. States get $4,000 for every child adopted beyond their best year's total, plus a payment of $4,000 for every child aged 9 and older and $2,000 for every special needs child adopted above the baseline year. States receive additional federal funds if they exceed their prior number of completed adoptions and federal technical support to help them reach their adoption targets, *not* their targets for discharging children to their homes. The money is paid when the adoption is finalized, so there is an incentive to place a child with little concern about whether the placement will really last. In fact, if the adoption fails and the child is placed again, the state can collect another bounty. States that do not comply with the law's provisions will be denied a portion of their funds that finance foster care and other child welfare services. Some states pay incentive funds to parents. The law no longer requires reasonable efforts to prevent placement, but it does not prohibit them. It is up to the states to decide.

Adoption is not the panacea that Congress had hoped for. Small increases in adoptions occurred until 2000, but then the increases stopped. The number of children taken from their parents, which increased every year, canceled out the increase in adoptions but one since ASFA was passed.[75] Many adoptions took place before ASFA was passed, 80 percent of them by foster parents and relatives. But ASFA put more pressure on states to complete adoptions. In their eagerness to get children adopted, caseworkers sometimes do not tell adoptive parents about problems the child has had, which leaves adoptive parents unprepared for the problems they will have to deal with. A disproportionate number of children from broken adoptions end up in group homes and residential treatment centers.[76] Lamont Wilder, a black child, was sent to a white adoptive home in Minnesota. They were unable to handle his behavior problems, and he was sent back to a foster home in New York City, and eventually to a treatment institution.

Disrupted adoptions are higher among older children, who often have severe behavior problems and are likely to have retained emotional ties to their biological parents. (Many adolescent run-aways from foster homes return to their parents.) Studies have shown that adoption disruption rates rise dramatically with age at adoptive placement, with disruption rates for older children reaching well into double-digit percentages within the first two years of adoptive placement alone.[77] The law does not require follow-up after a year, so no one knows how many adoptions fail after a year. Almost two-thirds of children awaiting adoption from foster care are at least six years old.[78]

Some horror stories have surfaced about failed adoptions. In New Jersey, four adopted boys in an adoptive home were being starved on a diet of peanut butter and plaster while the couple was being evaluated for the adoption of a seventh child. The family had received more than $30,000 a year in incentive payments from the state. In Houston, Texas, a couple was allowed to adopt six severely handicapped children. "Despite many complaints of abuse and rat-infested conditions in their home, the state acted to remove the children only after the couple beat one to death in 2000. In an internal review the state agency found it had not violated any of its own procedures in approving the adoption."[79]

Darlene Kuster, a welfare rights activist in Idaho, reports that the ASFA "has been a real windfall for the child-hungry middle class."[80] The Idaho legislature has expanded the reasons considered "cause" to take children away from their parents. Homelessness alone is considered "neglect." Homeless women are afraid to even apply for Medicaid for their children. The clock on termination of parental rights begins to tick as soon as the kid is out of the home, and the CPS caseworkers always check the "adoption" option rather than the "reunification" option on the "Goals" part of the form. So the case is always filed initially with the assumption that no case plan is really necessary.[81]

Kuster says that the overwhelming majority of poor women are white. Adoptive couples especially desire white babies. She and other activists "accompany women of kidnapped babies to the Department of Health and Welfare and the Public Pretender as advocates and witnesses."[82] They advise women never to disclose homelessness to the Department of Public Welfare (DPW), and they tell women in shelters that if shelter staff threaten to report them to DPW, they should leave the shelter. They collect women's stories and lobby legislators.[83]

One of the unintended consequences of the ASFA, according to researchers at the University of Chicago, is that family reunification rates have slowed down.[84] Richard Wexler, the director of the National Coalition for Child Protection Reform, had this to say about the law:

> Although ASFA encourages states to do a lot of bad things, by and large, it does not require them. In theory, the mandates of ASFA can be met just as easily with a renewed commitment to keeping families together as they can by embracing the "take the child and run" approach. There is nothing in AFSA that prohibits states from providing rent subsidies so children are less likely to lose their parents because those parents lack decent housing. And there is nothing to prohibit states from providing day care so single working parents do not lose their children because of "lack of supervision."[85]

Richard Gelles, dean of the University of Pennsylvania School of Social Work, who helped draft the ASFA, has said, "Initially this was just supposed to be a safe families bill, not really an adoption bill at all. The adoption component was a way of sanitizing the bill, to make it more appealing to a broader group of people. Adoption is a very popular concept in the country right now."[86] Gelles admits that ASFA might be differentially applied to poor, low income, and minority families. He says,

> When you err on the side of safety...you're going to make mistakes in terms of sweeping up children into the system who might not belong in the system and those children are almost always going to be from poor families, from minority families, from Spanish-speaking or non-majority-language families.[87]

Even before ASFA was passed, state efforts to expedite termination of parental rights were creating a generation of "legal orphans" with no ties to birth parents but without adoptive homes either. "Thanks to ASFA, the problem is spreading. In New Jersey, between 1997 and 1999 almost four children had parental rights terminated for every one actually adopted. A study of urban counties in Nebraska found that more than a year after parental rights were terminated, fewer than half the children had permanent homes."[88]

Some people think that ASFA was a stealth movement to try to create orphanages for children. Richard Gelles said that because the foster care system is already dangerously overloaded, "orphanages" would be "plausible and cost effective placements."[89] Edward Banfield, in his 1974 book *The Unheavenly City* proposed "as a thinking exercise" that we consider placing the children of the poor in institutions. Newt Gingrich invoked the nostalgic image of Boys Town in his call for orphanages. Protests against this silenced further open discussion of the idea but, according to Richard Wexler, "The Republicans knew full well there's never going to be enough middle class adopted to go around. The Republicans only started talking about adoption after their pollster, Frank Luntz, told them they could get what they wanted in terms of orphanages—but they had to stop using the term orphanage."[90]

Many people are looking into adopting foster children because they cannot afford international adoption, which can cost up to $30,000. The only offset of these costs is the Federal Adoption Tax Credit, which allows families adopting internally an income tax rebate of $12,150. People who adopt special needs children get the full credit, even if the actual expenses were less. Individuals who adopt special needs children are not eligible if they earn more than $182,180; individuals earning more than $222,180 are ineligible for either program.[91] The Adoption Tax Credit instituted to encourage domestic adoptions has probably been more beneficial for international adoptions. Perhaps that is why recent federal legislation has now made provisions for families who are adopting special needs children to receive the tax rebate without demonstrating adoption-related expenditures.[92]

INTERNATIONAL ADOPTION

As the supply of adoptable babies in the United States has gone down and birth rates in Western industrialized nations have declined, people have been turning to international adoption where birth rates are high and there are few prospective adopters for the many homeless children. Some families prefer to adopt overseas rather than domestically because the prevalence of open adoption has made them fearful of contact with birth mothers.

Wars create orphans and homeless children, and that has led to an increase in international adoptions. "Historically, Americans have adopted children left parentless by war: 8,000 Japanese and European orphans were adopted in the late 1940s; thousands more came from Korea a decade later."[93] The numbers of overseas adoptions increased dramatically until 2004, when they began to decline. In 2004, there were 22,884 international adoptions. By 2008, that number had dropped to 17,438, according to the State Department. Adoption experts predicted the total for fiscal 2009 would drop below

12,000. The decline was due to new restrictions by foreign governments and diminishing financial resources among prospective parents.[94]

China, Russia, and Guatemala had provided two-thirds of all foreign adoptions, but China and Russia have both imposed restrictions, and Guatemala has completely closed down its international adoptions, at least temporarily.

China

China's one-child policy and the Chinese preference for boys resulted in many girl babies being placed in orphanages. Between 1989 and 2008, China sent 71,403 children to the United States, almost all of them girls. That was more than any other country. But China's program began to slow in 2006. People speculated that the delay was because in the lead-up to the Beijing Olympics, China did not want to be seen as unable to care for its own.

China, troubled by publicity in the late 1990s over gay parents in the UnitedStates raising Chinese children, now requires all applicants to sign statements that they are not gay or lesbian. It also does not allow more than 8 percent of the country's children who are adopted to be placed with single people. China also banned adoptions by people older than the age of 50, anyone with a history of mental illness, low-income people, people who are overweight, and people who have been married less than 2 years.

Lillian Zang, executive director of China Adoption with Love, based in Brookline, Massachusetts, commented on the recent decline in adoptions in Massachusetts:

> Massachusetts is particularly hard-hit by the Chinese policy because of the high number of educated single women, as well as gays and lesbians, who seek to adopt from this state. Calling it a "blue state, red state" phenomenon, she speculated that liberal urban centers are more likely to be experiencing a drop in adoptions from China.[95]

Zang predicted a dramatic decline in Chinese placements across the country in the next decade because there will be fewer children available. "Chinese officials are encouraging the country's citizens to adopt. They have also launched an aggressive campaign to alter the traditional Chinese rural preference for male over female babies, a preference that resulted in the abandonment of many newborn girls."[96]

After the 2008 earthquake in China, inquiries to adoption agencies about adopting Chinese children more than tripled. The earthquake had killed at least 68,109 people and left an estimated 4,000 children without parents. Joshua Zhong, cofounder of Chinese Children Adoption International, said that many of the children might not be orphans once parents or other relatives are found. A Chinese adoption official at China's Ministry of Civil Affairs, said, "We intend to give priority to domestic adoption…over overseas adoptions."[97] The process for adopting Chinese children used to take a year and was efficient, transparent, and affordable, but the process now takes 31 months and is expected to get longer.[98]

South Korea, Ukraine, and Russia

Russia, Ukraine, and South Korea, all facing declining birthrates, are encouraging domestic adoption.[99] South Korea, once a world adoption leader, has tightened its rules in response to baby-trafficking cases and internal pressure to care for its own orphans.[100] The booming economy has changed social attitudes toward orphans. And with a birth rate of just 1.1 children per woman, below the level required to keep the population steady, the country needs to hold onto its people. In the summer of 2007, protesters gathered in downtown Seoul with placards that read KOREAN BABIES NOT FOR EXPORT. Today Seoul offers tax breaks, cash incentives, and extra vacation days to families who take in domestic orphans. The measures seem to be working: 2007 was the first year since the Korean War that more South Korean children were adopted at home (1,388) than overseas (1,265).[101] It plans to end its adoption program by 2015.

Ukraine banned prospective parents from selecting specific orphans before traveling to the country, in response to a scandal about an adoption facilitator in California, Yunona USA, that put photos of children on the Internet that were not actually available for adoption. Ukraine announced a moratorium on new adoptions to the United States in 2005, saying it had lost track of hundreds of adopted children.

In 2005, the Russian government said it had evidence linking the unlicensed adoption of orphans to the death of Russian children in American homes, and it tightened the rules about international adoption, requiring follow-up reports on adopted children.[102] It later closed and then reopened its program, with a new, strict emphasis on the health of potential parents, and fewer children being adopted. In recent times, Russia routinely sent upward of 4,000 children a year to the United States, but in 2008 that figure fell to 1,861. In January 2009, Russian leaders called for adoptions to the United States to be curtailed or halted, upset by the acquittal of a Washington-area father whose adopted son died of heatstroke after being left in a car.

Guatemala

Guatemala has been the largest source of babies for American families after China. It sent 4,135 children to the United States in 2006,[103] but it passed a law to tighten adoptions in December 2007 to comply with the Hague Convention, an international agreement designed to protect adopted children from human trafficking. At the time the law was enacted, there were 3,700 children who had already been matched with prospective parents. In response to pressure from the U.S. State Department, Guatemala made an exception in the law for these children to allow the adoptions to be completed.

Guatemala's adoptions were popular with U.S. parents. They were drawn by the few-questions-asked system that dispatched infants in a matter of months. Gays, singles, and unmarried couples were welcome. Inspired by the lack of regulations, a ruthless class of jaladora (pullers) began trolling the city slums and impoverished countryside, sometimes buying babies cheap (or, allegedly, stealing them) and selling them dear. Foreigners shelled out upward of $35,000 for a Guatemalan child, with shadowy foster homes and crooked bureaucrats playing midwife to the exchange.[104]

The new law practically eliminated the participation of notaries and created the National Adoption Council, an oversight agency that requires all orphanages to register with the agency. The law prohibits birth parents from being paid for giving a child up for adoption. Biological parents will have to wait at least six weeks after birth before deciding whether to put the child up for adoption.[105] Guatemala complied with Hague provisions and lifted the ban on adoptions in 2010.

Vietnam

When fewer children were available from China and Guatemala, growing numbers of U.S. citizens turned to Vietnam to adopt. They adopted more than 1,200 Vietnamese children over the 18 months ending in March 2008. In 2007, adoptions quadrupled from a year earlier. But in April 2008, Vietnamese officials announced that it was stopping all U.S. adoptions after a U.S. Embassy report alleged that there was widespread corruption, fraud, and baby selling in Vietnam. The report "outlined rampant abuses, including hospitals selling infants whose mothers could not pay their bills, brokers scouring villages for babies, and a grandmother who gave away her grandchild without telling the child's mother."[106]

The Embassy report said that there was a suspicious surge in the number of babies listed as abandoned, making it impossible to confirm the children were orphans or that their parents knowingly put them up for adoption, as required by U.S. law. The report said that some American adoption agencies paid orphanage officials as much as $10,000 per referral, while others took them on shopping sprees and junkets to the United States in return for a flow of babies.[107]

Vu Duc Long, director of Vietnam's International Adoption Agency, called the U.S. allegations "groundless." He threatened to scrap a bilateral agreement with the United States but said they would continue to process the current applications of families matched with babies.

On October 15, 2008, the governments of Vietnam and the United States jointly announced that intercountry adoptions were suspended until a new bilateral agreement is reached or Vietnam accedes to the Hague Adoption Convention. Since then, there have been talks between Vietnamese and U.S. officials. The government of Vietnam has stated its intention to introduce new adoption legislation and institute reforms in the adoption process, and it has indicated that the anticipated new legislation and implementing regulations may take effect in 2010.[108]

Romania

International adoptions in Romania soared after footage was released in the early 1990s depicting dire conditions at orphanages, which appeared on a Barbara Walters show. Approximately 20,000 children were adopted from Romania from 1990 to 2000,[109] but were halted when Romania banned adoptions by all foreigners except relatives of the children in 2005, without resolving the cases of 1,100 Romanian orphans and abandoned children for whom foreign families had registered adoption petitions before the ban. Approximately 270 families in the United States were in the process of adopting children from Romania before this law was passed. Romania was responding to pressure from the European Union (EU), whose representative for assessing Romania's EU membership was Baroness Emma Nicolson, described by Rep. Christopher Smith, a Republican from New Jersey, as "virulently anti-adoption." She was succeeded by a new representative at the EU, Pierre Moscovici, who stated publicly that he differed from his predecessor on the issue of international adoption. The European Parliament in December 2005 asked that Romania resolve international adoption cases registered during 2001–2004 "with the goal of allowing intercountry adoptions to take place, where justified and appropriate."[110]

Despite lobbying by parents who had applied for adoption, Congressional resolutions advocating changes in Romania's adoption laws, and attempts by President Bush to raise the issue with Romanian President Traian Basescu, Romania stopped its international adoptions.

Cambodia

Cambodia, which once supplied large numbers of children to adoptive parents, stopped its intercountry adoptions in 2002 because of allegations of corrupt "baby laundering." The Immigration and Naturalization Service (INS) suspended visa processing for adopted children, citing suspicions that they were bought or stolen from their parents and put into orphanages with false paperwork to feed the growing American demand for babies. The United States halted adoptions from Cambodia in 2001.

Even after the shutdown, critics said that babies were still being sold in some Cambodian villages, "with parents often driven into poverty in a country recovering from three decades of conflict and where 45 percent of the people live on $1 a day or less."[111] An adoption study by the Netherlands in 2003 found that children were bought for between $20 and $100 from poor Cambodian parents by brokers. Then, foreigners would pay from $5,000 to $20,000 to adopt. U.S. immigration authorities forced an

American adoption agency to close because it had put children up for adoption who had been bought from poor families. The director of the agency's plea deal stated that in most adoptions she and her partner had made payments of up to $3,500 to Cambodian ministry clerks, employees, or officials to facilitate adoptions. It also said that several adoptive parents were told to make direct deposits of $2,250 into the Phnom Penh bank account of a Cambodian public official.

Before the United States stopped adoptions from Cambodia, approximately 400 families were caught in the middle of the adoption process. Some U.S. parents flew to Phnom Penh to wait until their adoptions were cleared. The Cambodian government had already sent them an "adoption decree" that allowed them to pick up the child, but without INS approval they could not bring them home.

A *New York Times* reporter investigated the case of a child who had been sold to an orphanage by the mother, who was given $50 and promised another $100 in a week, but never received the $100. The mother sold the child because she was pregnant again and having trouble paying the rent. The aunt said, "When she told me she sold her baby, I could not do anything but cry."[112] The aunt located the child and her 22-year-old daughter went to the clinic where the child had been sold, accompanied by a policeman. The family bought the child back who "now lives with her aunt, grandmother and cousins, the six of them supported by the cousin's garment-factory wages of between $40 and $70 a month."[113] They are still paying on the loan they took out to buy the child back. The mother, who had moved to the countryside, sold the child's brother. The aunt said, "We don't know where the baby boy has gone."[114] She said the promise of a better life in the United States should not eclipse love, even when staying in Cambodia means inevitable hardship. "I understand they have food over there, but I would not feel calm if I could not see my niece."[115]

Dale Edmonds, a New Zealand adoptive mother living in Singapore, adopted a child who she was told was 6 years old, but the child told her that she was actually 11, that she and her brother were born with different names than had been given to Edmonds, and she was told not to discuss her history. The facilitator told Edmonds that her children's birth mother had died in a rural province, when in fact the child insisted that her mother was living in Phnom Penh. Edmonds located the children's mother and sister. The birth mother did not object to the siblings' move to Singapore, and Edmonds and her husband, at the mother's request, adopted her other daughter. "'What matters most,' Edmonds says, 'is that her Cambodian-born children were stripped of their names and histories and essentially hidden from their birth family. I wanted to think our adoption was ethical,' she says, 'It hurt bitterly to have those beliefs challenged.'"[116]

The INS cleared some pending cases for adoption, but said they would not approve adoptions until Cambodia changed its laws. Prospective parents accused the INS and the U.S. Embassy of viewing their situation heartlessly. They engaged in a passionate letter-writing campaign to Congress. They picketed the INS building in Washington toting posters that bore plaintive faces of orphanage children, emblazoned with slogans like "The Only Family That Wants Me Is in the U.S." Few seem willing to consider the governments' assertion that some of these children have been bought or that birth parents could have been intentionally misled. At the very least, many insist that shady practices are sporadic rather than systemic and that a shutdown of adoption is unwarranted. Most remain convinced that their particular agencies, facilitators, and orphanages are not suspect.[117] Meanwhile, the babies remained in orphanages. One child got malaria and another died while the parents were waiting for them.

A South Carolina adoption agency director of Carolina Hope Christian Adoption Agency said, "An imperfect system doesn't mean that all adoptions should stop. It means that some safeguards need to be put in place."[118]

It is difficult to evaluate how widespread child trafficking is. Some transactions that are called trafficking involve practice of bribing officials that is a commonplace way of doing business in some localities, even though bribes to civil officials is a crime in Cambodia. Some birth parents are glad to have their children adopted by parents who they believe can give their children a better life. "There are Cambodians who will crowd a baby stroller pushed by American parents and stroke the cheek of the adopted child inside, lending tacit approval. 'Lucky baby,' they will say in Kmer, 'Lucky baby.' There are others who pointedly avert their gaze."[119]

Most adoption agencies are probably ethical and are careful to know the child's parentage and history, but there are some unethical facilitators who are in it only for the money. Probably there is no way for adoptive parents to know with absolute certainty that the parents of their child were lied to, or worse, had their babies stolen, unless they have direct contact with the child's mother. Some birth parents lie when they give their child to an orphanage, saying that the child is an orphan.

Africa

Adoption agencies report that U.S. families increasingly are asking about adopting children from Africa. Changing racial attitudes are partly responsible, as well as the celebrity effect of Angelina Jolie, who adopted a girl from Ethiopia, and Madonna, who adopted a boy from Malawi. Also many churches are telling parishioners about the needs of orphans in Ethiopia and elsewhere in Africa. Ethiopia and Liberia are emerging as popular countries to adopt from, although the number of children they send here remains relatively small.[120] South Africa and Kenya have also allowed a few children to be adopted, but many African nations are closed to international adoption. Some countries resist adoption because of cultural beliefs and traditions, and some have lengthy processes that make it difficult to adopt. Adoption in Malawi is allowed only after 18 months of fostering a child in Malawi.[121] (When Madonna applied to adopt a second child in Malawi, a judge informed her that prospective parents must be resident in Malawi for 18 to 24 months before adopting.) [122]

The AIDS epidemic in sub-Saharan Africa has created an orphan crisis. A 2004 UNICEF and USAID report said that 12.3 million children have lost one or both parents to AIDS, and orphan numbers are projected to rise to 18.4 million by 2010. [123]

OPEN INTERNATIONAL ADOPTION

Open international adoptions could be arranged if an organization wanted to do it. Open adoption has occurred in the Marshall Islands, where many U.S. servicemen stationed there adopted children of native families. Traditionally, adoption in the Marshall Islands was practiced within the clan or tribe. The concept of terminating parental rights was never instituted, and the child had a relationship with both birth and adoptive families, often returning to the birth family in the birth parent's old age. The adoptive family, typically with more resources, was expected not only to care for the child but also to provide assistance to the child's birth family. The gift of the child was reciprocated by the adoptive family with ongoing assistance to the birth family. [124]

U.S. servicemen had adopted more than 140 children between 1990 and 1998, with some degree of openness. The birth mothers expected the children to return to Marshall Islands after attaining adulthood, and they also expected to stay in touch with the adoptive families. However, within several years of the adoption, only 28.8 percent believed their children would return. Promised gifts and letters stopped or had not come at all, although some did continue contact. Some adoptive families had sent photos and aid packages, made visits back to the Marshall Island, and even helped birth families visit the children in their adoptive homes.

Every birth parent wanted to stay in touch but some had no way of being contacted or making contact. They were very poor and many were intimidated by the prospect of writing a letter, especially in English, or sending items through the mail. Most of them could not afford to make an international phone call. Many moved frequently and left no forwarding address. "When the correspondence dwindles, some birth mothers may not be assertive enough to complain to the 'right' people—such as the local liaison that facilitated the adoption—or they may feel powerless to do anything to correct the situation." [125]

The authors of this study conclude that to facilitate contact between birth and adoptive parents, adoption facilitators or the government should provide translation and repository services and calling cards or Internet credit for e-mails. "In the meantime, the Marshallese birth families should be provided with safety net services such as food and medical programs as well as long term capacity building programs such as access to basic services, education, and economic self-sufficiency opportunities." [126] That is also good advice for this country and for all countries that supply children for adoption.

The Hague Convention on Intercountry Adoption

The Hague Convention sets minimum international standards for adoptions that occur between countries, to insure greater protection from exploitation of children, birth parents, and adoptive parents. The international treaty was approved by 66 nations in 1993 at the Hague. The United States signed it in 1994, but did not issue final rules until 2006. They ratified it on December 12, 2007, and it entered into force on April 1, 2008.

The Hague Convention requires the 75 participating countries to take specific steps to ensure that children have not been sold or stolen and that adoptive parents are suitable. It urges countries to try to find domestic homes for its children before looking abroad. It requires one central authority to be in place in each country so that adoptive parents get the most accurate information regarding adoption. The department of state is the U.S. Central authority. Private adoption agencies need to be accredited or approved. In the past, adoption agencies in the United States were licensed and supervised only by individual states.[127]

The Hague Convention has contributed to the decline of international adoptions. The U.S. government is more closely scrutinizing requests for U.S. visas for foreign children. Most child welfare advocates welcome the initiative, but some adoption experts claim that the State Department is sometimes too quick to reject adoptions from nations not meeting the Hague guidelines, as with Vietnam and Guatemala. "They fear that these rules may prove so rigorous and indiscriminate that they will severely curtail international adoptions as a vital escape route for children in troubled regions."[128]

The United Nations Children's Fund (UNICEF)

UNICEF has been a vocal proponent of keeping orphaned children in their home countries.[129] Alexandra Yuster, a senior adviser in the child-protection section of UNICEF, claims the organization advocates the inclusion of international adoption in the mix of potential solutions for countries seeking homes for orphaned children. But it is much more focused on helping birth families get adequate support from their governments so they can take care of their own kids. "That's our priority because that will help a much larger number of kids—as will promoting domestic adoption," she says.[130]

Some advocates blame the decline of international adoptions on the UNICEF policy. They argue that "the organization places misguided emphasis on maintaining cultural and geographic ties rather than on the child's overall well-being. That's true even when there is little chance of domestic adoption and virtually no public programs to provide care for abandoned children or struggling families."[131] Critics of international adoption argue that children have heritage rights and belong in their countries of birth, but children enjoy little in the way of heritage or other rights in institutions. UNICEF favors in-country foster care over out-of-country adoption, but foster care does not exist as a real option in most countries that allow children to be adopted abroad.

Adopting children from foreign orphanages carries the same risks as adopting children from the foster care system. Orphanages are overflowing with severely handicapped or older children who often bear deep physical or emotion scars, and that is also true of the U.S. foster care system. The U.S. Department of Health and Human Services recently found that 81 children adopted overseas were relinquished to foster care agencies in 14 states in 2006.[132]

CONCLUSION

Millions of the world's children are homeless or languishing in orphanages. Some people say that instead of adopting them, people should raise the standard of living in their native countries or contribute to a fund that helps the children. But it need not be an either-or choice. Both are necessary. Although countries are developing their capacity to care for their own children, there are children who would have no home if they were not adopted. Countries that say they will not allow intercountry adoptions because their children are "valuable resources" often do that for political reasons but do little or nothing to improve the living conditions of these "valuable resources." Underdeveloped countries take a long time to develop. Meanwhile, there are children who desperately need homes.

It seems to me that the Edmonds family who adopted Cambodian children has chosen the best of both worlds. The adoptive parents know their children's past and do not have any guilt about taking stolen children. The children know their origins and are in contact with their birth mother.

It is heartening to see the stigma of adoption lessening. It is time to put aside the idealization of the biological nuclear family. Families take many shapes besides that one—adoptive families, gays and lesbians, childless couples, single women and men, stepparents, grandparents and other relatives, and older people. Adoption helps people to break away from the obsession with biological reproduction and ethnic purity and to embrace the "other." Open adoption could even pave the way to that ideal society for children where children could choose who they want to live with, as in the Samoa described by Margaret Mead.

There is no reason to stigmatize adoption. There is no reason to stigmatize unwed parents. There is no reason to stigmatize mothers who choose to give their children to adoptive couple. But there is also no reason why children should be taken away from parents who want their children and would be able to parent them if given adequate social supports. That is as true for children who live in the United States as it is for children in other countries.

NOTES

1. Jack Goody, "Adoption in cross-cultural perspective," *Comparative Studies in Society and History*, New York: Cambridge University Press, 1959, pp. 55–78.
2. Meir Horowitz, "Child and youth legislation," in *Child and youth welfare in Israel*, ed. by Moshe Smilansky. Jerusalem: Henrietta Szold Institute for Child and Youth Welfare, 1960, p. 262.
3. Frederick Engels, *The origins of the family, private property, and the state*. New York: International Publishers, 1942.
4. Margaret Kornitzer, *Adoption in the modern world*. New York: Philosophical Library, 1952, p. 267.
5. T. Richard Witmer, "The purpose of American adoption laws," in Chap. 1 of *Independent Adoptions*, Helen Witmer et al. New York: Russell Sage Foundation, 1963, p. 20.
6. Ibid., p. 28.
7. S. B. Presser, "The historical background of the American law of adoption, *Journal of Family Law*, 1972, 11:446.
8. Marcel Proust, *Remembrance of things past: Within a budding grove*. New York: Vintage Books, 1982, pp. 744–745.
9. Deborah L. Jacobs, "Adult adoption a high-stakes means to an inheritance," *New York Times*, May 21, 2009.
10. Vern Carroll, ed. *Adoption in Eastern Oceania*. Honolulu: University of Hawaii Press, 1970.
11. Anthony Hopper, "Adoption in the society islands," in *Adoption in Eastern Oceania*, pp. 52–70.
12. J. L. Fisher, "Adoption on Ponape," in *Adoption in Eastern Oceania*, p. 303.
13. Margaret Mead, *Coming of age in Samoa*. New York: MentorBook, New American Library, 1949, p. 34.
14. Ibid.
15. "Margaret Mead: New Generation Coming of Age," in "Reiss: Rapid changes in sexual behavior," *The University of Iowa Spectator*, vol. 5, no. 5 (April 1972): 4–5. (Report of a speech by Margaret Mead.)
16. H. David Kirk, *Shared fate*. New York: Free Press, 1964, p. 129.
17. Adam Pertman, "A private matter no longer," *Boston Globe*, March 8, 1998, p. A1.
18. Elizabeth Barthelet, "Beyond biology," family workshop paper, February 8, 1994.
19. Ibid.
20. J. H. Hollinger, "Aftermath of adoption: Legal and social consequences," in *Adoption law and practice*, ed. J. H. Hollinger. New York: Matthew Bender, 1991, p. 13–35.

21. Burton Z. Sokoloff, "Antecedents of American adoption," *The future of children: Adoption*, vol. 3, no. 1, Spring 1993.

22. Bill Lohmann, "World of adoption; forced to give up her baby, she now opposes adoption," *Richmond Times Dispatch*, November 21, 2004, p. G-1. Accessed through LexisNexis June 9, 2006.

23. Ibid.

24. Ibid.

25. Ibid.

26. J. Paton, *The adopted break silence*. Acton, CA: Life History Study Center, 1954.

27. Sokoloff, "Antecedents of American adoption."

28. Otile McManus, "Birth mothers and the adoption triangle," *Boston Globe*, October 9, 1977, p. 57.

29. Dru Sefton, "Anti-adoption activists buck tide of public opinion," *Newhouse News Service*, August 4, 2004. Accessed through LexisNexis June 9, 2006.

30. Ibid.

31. Pertman, "A private matter no longer."

32. Sefton, "Anti-adoption activists."

33. Ibid.

34. Pertman, "A private matter no longer."

35. Ibid.

36. Ibid.

37. Esther B. Fein, "Secrecy and stigma no longer clouding adoptions," *New York Times*, October 25, 1998, p. 1.

38. Ibid.

39. Barthelet, "Beyond biology."

40. Ibid.

41. Tamar Lewin, "Unwed father fight for babies placed for adoption by mothers," *New York Times*, March 19, 2006. Accessed through LexisNexis June 9, 2006.

42. Ibid.

43. Kathleen Burge, "Mothers' past publicized during adoption process," *Boston Globe*, December 20, 1999.

44. Ibid.

45. Ibid., p. 19.

46. Ibid., p. 277.

47. Ibid., p. 301.

48. Ibid., p. 310.

49. Royal Ford, "At 43, Navajo native finally home," *Boston Globe*, June 2, 1996, p. 1.

50. Rohan Sullivan, "Australia rejects pressure for apology to Aborigines," *Boston Globe*, January 9, 1998.

51. National Public Radio, May 26, 2006.

52. "Yemenite Jews' babies taken, rabbi says," *Boston Globe*, September 18, 1997, p. A11.

53. *Journal of Public Health*, vol. 13, no. 3 (1992 Autumn): 291–305.
54. Rick Vecchio, "Pregnant teen's killing shocks Peru," *Boston Globe*, March 2, 2006, p. A9.
55. Andrew Jacobs, "Hunger for a son fueling abductions," *Boston Globe*, April 5, 2009, p. A2.
56. Fein, "Secrecy and stigma no longer clouding adoptions."
57. Ibid.
58. Henry S. Maas and Richard E. Engler, Jr., *Children in need of parents*. New York: Columbia University Press, 1959, p. 374.
59. Ibid., p. 377.
60. Trudy Bradley, *An exploration of caseworkers' perceptions of adoptive applicants*. New York: Child Welfare League of America, 1967, p. 190.
61. Ibid.
62. Bradley, *An exploration of caseworkers' perceptions*, p. 43.
63. Richard Sullivan and Ellie Lathrop, "Openness in adoption: Retrospective lessons and prospective choices," *Children and Youth Services Review*, vol. 26 (2004): 393–411.
64. Adam Pertman, "Vying to be among the chosen," *Boston Globe*, March 9, 1998, p. A1.
65. Ibid.
66. Elizabeth Barthelet, letter to *New York Times*, December 18, 1993, p. A24.
67. Charles Freid, letter to *New York Times*, December 8, 1993, p. A24.
68. Ron Nixon, "De-emphasis on race in adoption is criticized," *New York Times*, May 27, 2008, p. 16.
69. Ibid.
70. Ruth G. McRoy, Zena Oglesby, and Helen Grape, "Achieving same-race adoptive placements for African-American children: Culturally sensitive practice approaches," *Child Welfare*, vol. LXXVI, no. 1 (January–February 1997): 102.
71. Maas and Engler, *Children in need of parents*; Benson Jaffe and David Fanshel, *How they fared in adoption: A follow-up study*. New York: Columbia University Press, 1970; Henry Maas, "The successful adoptive parent applicant," *Social Work*, 5, 1960, pp. 14–20; Alfred Kadushin, "A study of adoptive parents of hard-to-place children," *Social Casework*, vol. 43: 227–233; Lillian Ripple, *A follow-up study of adopted children*. Chicago: University of Chicago Press, 1968; Bradley, *An exploration of caseworkers' perceptions*.
72. McRoy, Oglesby, and Grape, "Achieving same-race adoptive placements."
73. Christopher J. Mumola, *Incarcerated parents and their children*. Special report for the Department of Justice, August 2000, p. 4.
74. Victoria Law, *Resistance behind bars*. Oakland, CA: PM Press, 2009, p. 47.

75. U. S. Department of Health and Human Services, *Trends in foster care and adoption, FY 2002-FY 2008.* http://www/acf.hhs.gov/ programs/cb/stats_research/afcars/trends.htm. Accessed February 6, 2010.
76. Daniel Golden, "When adoption doesn't work," *Boston Globe,* June 11, 1989, p. 16.
77. Leroy Pelton, *For reasons of poverty: A critical analysis of the public child welfare system in the United States.* Westport, CT: Praeger, 1989, pp. 92–96.
78. U. S. Department of Health and Human Services. *The AFCARS report: Preliminary FY 2003 estimates as of April 2005 (10).* Washington, DC: Author.
79. Leslie Kaugman, "Cash incentives for adoption seen as risk to some children," *New York Times,* October 29, 2003.
80. Dalynn Kuster, "Babies for the rich," qwamyin@ivillage.com, posted on the Welfare Law Center listserv, workfare-wlc@igc.topica.com, May 1, 2000.
81. Ibid.
82. Ibid.
83. Ibid.
84. Fed H. Wilczyn, Kristen Brunner Hislop, and Lijun Chen, "Adoption dynamics and the Adoption and Safe Families Act. Chapin Hall Center for Children at the University of Chicago, November 2005. Accessed October 1, 2006 at http://www.rand.org/labor/ pdfs/2005_wulczyn.pdf
85. Richard Wexler, "Take the child and run: Tales from the age of ASFA." *New England Law Review,* vol. 36, no. 1, October 17, 2002.
86. Ibid.
87. "Failure to Protect," *Frontline PBS,* http://www.pbs.org/wgbh/pages/ frontline/shows/fostercare/inside/gelles.html. Accessed October 12, 2006.
88. Ibid., p. 145.
89. "Failure to Protect," p. 163.
90. Richard Wexler, personal communication.
91. Lifeline Children's Services, http://www.lifelineadoption.org
92. Peter C. Winkler, "Domestic and international adoptions," *Social Work,* vol. 52, no. 2, April 2007, p. 189.
93. Sara Corbett, "Where do babies come from?" *New York Times Magazine,* June 16, 2002, p. 46.
94. Erin Spiegel, "Adoptions of foreign children plunge," *Washington Times,* March 8, 2009.
95. Patricia Wen, "China's policies lead to drop in Bay State adoptions," *Boston Globe,* May 1, 2006.
96. Ibid.

97. Wendy Koch and Calum MacLeod, "Adoption agencies report swell of interest in earthquake orphans," *USA Today*, May 29, 2008.
98. Pat Wingert, "Wanted: A bundle of joy," *Newsweek*, October 13, 2008.
99. Ibid.
100. Ibid.
101. Mac Margolis, Mike Elkin, Anna Nemtsova, Alexandra Pollier, and B. J. Lee, "Who will fill the empty cribs? International adoptions are on the decline, despite growing demand and an endless supply of orphans," *Newsweek*, February 4, 2008.
102. Debbie Elliott, host of "All Things Considered," National Public Radio, January 8, 2006.
103. Juan Carlos Llorca, "Guatemala tightens adoptions, leaves pending cases alone," *Boston Globe*, December 12, 2007, p A3.
104. Margolis et. al., "Who will fill the empty cribs?"
105. Ibid.
106. Chris Brummitt, "Vietnam puts stop to all US adoptions," *Boston Globe*, April 29, 2008, p. A4.
107. Ibid.
108. Joint Council on International Children's Services, May 1, 2009. http://www.jcics.org/Vietnam.htm. Accessed February 6, 2010.
109. Alison Damast, "Family waits for word on Romanian adoption," *The Stamford Advocate*, May 27, 2006. Accessed June 9, 2006, at lexis-nexis.com/universe/document?_m=c1018613ce6b780cb34c9 9c4b7ec360...
110. Jeffrey Thomas, "Congressional resolution urges Romania to amend adoption ban," *Federal Information and News Dispatch, Inc.* Washington DC, April 11, 2006. Accessed June 9, 2006 at lexis-nexis. com/universe/document?_m=aa5f08cb3442c27a5c4ebb8e&...
111. Miranda Lettsinger, "Foreign adoptions of Cambodian children continue despite complaints of babies sold or stolen," *Associated Press Worldstream*, August 24, 2004. Accessed June 9, 2006 at lexis-nexis.com/universe/document?_m=41255253dd4901a5a84e 5f92d6fbb249...
112. Corbett, "Where do babies come from?" p. 47.
113. Ibid.
114. Corbett, "Where do babies come from?"
115. Ibid.
116. Ibid., p. 83.
117. Ibid., pp. 74, 82.
118. Corbett, "Where do babies come from?"
119. Ibid., p. 44.
120. Wendy Koch, "Cuts in foreign adoptions causing anxiety in USA: Rules protecting kids create barriers for some," *USA Today*,

August 12, 2008. http://www.usatoday.com/news/world/2008–08-12-foreign-adoptions_N.htm Accessed February 6, 2010.

121. Jini L. Robi and Stacey A. Shaw, "The African orphan crisis and international adoption," *Social Work*, vol. 51, no. 3, July 2006, p. 205.

122. Ryan Parry, "No mercy: Madonna screams out in agony as her adoption bid fails," *The Mirror*, April 4, 2009.

123. UNAIDS, UNICEF & USAID, "Children on the brink 2004: A joint report of new orphan estimates and a framework for action," 2004.

124. Jini Roby, Jamie Wyatt, and Gregory Pettys, "Openness in international adoptions: A study of U.S. parents who adopted children from the Marshall Islands," *Adoption Quarterly*, vol. 8, no. 3, 2005, p. 50.

125. Ibid.

126. Ibid., p. 68.

127. Office of Children's Issues, United States Department of State, *Intercountry Adoption*. http://adoption.state.gov/ Accessed February 6, 2010.

128. Margolis, et. al., "Who will fill the empty cribs?"

129. Ibid.

130. Pat Wingert, "When there's no place like home: Children's advocates can't agree on how much to emphasize intercountry adoption as a solution," *Newsweek*, February 4, 2008.

131. Ibid.

132. Margolis et al., "Who will fill the empty cribs?"

CHAPTER 8

The Punitive State: Dimensions of Incarceration in the United States

Marguerite G. Rosenthal

For most of the twentieth century... [the] view of prisons as exotic institutions was justified by an incarceration rate that covered a small fraction of the population. The prison boom, however, has overtaken the usual social science analysis. Researchers now observe that incarceration is a pervasive event in the lives of poor and minority men. *Punishment has become normalized...the criminal justice system has now become a fixture in the passage to adulthood for minority youth with little economic opportunity.*

—*Pattillo, Weiman, and Western, 2004. p. 3, emphasis added.*[1]

INTRODUCTION

The United States is often described as a welfare state laggard. This term and its companion, "the reluctant welfare state," refer to the fact that, compared to other industrialized (especially Western European) countries, the United States provides fewer and less comprehensive health, social, educational, and vocational programs and supports for its population. There are few universal programs (no universal health care, a not-quite-universal public pension system that is under attack, and time-limited social assistance, to name just a few examples).

An aspect of U.S. "exceptionalism" that is often ignored in comparative welfare state discourse is the far-reaching arm of its criminal justice system. The United States incarcerates an extraordinarily high number and proportion of its population, and, at the same time that welfare and educational programs have been contracting, prisons and jails and their attendant supervisory programs—probation and parole—have been expanding. In the context of a tax-resistant political climate, not only has incarceration consumed large proportions of federal, but especially state, budgets that might otherwise be spent on supportive public programs, but has also been carried out in an increasingly punitive manner that has for all intents and purposes abandoned rehabilitation as a goal.

This chapter addresses several aspects of recent American criminal justice policies, including the growth of the prison population over the last 30 years, the disproportionate incarceration of African American males, the acceleration of imprisoning women, prison conditions and outcomes, resource consumption associated with the criminal "justice" system, and the growth of the privatized prison system (an almost exclusively American approach). A brief comparison of U.S. criminal justice policies with those of other Western countries shows that in penal policy, too, the United States stands alone.

THE DRAMATIC GROWTH OF INCARCERATION IN THE UNITED STATES

Over the last 30 years, the United States has seen unprecedented numbers of people imprisoned, and the rates of the incarcerated—particularly of minority men—have skyrocketed.

The prison population in county, state, and federal jails and prisons numbered 2,250,000 in the year ending June 30, 2006 (the latest official data available). Of these, 191,080 were in federal custody, 1,365,438 in state or state-contracted prisons, and nearly 944,000 were serving sentences in local or county jails.[2] In 2005, nearly 35 percent of admissions to state prisons were for parole violations.[3] The Sentencing Project puts the current total at 2.3 million.[4] Although the recent recession's impact on state budgets has led to some states' resorting to early release programs, the trends have consistently been upward. As columnist Adam Liptak points out,[5] the United States has less than 5 percent of the world's population but almost a quarter of its prisoners; China, with four times our population (and not known for its kindness to criminals—for instance, it leads the world in executions) has somewhat more than half the number of prisoners. The U.S. prison population exceeds that of *all 26 European* countries, including the Russian Federation, by 400,000.[6] One-third of all prisoners are in the federal system and two populous and "tough on crime" states, Texas and California.[7]

The changing rates of incarceration—the number in state and federal prisons per 100,000 in the population—are very telling. In 1929, the rate was 79; by 1939, it had risen to 137: thereafter, it fluctuated between just under 100 to the 130s until 1981 when the rates began a steady rise to 217 in 1986, 332 in 1992 and, including the jail population, to 751 currently (excluding people in jail, the rate was 496:100,000 in 2006).[8] Men are 14 times more likely than women to be incarcerated, but the rate of women's incarceration has been rising faster than men's since 2000.[9] This is particularly stunning when we consider that the incarceration rate for women in 1970 was close to zero, rising to approximately 80:100,000 in 2000. There were 969 of every 100,000 men compared to 67 of every 100,000 women in federal or state prison. Currently, 1 of every 265 women is locked up.[10]

There has also been a dramatic increase in the number of prisoners serving life sentences. In 1984, there were 34,000 lifers, but by 2008, this figure had mushroomed to 140,610 or 1 in 11 prisoners (but 1 in 5 in California), almost all of whom are men and nearly half are African American; 42,000 have no possibility of parole, and almost 7,000 juveniles are serving life sentences, 26 percent of whom without the possibility of parole.[11] No other Western country treats juveniles this way. Again, a disproportionate—nearly half—of these youth are black. Needless to say, the United States stands alone among Western countries in continuing to put people to death.

Prison building has expanded dramatically, particularly in the states of Texas, Florida, California, and New York (among others). In the 10 states with the biggest increases, counties housing prisons went from 13 percent in 1979 to 31 percent in 2000.[12] Writing in the *New York Times,* California prisoner Kenneth Hartman put it this way: "Private airplane pilots tell me it's easy to navigate at night from San Diego to Los Angeles and on up the Central Valley to Sacramento by simply following the prisons' glowing lights."[13]

Racial disparities in the United States are particularly stunning. In 2006, black men were incarcerated at a rate 6.5 times greater than white men (4.8 percent of black men, 0.7 percent of white men, and 1.9 percent of Hispanic men were in state and federal prisons or local jails); almost 12 percent of black men between the ages of 25 and 29 were imprisoned.[14] Incarceration rates in impoverished neighborhoods are staggeringly high. It has been estimated that 75 percent of African American males living in Washington, DC spend time in jail or prison at some point during their lives.[15] Noted criminologist Bruce Western has calculated that a black male high school dropout born in the late 1960s had a nearly 60 percent risk of being imprisoned by the time he reached his early 30s. Even if he graduated from high school, he had a 20 percent chance of going to prison.[16] Human Rights Watch reports that in 11 states, black men are 12 to 26 times more likely to be incarcerated than white men; in Washington, DC, those rates are 49 times greater than for whites, and many if not most of these imprisonments are drug-related (see below).[17] As for women prisoners aged 35–39, the rate for whites is 1:355, for Hispanics, 1:297 but for blacks, 1:100.[18]

ECONOMIC COLLAPSE AND HARSHER SENTENCING POLICIES HAVE LED TO MORE IMPRISONMENT

Although crime rates rose dramatically between the mid-1960s and mid-1970s and accounted for some of the growth in the prison population, most of prison expansion happened later as a result of changes in laws and policies. A much more punitive response to crime, including prison sentences for drug possession, mandatory sentencing policies that have lengthened prison terms, and "three strikes" laws (where persons convicted of a third crime, no matter the degree of severity, receive an automatic sentence of anywhere from 25 years to life) account for as much as 88 percent of the increased prison population.[19]

These policies have particularly targeted black men whose legitimate earning capacities have been severely eroded. Inner city jobless ghettos were the incubators of mass incarceration, with violence associated with increased drug activity. Western refers to these events as the "disappointed promise of the civil rights movement"[20] and concludes that the aggressive approaches that incarcerate so many young men, especially young black men, are a repressive response by ruling white elites to that movement. Associated with this backlash was the election of Republican governors after 1980; harsh treatment, even for nonviolent offenders, characterized those Republican states.[21]

IMPRISONING NONVIOLENT AND DRUG OFFENDERS

Unlike those in other countries, U.S. policies (both federal and state laws) lead to the incarceration of nonviolent offenders. Thus in 1980, 41 percent of those in prison had been convicted of nonviolent crimes, increasing to 54 percent in 1990, and they accounted for 51 percent of prisoners in 2000. In 2005, 42 percent of prisoners in state prisons were evenly split between those convicted of drug and property crimes; another 8 percent were locked up for public order offenses.[22] (It should be noted, though, that because of plea bargaining, it is likely that some convictions for nonviolent offenses may, in fact, have been originally included charges of violent actions.)

Approximately 20 percent of state prisoners, but 55 percent of federal prisoners, are imprisoned for drug offenses. Drug offenses are among the most typical reasons that women are in prison.[23]

Drug offenses, in fact, are the principle reason that the federal prison population shot up in the 1990s, and the numbers in federal prisons for drug offenses continue to rise. Simple possession (i.e., possession of drugs for one's own use—a victimless crime) accounts for 28 percent of all drug-related admissions to state prisons, and even the majority of those imprisoned for trafficking were low-level operators.[24] Most disturbing are the extreme racial disparities in sentencing for drug offenses. Official reports, including results from the Federal National Household Survey on Drug Abuse, found that there are significantly more white than African American men who use drugs (i.e., 10.3 million versus 1.8 million in one 1997 month), but because federal law is harsher on crack cocaine use than powder (the latter used more by whites) and because of police and prosecutorial discretion, African American men are very much more likely to be imprisoned.[25] Some mitigation of these trends may be in the offing. A Supreme Court ruling in 2007 relieved federal judges from rigid sentencing guidelines in drug cases that have had a disproportionate effect on African Americans and in May, 2009, a federal district court judge ruled that convictions in crack and powder cocaine cases should be equivalent.[26] In Congress, the U.S. House Judiciary Subcommittee in July, 2009 supported legislation proposing to equalize federal sentences for the two forms of cocaine.[27] There has been a recent reversal in sentencing practices: from 1999 to 2005, there was a drop of 21.6 percent in the numbers of blacks in state prisons for drug offenses, while there was an increase of 42.6 percent of the numbers of incarcerated white drug offenders. Explanations include a decline in racial profiling, less open drug dealing, a drop in the crack trade, greater use of diversion programs such as drug courts, and more aggressive law enforcement efforts targeting the production and use of methamphetamines, activities conducted primarily by whites.[28]

Unemployment, Crime, and Punishment

The dramatic rise in the numbers and rates of the incarcerated in the United States is policy-driven. In the 1990s, during the period of economic boom, the crime rate fell dramatically, according to U.S. Department of Justice's National Institute of Corrections; nonetheless, the incarceration rate continued to rise. The FBI has found a positive correlation between property crime and unemployment, and a longitudinal study concluded that low wages played an even more significant role in crime trends than did unemployment.[29] Violent crime declined steadily in the 1990s, falling from a high of 758:100,000 in 1991 and 1992 to 507:100,000 in 2000 and 475:100,000 in 2003 (murder rates have increased by almost 2 percent since 1999, a factor related primarily to urban gang violence). Analysts dispute whether the steep rise in incarceration during the same period explains the drop; Bruce Western claims it accounts for 10 percent of the drop at most.[30]

Extraordinarily and chronically high rates of unemployment characterize urban, minority populations in the United States. Bruce Western's analysis of the true extent of joblessness among young black men in the late 1990s—the era frequently cited as a time when the country achieved nearly full employment—shows clearly that for this population, there was no employment miracle. In fact, factoring in as unemployed the 1 in 3 who were incarcerated in 2000 shows that their true unemployment rate was 32.4, not 23.7 percent; for Hispanic young men, with 30 percent of joblessness attributable to incarceration, the real rate was 14.3 percent, not 10.3 percent.[31] Of course, this was also the time when tough laws were implemented (see figure 8.1). Young minority ghettoized men, many of whom drop out of school and have few skills, are almost destined to spend time in prison. Minority communities are heavily policed, resulting in more scrutiny and more arrests than in white

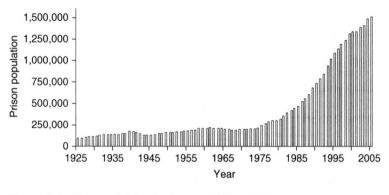

Figure 8.1 State and federal prisoners (1926–2005)
Source: Sentencing Project Homepage (www.sentencingproject.org)

neighborhoods, and minority men are targeted by the police. (Racial profiling has recently gained attention anew as the result of the arrest of Harvard professor Henry Louis Gates, Jr. in his own Cambridge, Massachusetts home.) As noted earlier, African Americans are incarcerated for drug crimes at levels much higher than the whites. Drug addiction itself is related to unemployment and hopelessness.[32] And unemployment rates are raised by the vast population of former prisoners who have great difficulty finding work because of lack of education and job skills, the de-skilling that takes place in prison, and significant discrimination on the part of employers.[33]

VIOLENCE IN AMERICA

Crimes of violence are higher in the United States than in other industrialized countries, at least partly caused by readily available guns and weak gun control policies. Even with a sharp decline in the murder rates in the United States in the late 1990s, those rates were still about four times greater than the average of European countries.[34] It is important to remember, though, that only approximately half of prison sentences are for violent offenders.

UNDOCUMENTED IMMIGRANTS, REFUGEES, AND PATRIOT ACT DETAINEES

As the U.S. economy has faltered, immigrants have become an easy target to blame for wage decline and unemployment among U.S. citizens, particularly the unskilled. Add to this the scare tactics orchestrated by the Bush administration after 9/11 and its predilection for rewarding its friends with lucrative contracts—in this case private prison corporations—as well as its creating a law enforcement/militarized cultural environment, and we come to the present situation where there has been an escalation in severe tactics used to keep migrants and refugees—particularly nonwhite ones—out and to imprison and deport thousands more. The passage of the Patriot Act was followed by broad sweeps of Muslim communities and detaining thousands. Immigrant detention is escalating faster than any other form of incarceration. The continuing failure of the U.S. Congress to reform our immigration laws has resulted in the brutal targeting, arrest and treatment of the undocumented, including factory raids and warrantless home intrusions, affecting many of the more than 11 million undocumented immigrants among us.

It is estimated that 440,000 migrants—more than 30,000 per day—were held in detention facilities in 2009, 3 times the number 10 years earlier.[35] The Immigration and Customs Enforcement agency of the Department of Homeland Security (ICE) holds 57 percent of detained immigrants in 312 county or city jails or in federal prisons and 43 percent in private prisons. It pays approximately $95/day for each detainee or approximately $1 billion each year to public and privately owned facilities. Cash-strapped local governments thus have an incentive to provide jail space for this population, and the private sector is profiting hugely. Immigrant detention, in fact, is the fastest growing sector in the private prison business.[36]

In 2008, following a tour of the U.S.-Mexican border and visiting a facility in Arizona—but having been denied access to others in Texas and New Jersey—the United Nations' Special Rapporteur on the human rights of migrants, Jorge Bustamante, issued a strong rebuke of the United States' treatment of immigrants. Bustamante charged the United States with violating international commitments for humane treatment of immigrants, especially of women and children, and he particularly pointed to overuse of and substandard conditions in detention facilities, overly long detentions, and lack of sufficient legal protections.[37] This last point is emphasized by Si Kahn in his review of the book, *American Gulag*. Detainees are technically not sentenced or awaiting trial, and unless they have been charged with a crime, they are not subject to the legal system available to American citizens. Instead, their fates are subject to the arbitrary decisions of ICE (formerly INS) bureaucrats, not judges.[38] A friend who does humanitarian work in the Arizona desert reports that as many as 70 people apprehended by the border control in a single day are given a "hearing" *en masse* in front of an ICE hearing officer before they are shunted off to detention. She recently witnessed an unusually brave man who had previously been deported—someone who now faces criminal charges for again illegally coming into the country—challenge his situation, stating that he had lived productively in the United States for 15 years, had a wife and children—all U.S. citizens—from whom he's now forcibly separated and whom he can no longer support.[39]

The official purpose of detention is to facilitate deportation, and although a 2001 U.S. Supreme Court issued a decision that migrants were to be summarily returned to their country of origin and not kept in detention for lengthy periods, many continue to be detained after they have been ordered to be deported—1,200 in March, 2005.[40] *New York Times* reporter Nina Bernstein has written repeatedly about the tragedies suffered by immigrant detainees. In January, 2010, she revealed that 107 immigrants have died in custody since 2003, many of them apparently because of disregard of their medical conditions and the denial of medical care.[41]

Parents, and especially mothers, face wrenching circumstances. On the one hand, their children can be inappropriately locked up with them; on the other, the children—especially if they have been born in the United States and are thus citizens—may be placed in foster care if no "legal" party agrees to care for them. Parents can be deported, leaving their children behind. Or, if their detention exceeds 15 months while their children are in foster care, termination of parental rights proceedings must begin, as prescribed by the Adoption and Safe Families Act (ASFA), and they may lose their children permanently. In some situations, informal foster arrangements can also result in immigrant parents' losing their children permanently.[42]

CONDITIONS IN PRISON

Recent prison riots have called some, if fleeting, public attention to the chronic overcrowding and the oppressive, threatening atmosphere that pervade American prisons. Even previously mouthed lip-service about rehabilitation and treatment, common in the post-World War II era, have been all but forgotten.[43] Control and punishment, combined with labor at subminimal wages, dominate prison complexes today. Jason DeParle summarizes the bipartisan Commission's report on Safety and Abuse in America's Prisons 2006 *Confronting Confinement* this way:

> America's prisons are dangerously overcrowded, unnecessarily violent, excessively reliant on physical segregation, breeding grounds of infectious disease, lacking in meaningful programs for inmates, and staffed by underpaid and undertrained guards in a culture that promotes abuse.[44]

A federal judge is quoted as saying that the prisons in Texas were pervaded by a "culture of sadistic and malicious violence" and that violence and intimidation are rampant in the nation's prisons.[45] In men's prisons, prisoner-on-prisoner rape is all too common and has become widely recognized. Prisoners have less ability to challenge these conditions than they once had; the Prison Litigation Reform Act of 1996 has succeeded in halving the number of prisoners' civil rights complaints.[46]

Women prisoners face a unique set of abuses and humiliations: sexual harassment, exploitation, and rape by male prison guards are all too frequent occurrences.[47] Approximately 65 percent of women prisoners are mothers of minor children, and one-third were raising their children alone at the time of their incarceration. Maintaining relationships with their children is made very difficult because of the lack of transportation and/or the unwillingness of caretakers and child welfare workers to bring children for visits.[48] Some women find visitation procedures—children being searched, their having to wear prison garb in their children's presence, meeting in noisy and impersonal surroundings—so unpleasant that they prefer to forego visits.[49] If a woman's child is placed in foster care—as is often the case—the mother faces losing custody permanently after 15 months, in accordance with provisions of ASFA. But even when children are raised by the prisoner's family member, she faces rejection for her failures, and some family caretakers refuse to return the children to their mothers when they are released.[50]

As for prison labor, an extreme example is the situation in Oregon where, in 1994, an approved ballot referendum mandates that all prisoners work for 40 hours per week.

The impact on unionized public sector, and especially on private sector, jobs has been enormous. In institutions around the country, prisoners book airline flights, pack and ship Microsoft software, and repair auto parts for a fraction of what "free world" workers make. Twenty-one thousand federal prisoners worked for Federal Prison Industries, a quasi-public for-profit company that sold $678.8 million in goods and services in 2002, $400 million to the Department of Defense. Prison workers are paid next to nothing for their labor—12 to 40 cents per hour for federal prisoners who work for UNICOR, the federal prison industries company.[51] Prison labor programs are not organized to provide job training or rehabilitation for prisoners but rather serve the needs of employers; those most likely to be chosen for work are those with the most skills.[52]

Treatment, whether for drug addictions or mental illness or health problems, is almost nonexistent in the prisons. Drug treatment slots were halved in the 1990s and are available to only 10 percent of those who need them.[53] A qualitative research study done by three of the author's students several years ago revealed that women in Framingham State Prison (the women's facility in Massachusetts), most of whom had drug involvement upon incarceration, received no treatment for their addictions until they reached their prerelease program.[54] Prisons have replaced state mental hospitals as the institutions for confining most of the country's mentally ill. The American Psychiatric Association has estimated that perhaps 20 percent of the prison population is mentally ill and a quarter of them are actively psychotic, yet there are barely any qualified mental health staff working in prisons and, instead, the most disturbed are seen as disruptive and are often isolated in solitary confinement.[55]

The state of prison health care is not only appallingly bad, but it also threatens public health since most prisoners eventually leave prison and share their diseases with the population at large. Prisoners come to prison in poorer health than the general population. HIV and AIDS, Tuberculosis and Hepatitis C are all communicable diseases that spread rapidly in prison, yet many if not most prisons have inadequate medical personnel and budgets to purchase needed medications. Medical care, determined by the U.S. Supreme Court to be constitutionally required for the incarcerated, is the largest single per prisoner cost, and yet many go untreated—particularly those who are served by privatized prison health companies.[56]

Education, too, has gone by the board in most prisons. Pell grants (federal grants available to low-income students to support college education), once available to prisoners, were cut off by Congress in 1994. Before the cutoff, approximately 300 colleges throughout the country offered courses in prisons. Now, despite the huge increase in the numbers of prisoners, only about 25 do so. One study found that 7 percent of prisoners from one institution who took college classes became recidivists, compared to 30 percent who did not, yet providing the opportunity to take college classes is seen as coddling, even rewarding, prisoners with benefits not available to others in the free world population. Despite a more than tripling of the numbers of state prisoners between 1979 and 1995, the number of educational staff remained virtually the same.[57]

Finally, the invention and spread of the "supermax" prison, from one in 1984 to at least 30 in 2001, emphasize the extreme of punishment in contemporary America. The details are gruesome and include long-term (measured in years) isolation, sensory deprivation, restricted communication with the outside world, high-tech scrutiny (video cameras), and little to no psychiatric attention for the mental problems and stress that precede or are the consequences of these practices. Prison officials claim that these prisons or units are necessary to isolate the extremely disruptive, including gang members, but administrative convenience may be the real reason for their overuse. Many acutely mentally ill prisoners, particularly those who are disruptive, are spending their lives in supermax cells. Statistics for the current numbers of supermax prisons and prisoners are hard to come by, but in 2001, it was estimated that 20,000 state prisoners were locked up in these tortuous conditions.[58] One can take a "virtual tour" of Virginia's supermax prison online. That such prisons are touted with pride by state prison authorities should, instead, be greatly decried.

PRIVATE PRISONS: A "LIBERAL" CORRECTIONS MODEL

In the United States, juveniles have been confined in private, nonprofit facilities for more than 100 years, though the pattern of increased reliance on the voluntary sector has grown since about 1970, now accounting for two-fifth of the juvenile correctional population.[59] Confining adults to private facilities can be related to the pervasive tight-money, antigovernment but pro-business economic and political environment that has dominated U.S. policy-making since the Reagan era of the 1980s. The result has been an ideological shift that favors privatization, even when it is not shown to be more effective or efficient.

Contracting with private facilities began at the federal level with Immigration and Naturalization Service's use of private facilities for detention of undocumented immigrants in the 1970s; the practice has now spread to the states, particularly in the South and rural West. The use of private prisons has been trending steadily upward, with 7.2 percent of all federal and state prisoners (excluding immigrant detainees), a total of 112,000, in contracted private facilities at mid-year 2006. Approximately 76 percent are in state-contracted private prisons. New Mexico houses 43 percent of its prisoners in private facilities, while Wyoming does so for 38 percent, and Hawaii, 30 percent.[60]

The growth of prisons-for-profit coincided with the rapid expansion of the prison population that coincided with the denigration of public services. In some cases, these facilities were built rapidly, and shoddily, to provide cells for overcrowded public corrections systems. The claim was that these prisons could be built and run for less money than the public ones, as much as 20 percent according to a report.[61] A big incentive was flexibility in hiring—in other words, union-busting. Because of the escalating numbers of prisoners, both states and the federal government were running out of space, and they turned—or were persuaded to turn—to the private, for-profit sector to provide needed prison space. A particularly troubling aspect of relying on private prisons to relieve prison overcrowding is that many prisoners get transferred out of state (Vermont sends prisoners to Kentucky, Alabama sends them to Mississippi, and Hawaii to Arizona, for instance), making family visiting virtually impossible and threatening even further the chances for successful post-incarceration adjustment.

PROMISES NOT KEPT

Two giant corporations dominate the U.S. private industry, Corrections Corporation of America (CCA) and the Geo Group (formerly the Wackenhut). (Geo is a huge, international corporation that contracts for a variety of security services, including guarding U.S. embassies abroad.) Together they comprise 75 percent of the private prison market. There are also several smaller companies that operate on local or state levels.[62] There are several health care companies (Corrections Medical Services and Prison Health Services) that contract with states and local jails to provide health care of a treacherous sort to prisoners throughout the country.[63] Private prison companies have promised to save money, and they also promised better care. But, they have done neither. Evaluations have found little to no difference in costs.[64] Financial difficulties have dogged CCA.[65] Add that private prisons generally refuse to accept more difficult prisoners and that they have a financial incentive to retain prisoners by controlling reports about prisoners' behavior, and it is clear that these prisons have not fulfilled their financial promises.

More serious is the track record of U.S. private prisons. Private prison corporations seek to make money for their investors. They do so by cutting costs, hiring untrained staff, and generally looking to the bottom line. Abuse of prisoners, escapes, prison violence (including prisoner-on-prisoner,

192 ❖ MARGUERITE G. ROSENTHAL

prisoner-on-guard and vice versa), restricted and malfeasant health care, providing rotten food, and other prison management problems are characteristic of the private prison industry.[66] For example, one study found 49 percent more prisoner-on-staff and 65 percent higher prisoner-on-prisoner assaults in private medium and minimum security prisons than in public ones.[67] A particularly notorious example is that of the CCA-operated Northeast Ohio Correction Center in Youngstown, Ohio where, in only 14 months, there were 13 stabbings, 2 murders, and 6 escapes that ended in violence, and there are many other documented examples of brutality and incompetence perpetrated in CCA-run facilities.[68]

POLITICAL AND ECONOMIC DIMENSIONS

Private prison interests have actively lobbied state legislatures and public officials to favor privatization, including contributing substantially to political campaigns (particularly but not exclusively in the South). An advocacy organization that documents campaign and other contributions has reported that, between 1998 and 2000, 2,250 checks were written to 830 recipients, $1,125,598 to individual candidates, and $96,432 to political parties.[69] Political campaign contributions by prison interests—and it must be stated that public prison unions, especially in California, have done likewise—have a corrupting influence because they not only push for private prisons, but they also encourage sentencing policies that will keep the prisons full. Both CCA and Wackenhut (now Geo) have been important contributors to the American Legislative Exchange Council, an organization that develops policy for and supports conservative state-level politicians and has encouraged get-tough crime policies.[70]

Too many public officials—desperate to create jobs in their economically depleted areas—have looked to prison-building as a source of job creation, both in construction and, in the longer term, for prison guards and upkeep—an idea that private prison companies have exploited. In the rural South, this argument has been appealing since so many traditional forms of employment—tobacco, cotton, textile, and furniture production—have largely disappeared. But it is not at all certain that, in the long run, prisons are money-makers for local jurisdictions. Private prison companies have received huge public subsidies (e.g., $68 billion in tax-free bonds) to help them build, and then there are hidden costs, for instance coping and intervening with the increases in alcoholism, divorce, family violence, and racist acts that result with prison guard work. Prisons incur expensive unintended costs for the communities in which they are located.[71]

CIVIL LIBERTIES AND PRISON PRIVATIZATION

The writer has a profound disagreement with the idea that private corporations and individuals are allowed to earn profits from the mistakes and miseries of others. There are real legal and civil liberties questions that are fundamental to this arrangement as well: there is a strong argument to be made that a private entity should not have the right to restrain an individual's liberty. As Richard Harding puts it,

> There is a view that, however well regulated, accountable, and success-
> ful the particular regime turns out to be...prison privatization is nev-
> ertheless unacceptable. This is the fundamental moral criticism, that
> imprisonment is an intrinsic or core state function that by definition
> cannot legitimately be delegated in any of its aspects to a nonstate
> agency without undermining the very notion of the state and its
> responsibility to and for its citizens.[72]

Long-Term Consequences of Imprisonment

Recidivism

A U.S. Department of Justice study of persons released from prison in 1994 revealed very high recidivism rates. Within 3 years from their release, 67.5 percent of the prisoners were rearrested for a new offense, 46.9 percent were convicted for a new crime, and 25.4 percent were resentenced to prison for a new crime. However, almost 52 percent of those resentenced to prison were for technical violations of their parole or release. Tellingly, those with the highest (almost 74 percent) rearrest rates were those who committed property crimes; 66.7 percent of released drug offenders were rearrested within 3 years of discharge.[73]

Unemployment and Employment Discrimination

A serious consequence of the longer terms now served by prisoners is that former prisoners are likely to have frayed ties with their families and communities. Most prisoners do not participate in drug treatment, vocational or educational programs before their release from prison.[74] As discussed earlier, incarcerated young men enter prison with high unemployment rates and low levels of education and skills. Whatever skills prisoners may have had when they entered prison are lost, particularly if they have long prison terms. And behaviors that are protective in prison—suspiciousness, aggressiveness, and self-isolation—are maladaptive to the world of work.[75] Employers are averse to hiring persons with prison records; one study found that 60 percent of surveyed employers in 4 metropolitan areas said they probably or definitely would not hire them, and approximately half of them said that they always or sometimes do criminal background checks on potential employees. Employers who are unlikely to hire those with criminal backgrounds also have entry requirements (high school degrees, work experience, and references) that just released prisoners are very unlikely to have. Many states require that particular jobs (for instance, those involving contact with children) are closed to anyone with a criminal record, and criminal background checks on applicants are routine. Although a formerly tight labor market somewhat improved their employment chances, former prisoners consistently fared less well in the eyes of employers than other stigmatized groups (particularly public assistance recipients).[76] Western summarizes the employment-related consequences for prisoners this way:

> Serving time behind bars reduces a man's wages, annual employment and total annual earnings. It also redirects the life course by relegating ex-convicts to a secondary labor market that offers neither job security nor economic mobility. There is, then, strong evidence that the poor economic performance we see in ex-inmates is attributable to imprisonment.[77]

These outcomes are tragic, since steady and remunerative employment is key to keeping people out of prison; it is no wonder that so many return to crime and end up back in prison.

Attenuated Family Ties

Prisoners are very frequently sent to facilities far from home. Visits from family and partners are rare because of distance and the lack of transportation, and family ties are often broken. Yet former prisoners who return to their families are less likely to recidivate.[78] Although marriage rates for incarcerated men between the ages of 22 and 30 are generally low, most—64 percent of whites, 81 percent of Hispanics, and 70 percent of blacks—are fathers. Indeed, in 2000, 2.1 million children—3 percent of the nation's total—had incarcerated fathers. The divorce rate for those who are married when they enter prison is high—approximately 50 percent—and divorce occurs quickly. Marriage is a stabilizing influence for men, but men who go to prison are less likely to have married than age-mates, and incarceration diminishes the chances that they will marry in the future. One study found that there was a 19 percent increase in the number of families headed by single black women as a result of the doubling of the number of black prisoners between 1980 and 1990.[79] And, of course, prisoners' partners and children experience stigma.

Men and women leave prison often not knowing where they will live (those with drug convictions are forbidden to live in public housing) or whether their families will have them back. Relations with children are particularly problematic, and family caretakers often discourage or even forbid the former prisoner from having custody or contact with his or her children. Social isolation, thus, is compounded for many leaving prison.[80]

Disenfranchisement

One consequence of imprisonment that has been getting some public attention recently—doubtless a result of the 2000 presidential election when many entitled to vote were falsely accused by Florida election officials as being former felons—is the barring former prisons from voting permanently (or if not permanently, then requiring compliance with arduous procedures to having voting rights restored). In some states, restoring voting rights is called "regaining citizenship." Almost 75 percent of those disenfranchised are not currently in prison; instead, they are either on probation or parole or they have been discharged completely from their sentences but, nonetheless, they cannot vote.[81] In November, 2004, 5.3 million were barred from voting and another 600,000 who were in jail awaiting trial were unable to vote. Felony disenfranchisement prohibits 13 percent of African American men from voting yet, see below, prisoners are counted as residents of the mostly rural jurisdictions in which their prisons are located.[82] Current and former felons are very interested in politics and are acutely concerned that they are unable to participate in the political process. Given the large number of persons so affected, these lost voices are silenced from objecting to the terms and conditions of imprisonment.[83]

INCARCERATION'S IMPACT ON STATE BUDGETS

The massive increase in the prison population has had serious consequences for public budgets, and the result has been a curtailing of expenditures for critical human services and public education. Of course, prison expansion has taken place at the same time as both the federal and state governments have pulled back from social expenditures as a matter of ideology (e.g., Bill Clinton's famous statement, "The era of big government is over") and recent declining revenues as a result of tax cuts and reduced tax revenues associated with high unemployment rates. It becomes difficult, therefore, to pinpoint precisely the financial effect of harsh penal policies, but there is a trend: particularly at the state level, expenditures on prisons are beginning to outstrip other important state functions.

State general fund expenditures for corrections have risen 315 percent between 1987 and 2007 and totalled $44.06 billion—$1 in every $15 state dollar expenditures—in 2007. In 2005, the average per prisoner operating cost was $23,867, ranging from a high of $44,860 in Rhode Island to $13,009 in Louisiana. Differences are largely explained by how much employees are paid in salary and benefits. It is estimated that capital expenditures are $65,000 per prisoner bed.[84] Despite their deficiencies, medical expenditures are the biggest single cost factor in prisons where serious communicable diseases are common and, because of long and life sentences, the prison population is aging.

Overall state spending has been declining since FY 2002. Thus, rising expenditures for prisons and other corrections activities are consuming larger proportions of state budgets, with the consequence that many states have cut expenditures in health programs for poor children and families (SCHIP and Medicaid), subsidized child care and, in the case of 34 states in 2004, state aid to K-12 public education.[85] Higher education budgets have been hit hard. Despite greater demand, public support for higher education rose only 21 percent between 1987 and 2007. In the Northeast, state spending actually declined by 5 percent, and higher education has suffered even greater losses in California, Texas, and New York.[86] Public higher education has become more expensive for students, with public colleges and universities charging higher tuition fees, making a college education less affordable for poor students. In combination with harsh and discriminatory justice policy implementation, these increased costs account, at least in part, for the fact that in 2000, there were more than one-third of young African American men in prison than in higher education.[87]

THE IRONIES OF PRISON DEMOGRAPHICS

Counties with prisons are able to count the prison population in census tabulations, a policy that enables them to take advantage of population-based federal grants and subsidies in such areas as Medicaid, Adoption Assistance, and social service block grants. The consequence is an unfair disadvantage to the neighborhoods and families from which prisoners come, since assets are redirected that would otherwise be available to them were the grants determined according to county of origin instead of county of "residence" (the resemblance to the 3/5 clause in the original U.S. Constitution has resonance here).

U.S. Prison Corrections Policies in Comparative Perspective

As the following table shows, incarceration rates in the United States are extraordinarily disproportionate in comparison to other industrialized countries, approximately four times greater than the average of European countries (see table 8.1).

Apparently struck by the glaring differences between the American incarceration rate and those of other countries, researchers have begun to develop a literature devoted to studying the reasons for these disparities.[88] The interested reader is referred to the referenced sources, since only a brief summary of their significant findings are presented here. Finland's policies are presented in somewhat more detail because that country has undertaken a significant departure in a very humane direction from its past approaches.

Claiming that rising and declining crime rates in most Western countries do not explain why, except in the United States, England, New Zealand, and the Netherlands, incarceration rates have not risen substantially, Michael Tonry, a leading comparative criminologist, claims that cultural and political differences are primarily responsible for countries' varying responses to crime

Table 8.1 Incarceration rates and total numbers (years vary)

Country	Rate: 100,000 population	Total Incarcerated
United States	750	2,245,189
Russian Federation	628	889,598
Ukraine	346	160,046
Czech Republic	186	19,145
England & Wales	148	80,229
Spain	147	66,129
Turkey	112	82,742
Austria	108	8,991
Germany	93	76,629
France	85	52,009
Sweden	79	7,175
Norway	75	3,533
Finland	68	3,595
Italy	67	39,348
Denmark	67	3,626

Source: International Centre for Prison Studies, King's College London, "World Prison Brief," and published in Warren, p. 35.

and criminals.[89] Tonry summarizes the major reasons for less punitive responses to crime this way:

Prominent protective factors include consensus political systems, nonpartisan judges and prosecutors, Francophonic political cultures [includes Quebec's influence on Canada], and a predominant view that criminal justice policy falls appropriately within the province of expert knowledge and professional experience.[90]

At one extreme are the Scandinavian countries, with the lowest rates of incarceration, that adhere to a consensus model of policy development where professional commissions make recommendations for enactment by their parliaments. It is worth noting that, beginning in the late 1970s, women have constituted at least 35 percent of parliamentary seats in the Nordic countries, achieved through quota systems imposed by the political parties; perhaps their influence accounts for the relatively humane approach in their justice systems. Court personnel (the police, prosecutors, and judges) in these countries are appointed career professionals. Judges have discretion in sentencing decisions. As a general rule, imprisonment is reserved for violent criminals, and the longest sentence—life—in practice means approximately 12 years. Finland, Sweden, and Denmark make extensive use of "open" institutions for those who are sentenced to prison. Addictions are treated rather than criminalized (drug dealing, though, is considered criminal and results in imprisonment in most Nordic countries), and community-based approaches are common.

In contrast, the competitive two-party system in the United States leads to a much less rational approach to policy development, and crime-fighting is frequently employed as a campaign slogan in American elections where, in many jurisdictions, judges and prosecutors are elected and sentences are mandated by law.[91] To these differences, add the federal structure of American government and our culture of individualism, unregulated capitalism, extreme income and wealth inequality, money-influenced politics, lack of gun control and racism, and we have the general outlines of what contributes to American exceptionalism. Note that exceptionalism also includes the death penalty, abolished in all of Europe.

FINLAND: HUMANE APPROACHES TO CRIMINAL CORRECTIONS

Finland provides a dramatic example of a country that completely changed its incarceration policies and prison conditions. In the 1970s, the Finnish government, observing that its prison population was high in Scandinavian terms, adopted policies to increase the use of suspended sentences and early parole, with the result that there was a 40 percent drop in the rate of incarceration between 1976 and 1992. Finnish prisons are of two kinds: "closed" and "open," but descriptions reveal that both institution types resemble dormitories more than anything else. Closed institutions use video monitors rather than gates and locks for security, and prisoners are housed in rooms rather than cells. Guards wear civilian clothing and are unarmed (guns are kept locked in prison safes). Work and sports are part of the prison regime. In open prisons, guards and prisoners are on a first-name basis, home visits occur regularly as prisoners near the end of their sentences, and beforehand, they can live with their families in houses on the prison grounds. Finland incarcerates drug dealers and violent criminals, but it aims to rehabilitate prisoners through values-reorientation and inculcation of self-control. The Finnish population has expressed satisfaction with these humane justice policies.[92] This approach should be a model for the rest of the world to examine and emulate.

THE WAY AHEAD: FAINT GLIMMERS OF HOPE

The current state of corrections policies in the United States is alarming, even cruel. Too many are incarcerated for the wrong reasons and for too long in institutions that are unsafe and provide no rehabilitation. But there are a few reasons to think that some of the worst excesses of our systems of "justice" may be on the road to mitigation. Recent legal decisions and the recommendations of a House Judiciary Subcommittee, as discussed earlier, auger less disparity in drug sentencing. Faced with overcrowding and budget crises, several states have turned to early release programs. In Massachusetts, a broad effort to reform the criminal records check system that thwarts employment chances for former prisoners is bearing fruit. Although details are undefined, the Obama administration has announced its intention to overhaul and improve the immigration detention system, and it has stopped detaining families in the much-criticized CCA detention facility, the T. Don Hutto Residential Center in Texas.[93] Even more promising are the efforts of Senator Jim Webb who has introduced legislation entitled The National Criminal Justice Commission Act of 2009 that would, if passed, shine a light on the entire criminal justice system. Webb, an outspoken and forceful new member of Congress, provides this convincing explanation for his proposal:

> America's criminal justice system has deteriorated to the point that it is a national disgrace. Its irregularities and inequities cut against the notion that we are a society founded on fundamental fairness. Our failure to address this problem has caused the nation's prisons to burst their seams with massive overcrowding, even as our neighborhoods have become more dangerous. We are wasting billions of dollars and diminishing millions of lives.
>
> We need to fix the system. Doing so will require a major nationwide recalculation of who goes to prison and for how long and of how we address the long-term consequences of incarceration.[94]

We hope that Webb's call for a rational reassessment of incarceration policies will gain sufficient traction to move our country in a different direction. For now, the conclusion must be that the United States remains unique among Western industrialized nations in its harsh, reactionary, and self-defeating criminal justice system.

NOTES

1. Mary Pattillo, M., David Weiman, and Bruce Western, eds., *Imprisoning America: The social effects of mass incarceration.* New York: Russell Sage Foundation, 2004, p. 3.
2. William. J. Sabol, Todd D. Minton, and Paige M. Harrison, "Prison and Jail Inmates at Midyear 2006," U.S. Department of Justice, Bureau of Justice Statistics, March, 2008, p. 2. Retrieved August 11, 2009.
3. Ibid., p. 4.
4. The Sentencing Project Homepage. Retrieved from www.sentencing-project.org on July 30, 2009.
5. Adam Liptak, "Inmate count in U.S. dwarfs other nations," *New York Times*, April 23, 2008.
6. Jenifer Warren, *One in 100: Behind bars in America 2008.* Washington, DC: The Pew Charitable Trusts, The Pew Center on the States, n.d., p. 34. Retrieved from www.pewtrusts.org on August 11, 2009.

7. Sabol, et al., "Prison and Jail Inmates at Midyear 2006," p. 2.
8. Information Plus Reference Series, *Prisons and jails: A deterrent to crime?* Detroit, New York, San Diego, San Francisco, and other cities: Thomson/Gale, 2004, p. 27.
9. Sabol, et al., "Prison and Jail Inmates at Midyear 2006," p. 5.
10. Information Plus (extrapolated from U.S. Bureau of Justice statistics, Figure 4.1), 2004, p 28; Warren, *One in 100*, p. 6. For good visual graphs of incarceration rates by age, race and gender, see Warren, p. 6.
11. Ashley Nellis and Ryan S. King, *No exit: The expanding use of life sentences in America*. Washington, DC: The Sentencing Project, July 2009. Retrieved from www.sentencingproject.org on August 11, 2009.
12. Sarah Lawrence and Jeremy Travis, *The new landscape of imprisonment: Mapping America's prison expansion*. Washington, D.C.: Urban Institute, Justice Policy Institute, 2004. Retrieved from www. urban.org on June 3, 2004.
13. Kenneth E. Hartman, "The recession behind bars," *New York Times*, September 6, 2009, Week in Review, p. 6.
14. Sabol et al., "Prison and Jail Inmates at Midyear 2006," p. 9.
15. Donald Braman, *Families and incarceration*, Ph.D. Dissertation, Yale University, 2002, cited by Marc Mauer, "Comparative international rates of incarceration: An examination of causes and trends." Paper presented to the U.S. Commission on Civil Rights (June 10, 2003), p. 3. Retrieved from www.sentencingproject.org on October 18, 2004.
16. Bruce Western, *Punishment and inequality in America*. New York: Russell Sage Foundation, 2007, p. 25.
17. Human Rights Watch, "United States punishment and prejudice: Racial disparities in the war on drugs," *Human Rights Watch Report*, vol. 12, #2, 2000. Retrieved from www.hrw.org/ureports/2000/ usa on October 30, 2004.
18. Warren, *One in 100*, p. 6.
19. Mauer, "Comparative international rates," p. 6.
20. Western, *Punishment and inequality*, p. 79.
21. Western, *Punishment and inequality*, chap. 3.
22. Information Plus, 2004, p. 38; U.S. Department of Justice, Bureau of Justice Statistics, "Prison Statistics: Summary of Findings," n.d. (2009?). Retrieved from www.ojp.usdoj.gov/bjs/ on August 11, 2009.
23. U. S. Department of Justice, n.d.
24. Information Plus, 2004, pp. 38–39.
25. Information Plus, 2004, p. 40, extrapolated from Table 5.5; Solomon Moore, "Decline in blacks in state prisons for drugs," *New York Times*, April 15, 2009, p. A12; Human Rights Watch, "United States punishment and prejudice," 2000.

26. Eric E. Sterling, "Racially disproportionate outcomes in processing drug cases," Silver Spring, MD: Criminal Justice Policy Foundation, 2001. Retrieved on October 30, 2004 at www.cjpf.org/drug/outcomes2.html.

27. Derrick Jackson, "High court's sensible sentencing," *Boston Globe,* December 11, 2007. Retrieved from www.boston.com on September 12, 2009; National Public Radio, "High court rules on sentencing disparities," December 11, 2007. Retrieved from www.npr.org on September 12, 2009.

28. The Sentencing Project, "House Judiciary Committee passes crack cocaine sentencing reform," July 29, 2009. Retrieved from www.sentencingproject.org on July 30, 2009.

29. U.S. Department of Justice, National Institute of Corrections, "The unemployment/crime connection," 2004. Retrieved from http://www.nicic.org/Downloads/Other/OCJTP_db_crime.aspx on October 30, 2004.

30. Curt Anderson, "FBI finds violent crime down, except murder," October 26, 2004, *Boston Globe,* p. A2; Jason DeParle, "The American prison nightmare," *New York Review of Books,* April 12, 2007, pp. 33–36; Western, *Punishment and inequality,* p. 185.

31. Western, *Punishment and inequality,* pp. 89–90.

32. Elliot Currie, *Crime and punishment in America.* New York: Holt, 1998; Elliot Currie, "Treatment yes, but," *Nation,* Sept. 20, 1999. Retrieved from http://www.thenation.com/docprint.mhtml?i=19990920&s=currie on October 30, 2004.

33. Bruce Western and Katherine Beckett, "How unregulated is the US labor market? The penal system as a labor market institution," *American Journal of Sociology,* vol. 104, no. 4, January 1999, pp. 1030–1060. Retrieved from www.pressroom.com/-afrimale/western.htm on October 30, 2004; Western, *Punishment and inequality,* chap. 5.

34. Mauer, "Comparative international rates," p. 5.

35. Detention Watch Network, "About the U.S. detention and deportation system," Retrieved from www.detentionwatchnetwork.rg/aboutdetention on September 18, 2009.

36. Meredith Kolodner, "Immigrant enforcement benefits prison firms," *New York Times,* July 19, 2006.

37. Teresa Wantanabe, "US fails to protect immigrants' rights, UN report asserts 'Biased picture' cited in response," *Boston Globe,* March 9, 2008.

38. Si Kahn, "Gulag: An American tragedy," (Essay Review of *American Gulag* by Mark Dow, 2004). *New Politics,* vol. 42, Winter 2007, pp. 176–182.

39. Lois Martin, Personal Communication, September 11, 2009.

40. Kathleen Glynn and Sarah Bronstein, "Systemic problems persist in U.S. ICE custody reviews for indefinite detainees," Catholic Legal

Immigration Network, Inc. [CLINIC], 2005. Retrieved at http://www.cliniclegal.org/DSP/IndefDetExecSumFINAL.pdf
41. Nina Bernstein, "Officials hid Truth of Immigrant Deaths in Jail," *New York Times*, January 10, 2010.
42. Ginger Thompson, "After losing freedom, some immigrants face loss of custody of their children," *New York* Times, April 23, 2009.
43. Randall G. Sheldon, *Controlling the dangerous classes: A critical introduction to the history of criminal justice.* Boston, London, Toronto, Sydney, Tokyo, and Singapore: Allyn and Bacon, 2001.
44. DeParle, "The American prison nightmare," p. 34.
45. Human Rights Watch, "Prisoner abuse: How different are U.S. prisons?," May 13, 2004. Retrieved from www.hrw.org/en/news/2pp4/05/13/prisoner-abuse-how-different-are-us-prisoners on September 18, 2009.
46. DeParle, "The American prison nightmare," p. 34.
47. Victoria Law, *Resistance behind bars: The struggles of incarcerated women.* Oakland, CA: PM Press, 2009, pp. 59–76.
48. Ibid., pp. 43–50.
49. Nicole Dussault, Beth Dymeck, and Catherine Furlong, "Incarcerated mothers and attachment to their children," Salem State College School of Social Work (unpublished research paper), 2003.
50. Ibid.
51. Gordon Lafer, Captive labor: America's prisoners as corporate workforce, *The American Prospect*, September 1, 1999. Available at http://www.prospect.org/cs/articles?article=captive_labor.
52. The prison index: Taking the pulse of the crime control industry, excerpted and published, n.d. Retrieved from www.prisonpolicy.org/prisonindex/prisonlabor.html on September 15, 2009.
53. Joanne Mariner, "Criminalizing the mentally ill: Prisons as mental institutions," *Counterpunch*, November 5, 2003. Available at www.counterpunch.org/mariner11052003.html.
54. Dussault et al., "Incarcerated mothers."
55. Mariner, "Criminalizing the mentally ill."
56. Marguerite G. Rosenthal, *Prescription for disaster: Commercializing prison health care in South Carolina.* Charlotte, NC: Grassroots Leadership, 2004. Available at www.grassrootsleadership.org.
57. Lisa Leigh Connors, "College behind bars is rare today," *Christian Science Monitor*, April 14, 2004; Western, *Punishment and inequality*, p. 175.
58. Leena Kurki and Norval Morris, "The purposes, practices and problems of supermax prisons," in Michael Tonry, ed., *Crime and justice: A review of research*, vol. 28. Chicago and London: University of Chicago Press. 2001, pp. 392–393.
59. Douglas C. McDonald, "Private penal institutions," in Michael Tonry, Ed., *Crime and justice: An annual review of research*, vol. 16. Chicago: University of Chicago Press, 1992. This chapter focuses on

incarceration of the adult (including young adult) population in the United States The overuse of detention, juvenile correctional facilities, and other forms of out-of-home "placements" of youngsters—particularly young people of color—in the United States is another, though related, subject of enormous importance and concern, but it is beyond the focus here.

60. Sabol et al., "Prison and jail inmates at Midyear 2006," p. 4.
61. Bill Carey, "Prison plan: Is it practical or political," *The Tennessean*, April 21, 1997 as cited in Amy Cheung, "Prison privatization and the use of incarceration," 2004. Available at www.sentencingproject. org/doc/publications/inc_prisonprivatization.
62. Phillip Mattera and Mafruza Khan, *Corrections Corporation of America: A critical look at its first twenty years*. Charlotte, NC: Grassroots Leadership, 2003. Available at www.grassrootsleadership. org.
63. Rosenthal, *Prescription for disaster* and Marguerite G. Rosenthal, *Prescription for recovery: Keeping South Carolina's prison health public and making it better*. Charlotte, NC: Grassroots Leadership. Available at www.grassrootsleadership.org.
64. General Accounting Office, *Private and public prisons: Studies comparing operation costs and/or quality of service*. GAO/GGD-96-158, August 1996; James Austin and Garry Coventry, *Emerging issues on privatized prisons*, U.S. Department of Justice, Office of Justice, Bureau of Justice Assistance, 2001. Available at www.ncjrs.gov/pdf-files1/bja/181249.pdf; Douglas McDonald, Elizabeth Fournier, Malcolm Russell-Einhourn, and Stephen Crawford, *Private prisons in the United States: An assessment of current practice*, Cambridge, MA: Abt Associates, July 16, 1998. Available at www.abtassociates. com/reports/ES-priv-report.pdf.
65. Mattera and Khan, *Corrections Corporation of America*.
66. The Sentencing Project, "Prison privatization and the use of incarceration," 2004. Retrieved from www.sentencingproject.org on October 15, 2004.
67. Ibid.; Judith Greene, "Bailing out private jails," *American Prospect*, September 9, 2001. Available at www.prospect.org; Mattera and Khan, *Corrections Corporation of America*; Tara Herivel and Paul Wright, Eds., *Prison profiteers: Who makes money from mass incarceration*. New York: New Press, 2007.
68. James Austin, cited in Greene, "Bailing out private jails."
69. The Sentencing Project, 2004; Mattera and Khan, *Corrections Corporation of America*.
70. Edwin Bender, *A contributing influence: The private-prison industry and political giving in the south*, Helena, Montana: The National Institute on Money in State Politics, April 23, 2002. Retrieved from www.followthemoney.org. on October 19, 2004; The Sentencing Project, 2004, pp. 4–5.

71. Phillip Mattera and Mafruza Khan, *Jail breaks: Economic development subsidies given to private prisons*. Washington, DC: Good Jobs First, October 2001. Available at www.goodjobsfirst.org/pdf/jailbreaks.pdf.; Tracy Huling, "Building a prison economy in rural America," in Marc Mauer and Meda Chesney-Lind, Eds., *Invisible punishment: The collateral consequences of mass imprisonment*, New York: New Press, 2002.

72. Richard Harding, "Private prisons," in Michael Tonry, Ed. *Crime and justice: A review of research*, vol. 28. Chicago and London: University of Chicago Press, 2001, p. 266.

73. Patrick A. Langan and David J. Levin, "Recidivism of prisoners released in 1994," U.S. Department of Justice, Office of Justice Programs, Bureau of Justice Statistics, 2002. Retrieved from http://www.ojp.usdoj.gov/bjs/pub/ascii/rpr94.txt. on November 3, 2004.

74. Jeremy Travis, "Reentry and reintegration: New perspectives on the challenges of mass incarceration," in Mary Pattillo, David Weiman, and Bruce Western, eds., *Imprisoning America: The social effects of mass incarceration*. New York: Russell Sage Foundation, 2004.

75. Western, *Punishment and inequality*, chap. 5.

76. Harry J. Holzer, Steven Raphael, and Michael Stoll, "Will employers hire former offenders?: Employer preferences, background checks, and their determinants," in Mary Pattillo, David Weiman, and Bruce Western, eds., *Imprisoning America: The social effects of mass incarceration*. New York: Russell Sage Foundation, 2004.

77. Western, *Punishment and inequality*, pp. 125–126.

78. Western, *Punishment and inequality*, chap. 6.

79. Western, *Punishment and inequality*, p. 139.

80. Anne M. Nurse, "Returning to strangers: Newly paroled young fathers and their children," in Mary Pattillo, David Weiman, and Bruce Western, eds., *Imprisoning America: The social effects of mass incarceration*. New York: Russell Sage Foundation, 2004; Dussault et al., "Incarcerated mothers"; Todd R. Clear, *Imprisoning communities: How mass incarceration makes disadvantaged neighborhoods worse*. New York: Oxford, 2007.

81. Christopher Uggen and Jeff Manza, "Lost voices: The civil and political views of disenfranchised felons" in Mary Pattillo, David Weiman, and Bruce Western, eds., *Imprisoning America: The social effects of mass incarceration*. New York: Russell Sage Foundation, 2004.

82. DeParle, "The American prison nightmare."

83. Uggen and Manza, "Lost voices."

84. Warren, *One in 100*, p. 11.

85. Elizabeth McNichol and David Kamin, "Fiscal crisis is shrinking state budgets," Washington, DC: Center on Budget and Policy Priorities, February 2004. Retrieved from www.cbpp.org on October 26, 2004.

86. Warren, *One in 100*, p. 15; Justice Policy Institute, "Cellblocks or classrooms?: Funding of higher education and corrections and its impact on African American men," 2003, p. 9. Retrieved from www.justicepolicy.org on October 29, 2004.

87. Lawrence and Travis, *New landscape of imprisonment*.

88. Michael Tonry, "Determinants of penal policies," *Crime and Justice*, vol. 36, University of Chicago, 2007; Howard S. Erlanger and Marie Gottschalk, "Review Essay," *34 Law and Social Inquiry*, American Bar Association, Spring, 2009; David P. Farrington, Patrick A. Langan, and Michael Tonry, Eds., *Cross-national studies in crime and justice*, U.S. Department of Justice, Office of Justice Programs, Bureau of Justice Statistics, September, 2004. Available at www.ojp.usdoj/boj/.

89. Tonry, "Determinants of penal policies," p. 1. Except for the Netherlands, the countries with increased incarceration rates are "liberal" in Esping-Andersen's influential analytical model (Gøsta Esping-Andersen, *Three worlds of welfare capitalis*. Princeton, NJ: Princeton University Press, 1990).Liberal welfare states, unlike Continental Europe and Scandinavia, rely on means-tested and earned rather than universal social benefits. But even in these countries, prison is less commonly used for nonviolent crimes and sentences are considerably shorter than in the United States. Liberal states (Great Britain, Australia, New Zealand, and Canada, in addition to the United States) have also turned to privatized prisons to some extent (Harding, "Private prisons").

90. Tonry, "Determinants of penal policies," p. 1.

91. Tapio Lappi-Seppala, "Penal policy in Scandinavia," *36 Crime & Justice*, University of Chicago, 2007.

92. Mauer, "Comparative international rates"; Warren Hoge, "Finish prisons: No gates or armed guards," *New York Times*, January 2, 2003.

93. Nina Bernstein, "U.S. to reform policy on detention for immigrants," *New York Times*, August 6, 2009.

94. Senator Jim Webb's web page, http://webb.senate.gov/email/criminaljusticereform.html.

CHAPTER 9

Alternatives to Welfare

Betty Reid Mandell

Almost everyone agree that the present welfare system (TANF) is an inferior program and should be replaced. There are various proposals for an alternative to the current welfare system. First, I examine the philosophy that all able adult citizens have a responsibility to do socially useful work, but they should also have the right to an adequate income. The French social philosopher and journalist André Gorz and the Brandeis University social welfare professor David Gil, who have put forward visionary proposals for an ideal society based on the philosophy, hold this philosophy. Gorz maintains that automation and the electronic revolution have resulted in widespread unemployment and a flexible labor force, with few jobs remaining secure. As industrial jobs have shrunk and service jobs have increased, Gorz predicts that "more than 80 percent of us will earn our living by offering services to others."[1] Therefore, Gorz says,

> If we wish to maintain order, we may no longer reserve the right to an income to those citizens only who have jobs, nor even make the level of income dependent on the number of hours worked. Hence the idea of *an income that would be guaranteed to every man and woman independently of work done....* The right to an income can no longer be the same thing as the right to a wage.[2]

There are both conservative and liberal versions of a guaranteed income. The conservative economist Milton Friedman proposed a "negative income tax" that would guarantee a subsistence minimum to each citizen. "This would be accompanied by the abolition of all other forms of social protection: minimum wage, Social Security, compensation for unemployment and illness, dependents' allowances, etc.... Nothing would be allowed to shackle the free play of the labor market."[3] The Netherlands provides a minimum income for everybody with inadequate financial resources. People receiving National

Assistance are obliged to look for work, but those responsible for the care of children aged under five can be exempted from a work requirement.[4] Gorz objects to this system:

> It leads to a split-up of society, to a dual stratification that can go so far as a South-Africanization of social relations. The guaranteed minimum income continues to be the wage of social exclusion, for it consolidates a system dominated by capitalist relations of production and by what I have called the "working elite." The guaranteed minimum is a way of accepting this split-up, and of making it more tolerable.[5]

Further, Gorz says, a plan that is not linked to a payment that each citizen receives in return for participation in the social processes of production is that this grant is *conceded* to people and may therefore be withdrawn or reduced. Viewed as social welfare, the plan "would make the recipients dependent upon the goodwill of the administration of the politically powerful class of well-paid job holders who pay most of the taxes."[6]

Gorz says that his left-wing version of the guaranteed income is radically different:

> It starts from the fact that, as the amount of labor that society needs will keep diminishing, liberation from socially necessary labor is the only sensible goal. As a consequence, the labor savings implied in technological changes should be distributed in such a way that *all men and women can work, but work less and less without loss of income.*[7]

Gorz says that left proposals would not only guarantee an adequate income, but also guarantee the right to work. "It is not from work itself but from socially necessary work time that income must become independent."[8] To achieve this, he proposes to share the quantity of work that is socially necessary, which would reduce the work time of each worker. He estimates that an average work time of 1,000 hours per year is becoming a tangible prospect, which could add up to a total of 20,000 hours for 10 years of full time work, or 40 years of intermittent work.[9] A person could use the free time for a variety of activities—"to go back to college, or to acquire a new skill or trade, but also to build a house, raise children, join a band or write a book, become his or her own doctor of analyst, work as a volunteer in a commune or co-op or a Third World country — and this without ever losing his or her normal income."[10]

Gorz lists raising children as an optional free-time activity. His proposal lacks a gender analysis. Women generally regard care work as a required, not a leisure time, activity. Gorz says that it is impossible to measure the productivity of caregiving work. "Their effectiveness or success depends much more upon human qualities and emotional investment than upon a professional qualification certified by a diploma."[11] He does not see caregiving as *work* that has economic value as socially necessary work. If, however, he defined it as valuable work that deserves financial compensation, he would include it in those 20,000 hours of lifetime work. He implies that the lack of professional certification for caregiving indicates that it requires less skill than professional work. Yet good care work requires a great deal of skill, as Deanne Bonnar points out in her analysis of what is involved in the work.[12]

Another problem with Gorz's analysis is that he takes the present definition of "socially necessary" work as fixed. He does not differentiate between nonproductive work such as waging war and making munitions and useful work that improves society. There is much more of this useful work to be done than is being done now. Who knows how many work hours of how many people would be needed if all work were really socially useful?

David Gil looks at the problem from a different perspective. Although he believes that all able-bodied citizens have a responsibility to do socially useful work as well as a right to receive an adequate income, he defines caregiving as work that deserves adequate compensation. He differentiates between socially useful and nonuseful work: "activities judged to be counterwork (e.g., production of nuclear weapons...) should be phased out, and should not entitle people engaging in them to remuneration."[13] He addresses the problem of alienating work: "Work would have to be redesigned to become meaningful, rather than alienating, to all workers, and conducive to their integrated physical, mental, and emotional development."[14] High-quality, advanced education should be available to prepare people to understand all aspects of the work they choose to undertake. There should be life-long access to education. "Ideally, all socially necessary work should be made sufficiently attractive, to be chosen voluntarily by enough people. However, work, deemed socially necessary, which cannot be redesigned and humanized, and which is not chosen voluntarily by enough people, would have to be shared by all people on a rotation basis."

Gil proposes a universal children's allowance to eliminate poverty among children, paid out of public revenues to every child under a specified age (e.g., from birth to high school graduation). The allowance should be at the level of the actual cost of living decently. It would replace the dependency deduction for children under the prevailing tax code, which gives an unfair advantage to people with higher income. There should be similar income guarantees to prevent poverty for students in postsecondary and vocational schools, for retirees, for people with disabilities and temporary illness, as well as for people involuntarily unemployed temporarily, while seeking a new place of work.

These public income guarantees should eventually replace Social Security, federal and state public welfare programs, loan and grant scholarship programs, as well as food, energy, and housing assistance programs.[15]

Gil proposes universal, single-payer, health insurance. He also proposes universal child care:

> To assure equal rights and opportunities for women and men for meaningful work and career development, the care of children of all ages would have to be recognized as a shared responsibility of parents and society. Such shared responsibility would require public provision of high-quality child care services for pre-school children, as well as after-school centers for school-age children. Parents who choose to use these services for their children, on a part-time or full-time basis, in order to pursue occupations and careers, would have to forego all, or part, of publicly provided caretaker wages. Once public child care services and a system of caretaker wages would be established, all parents would be free to choose between caring for their children and pursuing occupations and careers, in the same way affluent parents are free to choose now.[16]

Gil proposes to achieve full employment by shortening the standard work time and redistributing work, and creating additional work by publicly sponsoring socially necessary production. An adequate minimum wage should be guaranteed to all workers. The allowances and income programs should be considered taxable income, to recoup parts or all of the amounts from households with higher overall income. Everyone and every household should be entitled to a tax-free income up to the level of the actual cost of living decently. Income above that level, regardless of their source, should be taxed at progressively increasing rates.

And how does Gil propose to achieve this utopian society? He concludes that "large numbers of people would have to undergo transformations of consciousness. They would have to realize that their economic, social, psychological, and security needs cannot be met within the established societal order, and that transforming that order into one conducive to everyone's human development would serve their real interests. Spreading such insights requires social movements working to facilitate critical consciousness concerning people's real needs and interests through non-violent, dialogical processes."[17] A large order indeed.

Solving the problem of care work will require equal participation in the work by women and men. This will require equalization of wages because, on average, men make higher wages than women. Most couples think it more advantageous for the partner with lower wages to do unpaid care work. Yet even if wages were equalized, there are still deep-seated cultural attitudes about what is "men's work" and what is "women's work."

GUARANTEED ANNUAL INCOME

"I'm sick and tired of being sick and tired," proclaimed Fanny Lou Hamer, at the 1964 Democratic National Convention. She was a member of the

Mississippi Freedom Democratic Party, whose delegates were struggling to be seated at the Convention. Hamer later worked on Martin Luther King, Jr.'s Poor People's Campaign and supported the welfare rights movement, which fought for a Guaranteed Annual Income, a universal program that would replace the stingy and stigmatized AFDC (Aid to Families with Dependent Children) program. The Guaranteed Annual Income never materialized; in fact, since the 1970s we have traveled a road of diminishing guarantees, culminating in the punitive and stigmatized TANF.

The National Welfare Rights Organization (NWRO), a welfare rights movement of the 1960s, called for a Guaranteed Annual Income of $6,500 a year, the amount that the Bureau of Labor Statistics (BLS) estimated at that time to be a minimally adequate amount for a family of four.[18] President Nixon had proposed a scaled-down guaranteed income, called the Family Assistance Plan, which would guarantee every family $1,600 a year, plus food stamps, and included a work requirement. NWRO fought against it because of the meager amount of money and the work requirement, and it was eventually defeated in Congress. It would have benefited the southern states more than northern states, as the amount was more than the southern states were currently paying in AFDC grants, but much less than most northern states were paying. Some people considered it to be part of Nixon's southern strategy to increase Republican support in the South, particularly small businesses owners, because the program would supplement low wages. The plan would have expanded the welfare state, but justified the proposed reforms on the basis of a conservative ideology, moving people from the "welfare rolls to the payrolls." Everyone receiving family benefits of working age would be required to accept work or training except those unable to work or mothers of preschool children. Labor union officials criticized the program because it subsidized low wages.

A work requirement was included in the AFDC program by the Work Incentive Program in 1967 (called WIN by officials and WIP, pronounced whip) by welfare recipients and their advocates. The plan required recipients to work if adequate childcare arrangements could be made. Expanded public day care facilities were to be provided, but they never materialized and the subsidies to private facilities were inadequate to the need. A follow-up study of the WIN program concluded that it failed to achieve its objective of putting welfare recipients to work. It said, "WIN will probably never do much more than deal with a revolving group of the most employable clients, most of whom may well have found employment even without WIN."[19]

The WIN work requirement was tightened even further by the Talmadge Amendment of 1971, which forced recipients to work and eliminated several components of the original program, including training, job search counseling, and family support.

Eva Bertram, professor at the University of California, Santa Cruz, commented on the origins of "workfarist" social policy:

> Between 1971 and 1975, congressional leaders quietly transformed the character and politics of public assistance in the United States.

Three legislative initiatives were passed in quick succession and with little debate—the Talmadge Work Incentive amendments (WINII), Supplemental Security Income (SSI), and the Earned Income Tax Credit (EITC). Although they drew little attention at the time, their combined impact was significant in two respects. First, by redefining the terms and target populations of income assistance, they established the elements of a workfarist approach to federal antipoverty policy, one that turned the ends and means of federal assistance away from traditional needs-based New Deal welfarism and toward the principle of rewarding, encouraging, and enforcing work. In addition, the initiatives helped to create the political capacity for subsequent retrenchment of traditional welfare programs, notably Aid to Families with Dependent Children (AFDC).[20]

HELP FOR WORKING FAMILIES

As welfare reform was being considered in Congress, policy makers put forth various proposals to reform welfare. Some feminists were in favor of a work requirement for welfare recipients, believing that the only route to liberation for women was to participate in the waged labor market, and that staying home to care for children put women at a disadvantage in the labor market. Some middle-class feminists subscribed to this position and saw no problem with forcing mothers to work in the low-wage labor market. Many low-income women took a different view. This was one source of the cultural tension within the "women's lib" movement of the 1960s and '70s. As Patricia Williams pointed out, "relatively privileged white women wanted to be liberated into the workplace; relatively exhausted and exploited black women wanted to be liberated *from* it."[21] In 1995, the year before the welfare reform act was enacted, the journal *Feminist Economics* published a symposium on a proposal to reform welfare by the feminist economists Barbara Bergmann and Heidi Hartmann, co-chairs of the Institute for Women's Policy Research.[22] Entitled "A Welfare Reform Based on Help for Working Parents" (HWP), they proposed to do away with the present AFDC program and substitute a program that would encourage job holding and would provide increased child care and health care benefits, food stamps, the Earned Income Tax Credit, and housing assistance. They argued that these benefits, particularly guaranteed childcare for low-income and some middle-income parents, would raise low-income parents out of poverty. To make it more politically attractive, their child care proposal included some middle-income parents, on a sliding scale fee basis. The HWP fall-back proposal for parents who do not work for pay or are unemployed included giving vouchers for necessities and $100 a month cash. They estimated that 60 percent of AFDC recipients would work, and the HWP plan would cost $86 billion a year in new spending. Their plan was circulated at the American Economic Association meetings in January 1995 and was endorsed by more than 70 economists at that time.

All of the respondents to the Bergmann/Hartmann proposal, including me, objected to the "fall-back" proposal of giving vouchers to unemployed parents. Linda Gordon said,

> There is no justification for the use of vouchers rather than cash for the rest of the support that unemployed mothers will need. Furthermore, no one can live on $100 a month for everything except food, rent, utilities, and transportation. It is not only an insult to suggest that AFDC recipients cannot budget their money as well as, say, old-age pension recipients; just as bad, it encourages others to label AFDC recipients as generically dishonest.[23]

In response to the unanimous criticism of vouchers, Hartmann and Bergmann said that their support for vouchers was "lukewarm at best." They agreed with those of us who believed that giving cash is more respectful of peoples' ability to make their own decisions, but they saw vouchers as "an expediency that might make giving 'handouts' to the able-bodied more acceptable to the public."[24] They planned to drop the emphasis on new vouchers and "will retain vouchers only where they are currently the prevailing form of assistance for low-income families (food stamps, housing assistance, and child care assistance.)"[25] They recommended making voucher programs less stigmatizing, as has been done with food stamps, which are now attained through Electronic Benefit Transfers (a credit card).

In response to Gordon's objection that $100 a month would not be enough to live on, Bergmann and Hartmann replied, "We suspect that many current AFDC families would relish having as much as $100 in discretionary income after basic needs were taken care of."[26]

Gwendolyn Mink objected to the HWP plan privileging waged work over the unwaged work of caring for children:

> The Bergmann-Hartmann effort to negotiate a middle way through contemporary welfare politics has some strategic value. It appeals to the "work ethic." It makes childcare and health care core issues of labor policy. It supports poor, especially single, parents who want to choose to work outside the home. In these respects, this middle way opens space for feminist interventions to secure family-friendly social provision in the wage-labor market. But the Bergmann-Hartmann middle way closes the possibility of making family security in all its dimensions the strategy and goal for welfare reform. It does this by neglecting the many ways in which caretaking is *work*—socially productive labor—and by turning family practices (e.g., child-bearing, nurturing, spending) into opportunities for social control.[27]

Bergmann and Hartmann replied that they "admit without shame or remorse that we do privilege (work). We acknowledge that families who add employment to their assistance mix will be better off, reflecting the values current in our society."[28] In my response, I agreed with Mink that care work should be valued in its own right. I said,

Reformers can concoct schemes that look good on paper, but they would do better to put their energy into saving the essential programs that exist, weak though they are. The Republicans' proposal for ending AFDC as an entitlement program and turning it over the states in a block grant would tear apart the meager safety net that exists for poor mothers and children. The first order of business is to save AFDC as a federalized program and improve it, raising the grants to at least the poverty level. After we do that, we can begin the long hard road to win universal health insurance and universal day care. After that, maybe we can begin to work for a guaranteed annual income, or at the very least a universal family allowance. Whatever we work for, it should be universal and not means-tested.[29]

In response, Bergmann and Hartmann said,

To all those like Mandell and Mink who think we cannot only keep welfare from losing its entitlement status and being blockgranted to the states... but also increase cash grants substantially (*up to* the poverty level), we say, "Get real!" Many others and we have in fact been working quite hard to protect the entitlements and prevent cutbacks in current benefits. But, increasing benefits without substantially reforming the welfare system, as Mandell seems to recommend, is politically not even on the charts. We judge it will be far more likely to get the increased funds needed for childcare and health care and to reward work. We believe the only way cash payments to the poor can be substantially increased is if they are part and parcel of universal cash benefits that would go to all families regardless of income (such as child allowances, child-support enforcement assurance, child tax credits, paid family leave, etc.)[30]

The Nation published an exchange on the Bergmann/Hartmann proposal. In my letter, I said, "Bergmann and Hartmann assume that these women will be tracked into low-wage jobs. They don't mention the importance of a college education and don't suggest raising the minimum wage, which would be the single most effective way to raise mothers out of poverty."[31] Sheila B. Collins, Helen Lachs Ginsburg, and Gertrude Schaffner Goldberg expressed concern in their letter about Bergmann and Hartmann's assumption that there will be jobs for two million welfare mothers, and asked, "Why doesn't a 'program to help working parents' include job creation and an increase in the minimum wage?" In reply, Bergmann and Hartmann say that their plan "does not seek to reform the low-wage labor market or guarantee full employment...We chose to attack the income transfer part of the poverty problem...(because) we believe it will take a long time to reform the low-wage labor market."

Finally, Bergmann and Hartmann chide their critics for their failure to rally round the flag of providing more resources to the poor. We advocate nearly doubling resources for the poor in the HWP. How about it, (respondents)...? Don't be misers, sitting back in your armchairs and hoarding your money till that day when we have full employment and decent jobs for all. Get out there and give some money to the poor while we're waiting. Are you really against doubling the resources for low-income families with children?[32]

Bergmann and Hartmann's proposal had no more chance of passage than did Mink's and my proposal to pay money for caregiving. The Republican-dominated Congress had been cutting child care, health care, food stamps, and housing assistance and showed no inclination to increase them.

Basic Income

A basic income is a proposal for a guaranteed annual income that has received a great deal of interest and discussion since the 1980s. In a 1993 article, Ann Withorn suggested that welfare rights activists consider it as an alternative to AFDC.[33] A basic income is an income paid by a government, at a uniform level and at regular intervals, to each adult member of society. Except for citizenship, it would be unconditional with no means test. European countries, where unemployment is high, have been particularly interested in it as a means of partially solving the unemployment problem. "Many countries have political parties that advocate a basic income, such as the Green Party of Canada, Green Party of England and Wales, Vivant (Belgium), De Groenen (The Netherlands), the Scottish Green Party, and the New Zealand Democratic Party."[34]

A network for supporters of basic income worldwide was formed in 1986 as Basic Income Earth Network (BIEN).[35] A United State network was founded in 1999, called the U.S. Basic Income Guarantee Network. (USBIG)[36] Among its supporters are Stanley Aronowitz, William DiFazio, Frances Fox Piven, Nancy Folbre, and Fred Block. In 2006 a bill written by members of USBIG to transform the Earned Income Tax Credit into a partial basic income was introduced in the U.S. Congress but did not pass.[37] Both the worldwide and the U.S. groups hold regular conferences. An electronic journal has been set up at *The Berkeley Electronic Press*,[38] which publishes papers on basic income, and it is available through libraries.

Discussion papers reveal a wide range of opinions on the purpose and structure of basic income. Conservatives like Charles Murray see it as a way to get rid of the existing welfare state, particularly entitlement programs like Social Security.[39] Liberal to radical advocates view the plan as a way to "free individuals from forced service by prohibiting any group from setting conditions on access to all resources."[40] Philippe Van Parijs writes that the Universal Basic Income (UBI) would be particularly beneficial to women:

> Given the sexist division of labor in the household and the special "caring" functions that women disproportionately bear, their labor market participation, and range of choice in jobs, is far more constrained than those of men...Some of them, no doubt, will use the greater material freedom UBI provides to reduce their paid working time and thereby lighten the "double shift" at certain periods of their lives. But who can sincerely believe that working subject to the dictates of a boss for forty hours a week is a path to liberation? Moreover, it is not only against the tyranny of bosses that a UBI supplies some protection, but also against the tyranny of husbands and bureaucrats. It provides a modest but secure basis on which the more vulnerable can stand, as marriages collapse or administrative discretion is misused.[41]

Despite his view of the basic income as liberatory, Van Parijs does not think it would be realistic to make it large enough in the beginning to take care of all of a person's basic needs. Although he favors the highest sustainable income, and believes that all the richer countries could afford to pay a basic income above subsistence, he does not believe that advocates of a UBI need to press for a basic income at this level right away.

> In fact, the easiest and safest way forward, though details may differ considerably from one country to another, is likely to consist of enacting a UBI first at a level below subsistence, and then increasing it over time...For households whose net earnings are insufficient to reach the socially defined subsistence level, this unconditional and individual floor would be supplemented by means-tested benefits, differentiated according to household size and subjected, as they are now, to some work requirements.[42]

Critics of basic income point out the potential work disincentives created by such a program and have expressed doubts about the government's ability to fund it. A German critic, Dr. Roswitha Pioch of the Max Planck Institute, points out that the basic income would go only to citizens of a nation, not immigrants. Globalization has made national boundaries permeable, and "the formation of a European Union increases the demand to legitimize why some should pay for others, who are of different nationality."[43] She advocates smaller solutions, such as the negative income tax or wage subsidies. "Smaller solutions turn out to have bigger advantages for the integration of foreigners in modern welfare states."[44]

In 2008, the online journal *Basic Income Studies* published a symposium on basic income and gender equality.[45] Barbara Bergmann argued that benefits of the welfare state promote gender equality more than a basic income. She said that welfare state provisions are targeted toward those with particular needs, "without requiring that huge sums be expended to deliver to everybody benefits of equal value."[46] A welfare state gives a large portion of benefits in the form of goods and services, or vouchers that can only be spent on these. "This insures that public money goes to fill publicly agreed-upon needs and that taxpayers' money is not spent on things of lower public priority or that are wasteful, such as gambling or larger cars."[47] Bergmann disapproves of anything that keeps women out of the labor force, as she believes that paid work is the only way for women to get ahead in the world. She disapproves of long maternal leaves, and thinks the long leaves that Sweden gives are probably at least partly responsible for the high degree of occupational segregation by sex in Sweden.

Bergmann says that in-kind benefits are less likely to deter labor force participation less than do cash benefits. In fact, some in-kind benefits, such as child care, encourage it. She believes that requiring lone mothers to work to get benefits minimizes public resentment. "Part of the public resents births to lone mothers as imposing taxpayer costs that births to married couples avoid. Such resentments are minimized when lone mothers are earners (i.e., they are not 'lazy') and the in-kind benefits they get are also available to other parents."[48]

Bergmann says that as men's and women's occupational opportunities have become more equal, "the purchasing of household services formerly performed by family members has been increasing...Household operations and child care activities would be further commodified—either financed privately or paid for by the government. Whatever household activities remained for family members to perform would be divided more equitable between men and women."[49]

John Baker disagrees with Bergmann. He argues that "basic income can be construed as recognizing and supporting care work as a form of worthwhile but noncommodifiable activity and that this should be combined with confronting the division of labour culturally and ideologically."[50] He addresses the gender inequality in care work directly: "The central principle of feminism...is equality between women and men. This equality should not, of course, be based on assimilating women to male norms but on eliminating gendered norms altogether...Affective relationships also include important inequalities of power."[51] Baker focuses on affective relationships, believing that Bergmann's focus on income and employment is too narrow. He argues that "a feminist strategy on care work must attack the gendered division of labour, but must also recognize and support care work in a way that acknowledges the limits to its commodification."[52]

The gendered division of caring labor hurts both men and women; it frustrates the care needs of many men while the lack of recognition for care frustrates the needs of many women, who also need care for themselves in their caregiving role. A basic income "can serve not as a *payment* for care work, but as a universal *support* for care work, providing everyone with a more effective opportunity to engage in it, whether by partial or complete withdrawal from the labour market."[53]

Anda Gheaus believes that women should be wary of Basic Income (BI) because it would increase gender inequality in care work and "would make it easier for both women and men to pursue gender-unjust preferences."[54] She argues that satisfying people's preferences in an unjust system is not a solution to the problem of gender imbalance in care work. "What is good for a person in an unjust context — particularly if the injustices are historic and systematic — is not necessarily what justice requires."[55]

Gheaus believes that BI would increase polarization between home-centered and work-centered women. She cites research that shows that if cash is provided instead of services such as child care, women's preference patterns become more polarized. More women become either career-oriented or home-oriented, and fewer try to adapt to combine home and career. A study in Britain showed that approximately a fifth of UK women have a constant preference for being homemakers, and the author of that study advocated policies that would give equal support to both categories of women. Gheaus says that, whether or not such policies are possible, we should not take women's preferences at face value because many preferences are adaptive to an unjust system, and the BI would perpetuate such a system.

It seems to me that Gheaus fails to distinguish between women (and some men) who genuinely prefer caregiving to any other vocation, finding it creative and fulfilling, and women who choose caregiving because it is better than the alternatives, either not finding a job or having to take a job that is alienating and low paid. They also may choose it because it is better for their children.

Almaz Zelleke favors BI as a means of alleviating poverty: "A universal, unconditional basic income could greatly reduce the poverty rate of the most vulnerable group in capitalist economies: single women and their children. For this reason if for no other, feminists should endorse a basic income."[56] Zelleke criticizes those who believe that caregiving and other domestic work are problems to be solved through commodification, that is, increased availability of child and elder care, house cleaning, and meal preparation services. Nancy Fraser calls this the "universal breadwinner model," which aims to achieve gender equity principally by promoting women's employment.[57]

Fraser believes that true gender equality requires redistributing what is primarily *women's* work—care work—as well as restructuring social institutions. "The key to achieving gender equity in a postindustrial welfare state...is to make women's current life-patterns the norm for everyone."[58] All citizens would participate in both kinds of work, rather than dividing paid employment and care work between workers and caregivers. Fraser believes that caregiving and household responsibilities "cannot be fully commodified or restricted to the confines of employment-comparable hours and tasks."[59]

Zelleke points out that caregiving is not comparable to a job with limited and definable hours and responsibilities.

When workers are off duty, they can enjoy leisure, but homebased caregiving is a job that can be round the clock, depending on the nature of the person cared for. Viewing caregiving as a job with an income risks entrenching the view that it is an individual, chosen responsibility, rather than either a mandatory activity that someone must undertake or, more properly, a universal responsibility in which all should participate.[60]

Caregivers need a regular income, but caregiving cannot be limited by financial considerations. Baker cites a study of caregivers and care recipients in Ireland that illustrates the importance of "love, moral obligation and the patent absence of alternatives that could meet the needs of their children, dependent spouses or parents."[61] This moral obligation is not confined to caring for relatives, as Deborah Stone shows in her study of home care workers.[62] Stone tells about a home care worker who was unhappy with agency policies that prohibit aides and nurses from giving any kind of help to their clients outside the prescribed care plan or their shifts, policies that were dictated by Medicare rules. "She was arguing with a public morality that conflicted with her personal morality, and which she believes is a higher morality."[63] She described her dilemma in caring for a patient with MS:

> I told the guy with MS, "Hey, if they cut you off, you won't go without a bath"...If he gets cut off, I don't know what he'd do...The man gets less than eight hundred dollars a month...and he can't afford to hire aides privately. "It's not right, it stinks," she declared, talking about the Medicare rule-tightening and budget cutbacks. Then she circled back to the man with MS. "I told him I'd stop by after work and do it. They can't stop you on your own time. After 3:30, you're a private citizen."[64]

Stone discusses the conservative attack on giving government help to people. Claiming that helping people "fosters dependence," the conservatives "encourage self-sufficiency" by forcing welfare mothers into low-wage jobs, and slash the safety net in other ways.

> The reigning public philosophy in post-Reagan America is: Help is harmful. Giving has too many bad consequences. Compassion is often a form of self-indulgence—it makes us feel better but worsens the problem. Helping people enables them to slack off their personal effort. Sharing opens the door to freeloaders. Government should teach personal responsibility. Self-reliance is the best way to live.[65]

This philosophy affects all caring professions. Doctors are prevented from spending time with patients because of the requirements of managed care and HMOs. This violates their professional standards and their own moral standards. A Medicare reform bill includes a cost-cutting policy called Relative Value Unit (RVU). It seeks to measure the productivity of a physician every hour of his or her day. "The more RVUs you accumulate, the more money you make."[66] Dr. Jerome Goopman opposes RVUs because they dehumanize medical practice. He says, "There are no RVUs for sitting with a confused third-year medical student. There are no RVUs for the humanistic core of medicine that drew me into this profession in the first place."[67] RVUs reward doctors who perform high-risk procedures that require great skill and produce large money at the expense of primary care physicians.

Cutbacks in Medicaid and Medicare take away care that people need. Psychotherapists are unable to give patients the listening time that troubled people need. One community psychiatrist said in a letter to the editor, "Mental health programs are designed to fail because reimbursements do not cover costs, and this is especially true for patients with special needs. A clinician (at one clinic) has to see 81 billable patients per week just to break even."[68]

Nearly 98,000 Americans die each year due to medical mistakes in hospitals. Part of the reason is that hospitals are understaffed. One study showed that the lower the nurse-to-patient ratio in hospitals, the higher rate of bedsores because there are not enough nurses to move patients in bed. Once bedsores get going, they can lead to serious infections.[69]

WAGE INSURANCE

In March 2001 Robert Litan, a Brookings Institutions economist, and Lori Kletzer, a University of California-Santa Cruz economics professor, wrote a paper advocating that the United States set up a program of wage insurance, combined with subsidies for health insurance, for workers who lose their jobs through no fault of their own. Wage insurance would take effect only after a laid-off person found a new job. "If the new position pays less than the job he lost, he would get half the difference between his new and old salaries, up to $10,000 annually, for two years. He would also qualify for subsidies on health insurance premiums until he found new work."[70]

The program was promoted as a way to compensate workers for losing jobs due to outsourcing. It was supported by Senator Charles Schumer of New York, Robert Rubin, the former Treasury secretary, and Robert B. Reich, the former secretary of labor, "who view global trade and open markets as sources of growth and dynamism, but see a need to protect workers whose lives are disrupted."[71] Some conservatives see it as a way to dismantle or weaken Unemployment Insurance, because "they don't like unemployment insurance where you're paying people not to work, so wage insurance gives them that incentive to support it, because it puts people back to work."[72]

The most vocal opposition to wage insurance comes from labor unions and groups aligned with organized labor. Labor leaders say that wage insurance would subsidize downward mobility by providing money to employers offering the lowest wages possible. Thea Lee, policy director at the AFL-CIO, says, "It's basically about getting workers to take bad jobs quickly. This seems to be giving up on the possibility of trying to get workers into better-paying jobs."[73] Labor leaders who have fought trade agreements in recent years say, "Using wage insurance to support free trade would simply add insult to injury."[74] Maurice Emsellem of the National Employment Law Project testified to the House Ways & Means Committee in 2007 in favor of improving Unemployment Insurance and against wage insurance. He said, "Rather than encouraging workers to forego their long-term interests for a wage insurance job, Congress should focus on more meaningful solutions that create genuine economic security and more family-friendly sustaining jobs in our economy."[75] He said that the wage insurance would make it impossible for workers to pursue the education and training they need to get a better job.

WAGES FOR HOUSEWORK (CARE WORK)

In the 1970s, Selma James started a movement called "Wages for Housework." Few people even knew about it, and few were interested.[76] Recently, however, the work of unpaid care is receiving popular and academic attention. There are several organizations that work on issues related to women's work and caregiving. We describe those in the appendix.

One of the most significant developments has been the unionization of care workers who care for seniors or disabled people. Beginning in 1987, Service Employees International Union (SEIU) organized thousands of home care workers in California. They were paid by the state In-Home Supportive Services (IHSS) program, which was started in 1973 as a way to reimburse low-income families for providing care to their relatives in their homes. Approximately 40 percent of homecare workers were immediate family members or related in some way. The program aimed to keep costs down by avoiding expensive long-term institutional settings and was funded by Medicaid. The agency followed a model pioneered by the disability rights movement, which allows people who need care to hire their caregivers and set the terms of employment, although they cannot negotiate wages.[77] In addition to organizing in California, SEIU has organized home care workers in Illinois and Oregon, and Massachusetts.

Before collective bargaining, prevailing wages for IHSS workers were approximately $6.15 an hour. Union organizing succeeded in raising wages substantially, and winning benefits for workers. This in turn led to reduced turnover. In their analysis of this program, Brandynn Holgate and Jennifer Shea point out that one difficulty with it is that "in pushing the discourse of care primarily into the market, this construction risks veiling the important familial and relational components inherent in care work because market norms do not allow for the concept of long-term reciprocity that comes with family relations."[78]

AFSCME (The American Federation of State, County, and Municipal Employees) has organized tens of thousands of day care workers across the country and has also organized home care workers. Although these have been major breakthroughs in paying low-income people (primarily women) for their care work, they do not of course pay parents for caring for their own children. Yet they have established a precedent for valuing care work in monetary terms.

Perhaps the hardest group to organize is household workers, who are isolated and not likely to have contact with each other. Yet India's household workers are organizing for their rights, helped by unions and advocacy organizations.

The effort is being made as the supply-demand ratio for domestic workers shifts in their favor. India's economic rise has spurred more and more families to hire more servants. Increasingly, household help is seen as a necessity for India's busy families, as well as a sign of status in this class-conscious country.[79]

Domestic worker organizations have begun holding street protests to demand salary increases, sick pay, and a weekly day off. The coordinator of one of these organizations said, "The heart of the issue is that society doesn't respect their labor as real work...Even the workers themselves took a long time to see that there was actual labor and dignity in their jobs."[80]

Children's Allowance/Family Allowance

The Children's Allowance, or Family Allowance, is a universal payment for children, irrespective of income. It is designed to equalize family income, since wages are not paid on the basis of the numbers of dependents. Advantages of the children's allowance are elimination of the stigma of assistance, relative ease of administration, special assistance to large families, and avoidance for the most part of the issue of work incentive since it supplements rather than replaces earnings. Some critics of the children's allowance object that it would raise the birthrate, but evidence from other countries indicates that it has no appreciable effect on the birth rate.

Currently 88 countries, worldwide, provide child or family allowances. Sometimes these allowances are integrated with or replaced by tax provisions, such as tax credits. In some countries, benefits are only available to families with children who have at least one parent in the work force, or higher benefit levels are offered to families attached to the labor force. At various times (not currently) they were initiated as pronatalist policies, as in England after World War II. As the European Union moves toward greater unity among its member states, family allowances are viewed as an instrument that can foster societal cohesion and progress.[81]

In some European countries (e.g., in Ireland) support for marriage and the family is stated in the constitution. Ireland has changed the name of Children's Allowance to Child Benefit. It is payable to the parents or guardians of children less than 16 years of age, or less than 19 years of age if the child is in full-time education, training, or has a disability. The monthly amount of the child benefit is 166 euros for 1 child, 332 euros for 2 children, 535 euros for 3, and 738 euros for 4.[82]

The children's allowance is usually sent to the mother, which is actually a form of wages for caregiving, and gives the wife more financial freedom than she might otherwise have. Several studies have shown that women "have a higher propensity than men to spend on goods that benefit children and enhance their capacities."[83]

Several years ago, I was a social worker at the Children's Aid Society in Cornwall, Canada. At that time Canada had a universal children's allowance that was sent to the mother. Once a month, my friend and her husband would cheerfully announce, "It's mother's day. Let's go out to lunch. It's our treat."

There is no more free lunch on mother's day. A conservative government used means testing as a way to cut back on benefits. Canada replaced its universal family allowance with a means tested Child Tax Benefit in 1998, a program similar to a Negative Income Tax. This was part of a conservative campaign to attack entitlement programs, following the lead of the United States. The Negative Income Tax has been used by conservatives in Canada to make substantial cuts via changes to the tax system.

ASSET BUILDING

The current fad in antipoverty policy is asset building. It is based on the philosophy that the poor, unlike middle-class people, have no assets on which to build a secure future, and they need help in building assets. It also assumes that poor people need to learn how to save for long-term goals. It follows the script of the "ownership society." It takes the form of "Individual Development Accounts (IDAs).

IDAs encourage savings efforts among the poor by offering them 1:1, 2:1, or more generous matches for their own deposits. IDAs reward the monthly savings of working-poor families who are trying to buy their first home, pay for post-secondary education, or start a small business. These matched savings accounts are similar to 401(k) plans and other matched savings accounts but can serve a broad range of purposes.[84]

Some form of Asset Building legislation has been passed in all but 6 states, and 30 states have included IDAs in their state TANF plans. Legislation supporting IDA programs nationwide has also been passed at the federal level in the Assets for Independence Act of 1998. IDAs are touted as helping families to achieve the American Dream. A demonstration project to study them was called The American Dream Demonstration. When people sign up for an IDA, they must attend "financial literacy" training. "Key to the success of IDAs is the economic education that participants receive."[85] IDAs are administered by community-based organizations in partnership with a financial institution that holds the deposits, and they are funded by public and private sources.

States are permitted to include IDAs in welfare reform plans and welfare-to-work grants but are not required to fund them. Public housing authorities who wish to expand their services must develop new self-sufficiency programs, as mandated by the Family Self-Sufficiency Program (FSS) of 1992 by Section 554 of the National Affordable Housing Act. When a family enters the FSS, they agree to a set of contractual goals that cover a period of five years. If the participant is receiving Section 8 housing benefits, escrow accounts are created as part of these contracts.[86]

The idea of creating a trust fund for every child is gaining in popularity. The plan calls for the government to contribute an initial deposit at birth, with low-income families receiving a supplement. The family could add to the fund, which would accrue interest tax-free, and the government would offer some matching incentive. Both Republicans and Democrats in Congress have supported asset building. Joe Biden advocated it during his presidential campaign, and Rahm Emanuel pushed relevant legislation in the House. Prominent conservative fans include the columnist David Brooks and former senator Rick Santorum, who find it compatible with the "ownership society." The plan is being tested in Maine, funded by private philanthropy, and Oklahoma has a pilot project. Several bills have been introduced in Congress. Other nations, such as Singapore, South Korea, and Canada, have conducted experiments.[87]

Liberal critics of the plan fear that it "represents a step down a slippery slope toward a privatized social safety net."[88] They also fear that it could divert money from current programs such as Head Start or primary education. Conservative critics see it as another expensive program that would add to other entitlement programs such as Social Security and Medicaid.

Britain enacted the Child Trust Fund in 2002, an endowment paid by the state to every child born in Britain. The government gives a 250-pound voucher to start each child's account. Children in families receiving Child Tax Credit may be entitled to an additional payment of 250 pounds. A maximum of 1,200 pounds each year can be saved in the account by parents, family, or friends. The government makes a further contribution of 250 pounds when the child is 7 years old, with children in lower income families receiving an additional 250 pounds. Once the child is 18 years old, he or she can decide how to use the money. Money cannot be taken out of the account once it has been put in until the child is 18 years old.[89] There are no restrictions on how the money is to be used—children make their own decisions about that. A survey of public attitudes found that young people were skeptical about very generous stakes and about the lack of any restriction on how the money can be used. Some people argue that advising, informing, and mentoring the account holders would solve the problem of "responsible" use, but one author counters, "from a morally neutral point of view, advice and mentoring cannot prevent a teenager from spending her lifetime savings on a holiday in Malibu."[90] While asset building helps the poor save for the future, it does not provide money for daily living expenses. Proponents are quite explicit in saying, "The answer...is not income redistribution. The primary challenge, instead, is to *expand the reach* of the tax code so that any Americans willing to work and save, regardless of income, have an opportunity to build assets."[91]

Conservatives regard asset building as a way to replace some, if not all, existing welfare programs. Liberals argue that it can at best be only a complement to existing programs, not a substitute. Sanford Schram attacks it as the latest way to blame the poor for their poverty, the neoliberal version of blaming the victim for being trapped in a culture of poverty. "Teach 'them' to save and they will become like 'us'—the personally responsible, middle class (white) people."[92]

NOTES

1. André Gorz, "S(he) who does not work shall eat all the same: Tomorrow's economy and proposals from the Left," *Dissent*, Spring 1987, p. 180.
2. Ibid., p. 181. Emphasis in the original.
3. Ibid., p. 182.
4. European Social Welfare Information Network, *The Netherlands Eswin Social Welfare Summary Fact Sheet*, http://websrvl.nizw.nl/eswin/Nleswin/nlswfs.htm, December 2, 2002, p. 17.
5. Gorz, p. 182.
6. Ibid., p. 184.
7. Ibid., p.183. Emphasis in the original.
8. Ibid., p. 182.
9. Ibid., p. 183
10. Ibid., p. 184.
11. Ibid.
12. Deanne Bonnar, "The wages of care," *New Politics*, Summer 2006, pp. 38–45.
13. David Gil, "Toward constructive alternatives to the welfare system," Unpublished ms., undated.
14. Ibid.
15. Ibid.
16. Ibid.
17. Ibid.
18. At that time, the Bureau of Labor Statistics annually published estimates of the amount of money that families needed to live in

different parts of the country. They gave estimates for three different income levels: a minimally adequate, a modestly adequate, and a higher income that allowed for a few luxuries. The BLS no longer does this, probably because their estimates were so much higher than the official poverty line and they could not rationalize this inconsistency. A nonprofit organization, Wider Opportunities for Women, publishes studies on the amount of money needed for a minimally adequate standard of living for a family, which they call a "Self-sufficiency Standard." Their study includes various sections of the country and is periodically updated.

19. U.S. Department of HEW, National Center for Social Statistics, "Child care arrangements of AFDC recipients under the Work Incentive Program November 1969," NCSS Report E-4 (11/69).

20. Eva C. Bertram, "The institutional origins of 'workfarist' social Policy," *Cambridge Journals*, http://journals.cambridge.org/action/display/abstract;jsessionid...

21. Patricia Williams, "Mrs. Obama meets Mrs. Windsor," *Nation*, April 27, 2009, p. 9. Emphasis in the original.

22. *Feminist Economics*, vol. 2, no. 2, Summer 1995, pp. 81–119.

23. Linda Gordon, "Thoughts on the Help for Working Parents plan," *Feminist Economics, vol. 2, no. 2, Summer 1995*, p. 93.

24. Barbara Bergmann, "Get real! Look to the future, not the past," *Feminist Economics*, vol. 2, no. 2, Summer 1995, p. 115.

25. Ibid.

26. Ibid., p. 116.

27. Gwendolyn Mink, "Wage work, family work, and welfare politics," *Feminist Economics*, vol. 2, no 2, Summer 1995, p. 98.

28. Bergmann, "Get real!..."

29. Betty Reid Mandell, "Why can't we care for our own children?" *Feminist Economics*, vol. 2, no. 2, Summer 1995, p. 103.

30. Bergmann, "Get real!...," p. 117.

31. Betty Reid Mandell, "Welfare that works?" *The Nation*, July 31/August 7, 1995, p. 114.

32. Ibid., Barbara Bergmann and Heidi Hartmann, p. 117.

33. Ann Withorn, "Women and basic income in the US: Is one man's ceiling another woman's floor?" *Journal of Progressive Human Services*, vol. 4., no. 1, 1993, pp. 29–42.

34. Wikipedia, http://en.wikipedia.org/wiki/Basic_income

35. BIEN: frequently asked questions (http://www.etes.ucl.ac.be/bien/BI/FAQ.htm)

36. The U.S. Basic Income Guarantee Network, http://www.usbig.net/about.html

37. Al Sheahen, "The rise and fall of a Basic Income Guarantee bill in the United State Congress," The US Basic Income Guarantee Network (USBIG), 2008, http://www.usbig.net/papers/179-Sheahen—rise&fall.doc Accessed February 4, 2010.

38. http://www.bepress.com/bis
39. Charles Murray, "Guaranteed Income as a replacement for the welfare state," *Basic Income Studies*, vol. 3, no. 2, Article 6. Available at: http://www.bepress.com/bis/vol3/iss2/art6 Accessed February 5, 2010.
40. Karl Widerquist, "Status Freedom," available at http://www.usbig.net/ Accessed February 5, 2010.
41. Philippe Van Parijs, "A Basic Income for All," *Boston Review*, http://bostonreview.net/BR25.5/vanparijs.html Accessed February 5, 2010.
42. Ibid.
43. Dr. Roswitha Pioch, "EU integration and basic income — Rethinking social justice in competitive welfare states," 2000, http://www.bepress.com/bis Accessed February 5, 2010.
44. Ibid.
45. *Basic Income Studies: An International Journal of Basic Income Research*. The Berkeley Electronic Press, December 2008.
46. Barbara Bergmann, "Basic Income grants or the welfare state: Which better promotes gender equality?" *Basic Income Studies*, December 2008.
47. Ibid.
48. Ibid., p. 5.
49. Ibid., p. 3.
50. John Baker, "All things considered, should feminists embrace basic income?" *Basic Income Studies*, December, 2008.
51. Ibid., p. 2.
52. Ibid., p. 6.
53. Ibid., p. 4.
54. Anda Gheaus, "Basic Income, gender justice and the costs of gender-symmetrical lifestyles," *Basic Income Studies*, December 2008, p. 1.
55. Ibid., p. 2.
56. Almaz Zelleke, "Institutionalizing the universal caretaker through a basic income?" *Basic Income Studies*, December 2008, p. 1.
57. Nancy Fraser, "After the family wage: A postindustrial thought experiment," in *Justice Interruptus: Critical Reflections on the 'Postsocialist' Condition*. New York: Routledge, 1997, pp. 41–69.
58. Fraser, p. 61.
59. Zelleke, p. 5.
60. Ibid.
61. Baker, pp. 5–6.
62. Deborah Stone, *The Samaritan's Dilemma*. New York: Nation Books, 2008.
63. Ibid., p. 139.
64. Ibid.
65. Ibid., p. 8.

66. Sam Allis, "Relative value unseen," *Boston Globe*, March 1, 2009, p. A9.
67. Ibid.
68. George Sigel, "Stepping up in a system designed to fail," *Boston Globe*, February 98, 2009, p. L8.
69. Ranit Mishori, "Don't let a hospital make you sick," *Boston Sunday Globe*, *Parade*, February 8, 2009, p. 12.
70. Mark Roth, "Wage insurance: A way to ease outsourcing angst?" *Pittsburgh Post-Gazette*, March 24, 2004.
71. Mark Thoma, "Wage insurance," March 18, 2007, http://economistsview.typepad.com/economistsview/2007/03/wage_insurance
72. Roth, p. 2.
73. Thoma.
74. Ibid.
75. Maurice Emsellem, "Testimony of Maurice Ensellem, National Employment Law Project, Hearing Before the U.S. Congress, House of Representatives, Committee on Homeland Security on the Transportation Worker Identification Credential, October 31, 2007 p. 12. 20071031111154–82971.pdf.
76. The term "housework" is misleading because, as Deanne Bonnar says, housework is only one part of caregiving, which she prefers to call "care work." The term most generally used is "caregiving."
77. Brandynn Holgate and Jennifer Shea, "SEIU confronts the home care crisis in California," *New Politics*, vol. XI, no. 2, Winter 2007, pp. 46–55.
78. Ibid, p. 52.
79. Emily Wax, "India's household workers push for rights, to organize," *Boston Globe*, November 9, 2008, p. A22.
80. Ibid.
81. The Clearinghouse on international developments in child, youth, and family policies at Columbia University, "Child and Family Allowances," http://www.childpolicyintl.org/familychildallowances. html Accessed February 6, 2010.
82. Citizens Information, "Child Benefit" http://www.citizensinformation.ie/catgories/social-welfare/social-welfare-payments/social-welfare-payments-to-families-and-children. Accessed February 6, 2010.
83. Judith Bruce and Cynthia B. Lloyd, "Finding the ties that bind: Beyond headship and household," in *Intrahousehold Resource Allocation in Developing Countries: Methods, Models, and Policy*. ed. Lawrence Haddad, John Hoddinott, and Harold Alderman. Baltimore: International Food Policy Research Institute and Johns Hopkins University Press, 1997, pp. 213–131.
84. Washington University in St. Louis, "Asset Building," http://gwbweb.wustl.edu/csd/Asset/idas.htm
85. Ibid.

86. Ray Boshara, Corporation for Enterprise Development, "Federal and State IDA policy overview," January 2000.
87. Rebecca Tuhus-Dubrow, "Cash on delivery: The movement to give every American a trust fund at birth, *Boston Globe*, February 1, 2009, p. C1.
88. Ibid., p. 2.
89. Child Trust Fund, http://www.childtrustfund.gov.uk Accessed February 6, 2010.
90. *Basic Income Studies*, vol. 3, no. 2 (2008), Article 8, http://www.bepress.com/bis/vol3/iss2/art8 Accessed February 4, 2010.
91. Ibid. Emphasis in the original.
92. Communication to bertha-swaa@yahoogroups.com listserv, January 15, 2009.

Current Safety Net Programs

The safety net programs that have the most political protection are those that include the middle class as well as the poor, such as Social Security and Medicare. Some programs have the political protection of powerful lobbies, such as food stamps and nutrition programs that are supported by the agricultural lobby. Medicaid has some protection from doctors, pharmacists, nursing homes, and middle-class people who need it to pay for their relatives' nursing home care. Programs that serve only the poor, such as TANF, fare badly in the political arena. Following is a description of the major government safety net programs in the United States:

Social Security (OASDI, Old Age, Survivors, and Disability Insurance) was enacted in 1935 during the Great Depression. It was won through grass roots struggles and was a response to growing unrest about unemployment. Aiming to get older people out of the labor market by providing them with pensions, it freed up jobs for younger workers and so helped to quell growing unrest.

It now provides income protection to 156 million workers and provides benefits to 44 million retirees, people with disabilities, widow(er)s, and children. Conservatives want to privatize it, but have so far failed. Treasury chief Henry Paulson vowed in 2006 to continue the fight to overhaul Social Security, "although his two predecessors were carried off the field after bruising political battles."[1] President Obama has talked about "looking at entitlements," and a commission composed of people in favor of privatizing Social Security, including Paul Peterson, is studying the matter. Polling data show that not having enough money for retirement is at the top of Americans' economic concerns, and they will no doubt resist privatization. People have seen the value of their 401Ks drop as the stock market collapsed.

Many women work part-time or drop out of the labor market when they have caregiving responsibilities. This often makes them ineligible for Social Security, which bases benefits on a 40-year work history, with the five lowest income years removed. At retirement age, women can choose between their own benefits or an amount equal to half their husband's—whichever is greater. A large majority of women pay Social Security taxes for years, but when they opt to take benefits as "dependents," they receive the same benefits they would have had had they never held a paying job at all.[2]

In the eyes of the government, caregivers thus deserve half the retirement income of wage earners. This penalizes almost two-thirds of American women. In 1993, only 36 percent of women drew Social Security benefits based on their own work records. Even by the year 2030, it is estimated that only four out of ten women will be earning more Social Security in their own right than as "dependents."[3]

Social Security is particularly important for women. "Nearly two-thirds of women 65 and over get a majority of their income from Social Security, and nearly one-third rely on Social Security for 90 percent or more of their income. Without Social Security, more than half of all elderly women would be living in poverty. But, even with Social Security, one of every five elderly women living alone is poor."[4] Married women who were homemakers are not covered by Social Security as homemakers. The government does not define caregiving as work; retired homemakers must rely on their husband's Social Security. Social Security is particularly important to women of color, as on average they have low lifetime earnings and long life spans. They also draw disproportionately on Social Security's benefits for disabled workers and for the families of workers who become disabled or die prematurely.[5]

In 2009, the Urban Institute published a proposal for a new minimum benefits for low lifetime earners. This would target workers with long careers with low lifetime earnings along with a modest credit that compensates workers for up to three years out of the labor market due to caregiving, unemployment, or poor health. The proposed minimum would start at 60 percent of the poverty threshold for a worker with 20 years of Social Security-covered earning, and increases to a maximum of 110 percent of poverty for those working 40 or more years. The caregiving and health credits, which are based on the average wage, count toward the work years required by the minimum benefit. The change is proposed to take effect in 2010.[6] The proposal would cover caregiving for children up to the age of four. This is similar to the proposals in other nations, with most nations providing the credit for children aged 3 to 4. Age limits for the child to whom the worker provides care vary from age 1 or under in Japan to age 16 or under in Switzerland and the United Kingdom. Most other industrialized countries integrate caregiving credits in their social security systems.[7]

Supplemental Security Income (SSI) is a means-tested federal entitlement program for the aged (65 or older), disabled, and blind. It was enacted in 1974 as part of President Nixon's efforts to reform the nation's welfare programs. It aimed to replace various state-administered programs, as a way to standardize the level of benefits. Benefits are well below the poverty level, a maximum of $637 a month for individuals in 2008 and $956 for a couple.[8] It is part of the Social Security Act (Title 16), and it is administered by the

Social Security Administration. The majority of elderly and disabled SSI beneficiaries are women (71 percent of the elderly and 57 percent of the disabled). Individual beneficiaries are not allowed to have more than $2,000 a year in assets, $3,000 a year for couples. Ten states provide a supplement to SSI. President Reagan kicked thousands of disabled people off SSI. Advocates fought that and were able to get two-thirds of them reinstated. It is very difficult to establish eligibility for SSI. Lawyers who help people with their applications say that many people have to appeal their denial twice, and two-thirds of them are accepted the third time they applied.

Medicare, enacted in 1965 as an Amendment to the Social Security Act, is a universal entitlement program that provides medical insurance and prescription coverage to people aged 65 or older. Part A covers hospital care, skilled nursing home care, and some home health care. Part B covers outpatient care. Both parts have some deductibles. Part D subsidizes the cost of prescription drugs and is administered by private insurance companies. The Bush administration introduced this in 2006, with the hope that this would be a foot in the door to privatization of the entire Medicare program.

In most plans, there are large deductibles. Medicare beneficiaries whose total drug costs reach $2,400 must pay 100 percent of prescription costs until $3,850 is spent out-of-pocket. As of 2008, there were 1,824 Part D plans, which makes choosing a plan extremely difficult. The federal government is not allowed to negotiate prices of drugs with the drug companies. The Veterans Administration (VA), which negotiates prices with drug companies, pays 58 percent less for drugs than Medicare Part D. Paul Krugman compared patients in the Medicare Advantage plans to the VA system and found that mortality rates in Medicare Advantage plans are 40 percent higher than mortality rates of elderly veterans treated by the VA.[9]

Medicaid, enacted in 1965 as an Amendment to the Social Social Security Act, is a means-tested health insurance program for low-income people. It is not a universal entitlement program like Medicare. Federal and state governments fund it jointly, with states providing up to half of the funding, and counties sometimes contributing. It is administered by states. State participation is voluntary, but all states have participated since 1982, when Arizona adopted the program. The federal government establishes basic guidelines, but each state runs its own program. While all states are required to provide some dental service to children, some states do not provide dental service to adults. Some states do not provide eyeglasses or prosthetic devices. In certain circumstances, homosexuals may be denied coverage. Medicare provides a wider range of health services than does Medicaid. Not all poor people are eligible or enrolled; approximately 60 percent of poor Americans are not covered.[10]

Medicaid has become a major budgetary issue for many states, and this has resulted in severe cutbacks. It gets some political protection from elderly people who need nursing home care. They and their relatives fight to pre-serve Medicaid payments. More than two-thirds of Medicaid payments go to the elderly. Some states require people who apply for nursing home care to allow the state to take their homes when they die. Lawyers help many people figure out ways to avoid this.

TANF

President Clinton signed into law the Personal Responsibility and Work Opportunity Reconciliation Act of 1996. The law cut funding for low-in-come programs by approximately $55 billion over the next 6 years, the heavi-est in food stamps, Supplemental Security Income, and assistance to legal immigrants. (Illegal immigrants were already ineligible for most programs.) Legal immigrants were cut off of most assistance programs, including food stamps and SSI, and other types of assistance. Some of the restrictions affect-ing immigrants were later eased up, but many immigrants are still ineligible for help.

The law replaced AFDC, emergency assistance, and the JOBS (Job Opportunities and Basic Skills) program with the TANF Block Grant. It gives federal money to the states to run their own programs, but the amount of money was essentially fixed. The federal government matched state spend-ing under the previous law. That is no longer the case. States can spend more than their federal allotment, but it is not matched by federal dollars.

In the past, states had to get a waiver from the federal government if they wanted to do something contrary to federal regulations. Now, however, states can set their own standards. They can define "needy" any way they like, and can even use different definitions for different areas of the state. They can set tighter time limits and establish new requirements such as de-nying aid to children born while the family is on assistance (the family cap), denying aid to two-parent families, or denying aid to parents who fail to im-munize their children or fail to keep them in school.

Tommy Thompson, director of the federal Health and Human Services Department in the Clinton administration, created one of the toughest wel-fare systems in the nation in Wisconsin when he was governor. Consisting almost entirely of forced work, it became the model for welfare reform na-tionwide. It caused a sharp rise in infant mortality in Wisconsin between 1997 and 1998. The rise was especially sharp, 37 percent, for African Americans, who are disproportionately represented on welfare in Milwaukee.[11]

Following are some of the features of the Act:

- There is a lifetime "drop dead" time limit of five years on cash assis-tance. States may exempt 20 percent of their caseload from the 5-year limit. States may set shorter time limits, regardless of whether the par-ents in the family can find employment. These percentages give states a perverse incentive to cut the rolls, since they will be able to meet work quotas more easily if there are fewer people to put to work. States can therefore meet their quotas by knocking people off the rolls, and they have done that.

- The law has a narrower definition of work and training than the previous program. It does not allow higher education, and allows only 12 months of vocational training. Officials prefer really short training programs.
- Although the law increased the need for child care because of expanded work requirements, child care funding fell far short of what was needed. The law also did not provide for transportation costs. The previous 1988 law required work for women whose children were more than the age of three, but it provided day care and transportation.
- People convicted of drug felonies are prohibited from receiving a TANF block grant or food stamps for life. However, the Obama administration removed that restriction on food stamps.
- The law required states to impose harsher sanctions than allowed under previous law on families where the parent does not "cooperate fully" in establishing paternity and collecting child support. States must reduce by at least 25 percent the payments made to any family not "cooperating fully," as well as eliminate assistance for an entire family if the head of the family declines to assign support rights to the state. The definition of "cooperating fully" is subject to various interpretations. For a time, Massachusetts was dropping families from the rolls if the mother was unable to provide such information as the father's Social Security number, his whereabouts, and place of employment, even when the mother did not have this information. A class action suit brought by legal services stopped the practice.
- The law denies most immigrants, including lawful permanent residents, access to many federal public benefit programs, and gives states the option to adopt similar restrictions for state-funded benefits.

The law is scheduled to be reauthorized in 2010.

State Children's Health Insurance Program (SCHIP) is a federally funded program enacted in 1997 as Title XXI of the Social Security Act. It provides money to states to provide health insurance for children whose families are poor, but earn more than the eligibility level for Medicaid. It was the largest expansion of taxpayer funded health insurance coverage for children in the United States since Medicaid began. States are given flexibility in designing their eligibility requirements within broad federal guidelines. The program is already facing funding shortfalls in several states. Attempts to expand funding for the program have met with political opposition. Congressional proposals to expand the program in 2007 were vetoed by President Bush, but at the end of 2007, Bush signed an extension of the program to cover current enrollment levels through March 2009. In February 2009, the Obama administration added up to 4 million children to the program to the 7 million children who were already receiving it.[12]

Community Health Centers One of the few concrete examples of President Bush's "compassionate conservatism" is his doubling federal financing for community health centers, enabling the creation or expansion of 1,297 in medically underserved areas.

> As governor of Texas, Mr. Bush came to admire the missionary zeal and cost-efficiency of the not-for-profit community health centers, which qualify for federal operating grants by being located in designated underserved area and treating patients regardless of their ability to pay.[13]

The clinics are lauded as low-cost alternatives to hospital emergency rooms, where the uninsured and underinsured often seek care. However, many areas of the country remain without access to affordable primary care. "The recession has only magnified the need as hundreds of thousands of Americans have lost their employer-sponsored health insurance along with their jobs."[14] The Obama administration allocated more than $2 billion in resources to community health centers in 2010, as part of the American Recovery and Reinvestment Act.[15]

Food Stamps (now called SNAP, Supplemental Nutrition Assistance Program) are an important supplement to people's income, and sometimes the only assistance available to unemployed people, aside from food pantries and food kitchens. It is means-tested, but all eligible people are entitled to it. Conservative legislators try to make it discretionary. Thanks to advocacy work by the Food Research and Action Center and state and local advocates, its entitlement status has been maintained and it has been increased recently. The nutrition title in the Farm Bill that became law in July 2008 invested an additional $10.3 billion in food stamps and other federal nutrition programs. This included a boost in the food stamp benefit level. The number of people receiving food stamps has grown from 26.3 million in April 2007 to 29.5 million in August 2008. Experts predict this number will rise by millions more in the months ahead.[16]

The American Recovery and Reinvestment Act (stimulus package) that was signed into law on February 19, 2009, contains an increase of $20 billion in food stamp benefits and increased cash assistance for needy families.[17] Starting in April 2009, a family of 4 on food stamps received an average of $80 extra. The U.S. Department of Agriculture calculates that for every $5 of food stamp spending, there is $9.20 of total economic activity, as grocer and farmers pay their employees and suppliers who in turn shop and pay their bills. Nationwide, enrollment in the program surged in March 2009 to approximately 33.2 million people, up by nearly 1 million since January and by more than 5 million from March 2008.[18]

School Lunch, School Breakfast, and **WIC** (Women, Infants, and Children program) are nutrition programs. WIC gives food to pregnant mothers and children up to age 5, as well as nutritional counseling. It is not an entitlement program, so is not required to serve everyone who needs it. The school lunch program is an entitlement program that provides free or low-cost lunch to school children and residential childcare programs. It provides school children with one-third or more of the recommended dietary allowance for key nutrients. Schools must apply to participate in the program. During the 2006–2007 school year, 30.5 million children participated in the program.

The school breakfast program is an entitlement program, but fewer schools participate in it than in the lunch program. President Lyndon Johnson signed it into law as the Child Nutrition Act in 1966. Some believe that the huge success of the Black Panther breakfast program in the early 1960s "shamed" the Johnson administration into providing free breakfasts in public schools. The Panthers would cook and serve food to the poor inner city youth of the area out of a San Francisco church, and eventually country-wide, which fed up to 10,000 children. More than 3 out of 4 schools that serve lunch also serve breakfast. In the 2006–2007 school period, 9.9 million children participated in the program. Most programs are means-tested, but schools have the option of providing a universal program, available to all children, if they supplement the program with state funds. Many children in very poor families get most of their food from these programs, but many children who are eligible do not participate. [19]

There is also a Summer Food Service Program, which combines a feeding program with a summer activity program.

These food programs also benefit farmers, which gives the programs political protection. People who created WIC realized that it would receive political protection by calling it a health program, rather than a welfare program. Also, the fact that WIC and the school lunch and breakfast programs benefit children gives them further protection. Children are the objects of compassion because they are not responsible for their poverty, while their parents are often considered to be responsible for their poverty.

Fuel Assistance (LIHEAP, Low Income Home Energy Assistance Program) is a means-tested federal program for low-income people, begun in 1981 and funded by block grants to states. It also helps with weatherization. Congress established the formula for distributing funds to States based on each state's weather and low-income population. The funds are never enough to meet the need, particularly in states with severe winters, and states struggle to get more money from the federal government.

Unemployment Insurance is a federal/state program to provide assistance to unemployed workers. Titles III and IX of the Social Security Act authorized the federal government to grant money to states to administer unemployment insurance (UI). States administer the program in a variety of ways.

A 2008 report by the Center for American Progress and the National Employment Law Project said that tighter rules on UI result in just

37 percent of unemployed Americans receiving jobless benefits today, down from 42 percent during the 1981–1982 recession and 50 percent during the 1974–1975 downturn. (European countries are more generous; 98 percent of French and 89 percent of German workers who are out of work qualify for benefits.)[20]

During periods of high unemployment, the federal government can increase the number of weeks that people receive unemployment benefits. The American Recovery and Reinvestment Act (stimulus package) that was signed into law on February 19, 2009, contained an increase in unemployment benefits and the length of time unemployed workers can collect. Economist Randy Albelda says that incentives for states to extend unemployment benefits to low-wage and part-time workers are particularly important to women.[21]

As a result of the stimulus bill, laid-off workers in nearly half the states could collect benefits for up to 79 weeks, the longest period since UI was created in the 1930s. But unemployment in this recession proved to be especially tenacious, and a wave of job seekers used up even this prolonged aid. By August 2009, tens of thousands of workers had already used up their benefits and the numbers were expected to soar, reaching half a million by the end of September and 1.5 million by the end of the year.

Payments averaged just more than $300 a week, varying by state and work history.[22]

Americans in 2008 received a maximum of 39 weeks of unemployment benefits, down from 65 weeks in the 1970s. And low-income workers—a category that tends to include women and those in part-time employment—are one-third as likely to receive UI as higher-income workers.[23]

The National Employment Law Project testified before the House Ways & Means Committee in 2007 in favor of a UI modernization bill, which would allow families to work part-time and collect UI benefits; currently they are unable to do so in most states.

> Part-time work has now become a necessity for many more workers to accommodate their family responsibilities or to find the time necessary to go back to school and improve their job skills. Today, one in six workers are employed part-time, and most of them are women workers. While working an average of 23 hours a week, only 23 percent of low-wage part-time workers collect jobless benefits.[24]

Maine recently provided UI to part-time workers, "and now more than 70 percent of those who qualify with the help of the new part-time worker protection are women workers"(collecting an average of more than $2,000).[24]

People who receive UI are required to look for work and to take any job for which they are qualified. States vary in their requirements, but in some states there is no allowance for maternity needs. During the NPR "On Point" radio program of November 19, 2008, a woman called in to say she had been fired from her job two hours ago. She was 9 months pregnant, and due to deliver in a week. She had maternity leave as part of the job, but now that she had no job, she does not know what she is going to do. "Can they do that?" she asked, then answered her own question, "I guess they can. They did it." She was advised to file for UI, but the work requirement presented difficulties. One of the guest speakers, an employment counselor in Tennessee, said that in his state there is no time allowed for maternity leave. The law requires a recipient to be available for work and willing to take any job for which (s)he is qualified. The host pressed him, "She is due to deliver in a week. Do you mean she would have to take a job on the day she delivers?" The employment counselor, in the manner of a true bureaucrat, simply repeated the same rule.

Unemployment coverage tends to be high where jobs pay well and unions are strong. The strongest state coverage is in New Jersey, Pennsylvania, and Wisconsin.[26]

Housing Assistance

Even with low wages, many poor people could afford housing if they had access to government-subsidized public housing. However, the federal government has been cutting back on building housing and on providing subsidies for housing since the early 1980s. The federal government chose to subsidize private housing for poor people through Section 8 vouchers rather than build housing because it did not want to interfere with private real estate interests. Real estate interests have decimated rent control in most cities, as rents continue to rise beyond the ability of low-income and even middle-income people to pay them.

While the federal government has been cutting housing for the poor, it has increased housing subsidies for the affluent through tax benefits for home ownership.

We discuss housing assistance in more detail in the chapter "Shelters for the Homeless: A Feeble Response to Homelessness."

The **Earned Income Tax Credit** program for the working poor has been more effective in reducing poverty than any other safety net program. It provides a refundable tax. In 2008, it gives up to $4,824 to families with 2 or more children who earn less than $38,646; up to $2,917 to families with one child who earn less than $33,995; and up to $438 to people with no children who earn less than $12,880. While it is a much-needed bonus to low-income people, it is also a bonus to employers of low-wage people as it supplements low wages. In 2007, 23.1 million families and individuals claimed EIC. Yet millions more eligible individuals did not file for the credit and ended up foregoing millions of dollars for which they qualified. The Center for Budget and Policy Priorities does extensive outreach program to tell people about the program.[27]

The **Child Tax Credit** is a federal tax credit worth up to $1,000 in 2008 for each qualifying child under age 17 claimed on the worker's tax return. A refundable additional amount is returned to some workers who owe no income tax. Liberal Democrats in Congress have worked to lower the income limit to include more low-income people and succeeded in lowering it from $12,050 in 2007 to $8,500 in 2009. The stimulus package lowered the income limit to $3,000, which will give cash to many more low-income parents. In a 2003 congressional debate, Democrats pointed out the essential unfairness of legislation that provides most of its benefits to the wealthy. The White House defended the decision of congressional negotiators to deny the increased child tax credit to millions of minimum-wage families, saying the new tax law was intended to help people who pay taxes, not those who are too poor to pay. Conservatives do not want to give parents cash for caring for their children.

Theresa Funiciello, the author of *Tyranny of Kindness*, advocated a refundable child tax credit as an alternative to TANF. Funiciello was at one time a welfare recipient. Her book is an angry denunciation of the bureaucracy that administers welfare. She argues that the money spent on bureaucratic administration of welfare should be given directly to welfare recipients, as is done with Social Security payments. She believes that a refundable child tax credit would be a more dignified program for low-income parents, without the stigma that accompanies welfare. The problem with this, as Gwendolyn Mink points out, is that it would not be enough to adequately support a family. Tax supports will only supplement other income.[28]

The Child and Dependent Care Credit is a tax benefit that helps families pay for child care they need to work or to look for work. It is also available to families that must pay for the care of a spouse or an adult dependent who is incapable of caring for himself or herself. For the year 2007, parents could claim as much as $3,000 in dependent care expenses per child (up to $6,000 for two or more children). However, families earning too little to pay federal income tax cannot use this credit. The credit is not refundable.

"Making Work Pay" Tax Credit was included in the American Recovery and Reinvestment Act. It provides a credit of up to $400 for individuals and $800 for married taxpayers filing joint returns.

American Opportunity Tax Credit expands the existing Hope Credit. Taxpayers can claim $2,500 tax credit for college tuition and related costs.

Workers' compensation in the United States began in 1911 during the Progressive Era when Wisconsin passed the first statutory system. Other U.S. jurisdictions followed suit. "Employees' compensation laws are usually a feature of highly developed industrial societies, implemented after long and hard-fought struggles by trade unions."[29] Workers' Compensation is a form of insurance that provides compensation for employees who are injured in the course of employment, in exchange for mandatory relinquishment of the employee's right to sue his or her employer for the tort of negligence. Although plans differ between jurisdictions, they can include weekly payments in place of wages, compensation for economic loss, reimbursement or payment of medical and like expenses, and benefits payable to the dependents of workers killed during employment. "In general, business groups seek to limit the cost of Workers' Compensation coverage, while labor groups seek to increase benefits paid to workers."[30] Parents who stay home to care for children are not eligible for workers' compensation if they are injured on the job, because the government does not define caregiving as work.

Veterans' Benefits. There are various veterans' benefits, including many VA hospitals that give good care. In general, World War II veterans were treated more generously than veterans of subsequent wars, although Congress has recently expanded educational benefits for veterans. There have been recent exposes of poor treatment in Walter Reed Hospital, and long waits to process disability claims. Some claims have not been processed for more than a year.

The Veterans' administration gets large discounts for wholesale purchase of prescription drugs. This is in contrast to Medicare, Part D, which is forbidden by law to buy prescription drugs at a discount.

Child Care

During World War II, women were encouraged to enter the waged labor market to help with war production. The Kaiser Company built shipyard 24-hour child care centers for working mothers, which cared for thousands of children. "At the close of the war, these Kaiser centers, along with 3,100 other federal and state funded centers serving from 600,000 to 1.6 million children, were dismantled. California is the only state where publicly funded center continued after the war."[31]

The 1996 welfare reform law eliminated the federal entitlement to child care assistance for families receiving or leaving AFDC, combined the principal preexisting federal child care funding sources into a single Child Care and Development Fund (CCDF) block grant, and increased state discretion in designing and operating child care programs. States can use the funds for all low-income families, not just those receiving AFDC/TANF assistance. There has never been a federal guarantee of childcare assistance. Rhode Island is the only state that has a statutory guarantee that all working families under a certain income level will receive childcare assistance.[32] During the Nixon administration, Congress proposed a universal day care program, but Nixon vetoed it. A Nixon aide said it "would Sovietize child care."

Childcare, even for TANF recipients, is never enough and much of it is of a low quality. Except for Head Start, a federal program, almost all of it is private. A few employers have day care facilities for their employees. Some cities have started prekindergarten programs, and Obama has mentioned the possibility of creating a universal prekindergarten program. Prekindergarten programs are generally half-day programs, as is Head Start. While that is some help for working parents, it is not sufficient. Truly adequate day care would have to be of high quality and for a full 24-hours.

The American Recovery and Reinvestment Act (stimulus package) that was signed into law on February 19, 2009 includes $4 billion for childcare for low-income families (more than half of which are single-mother families).[33]

General Assistance

There is no federal program for able-bodied unemployed people except for Unemployment Insurance and food stamps. If people have used up their UI benefits, or if they are not eligible for them, there is no federal cash assistance for them. Some states give small amounts of cash assistance, but most states have cut back or eliminated those programs. Michigan, Pennsylvania, Ohio, Illinois, and Los Angeles County ended General Assistance. Massachusetts ended it for the able-bodied unemployed during the administration of Governor Dukakis. It now gives some disabled and elderly people and children only approximately $300 a month. The food stamp program contained a work requirement for childless adults until the current recession, when the stimulus package removed the requirement.

NOTES

1. Greg Robb, "Paulson vows to stay on Social Security fight," *Market Watch*, http://www.marketwatch.com/News/Story.aspz?dist=news.
2. Ann Crittenden, *The Price of Motherhood*. New York: Henry Holt & Company, 2001, pp. 194–195.
3. Ibid., citing *How Well Do Women Far Under the Nation's Retirement Policies?* A report of the Subcommittee on Retirement Income and Employment of the Select Committee on Aging. 102nd Congress, Washington, DC, 1992, p. 12.
4. "Retirement Security," National Women's Law Center, http://www.nwlc.org/display.cfm?section=socialsecurity.
5. "Women of color and Social Security," National Women's Law Center, http://www.nwlc.org/display.cfin?section=socialsecurity.
6. Melissa M Favreaulot, "A new minimum benefit for low lifetime earners," Washington DC: Urban Institute Retirement Policy Program, March 2009, p. 1. www.retirementpoicy.org.
7. Ibid., p. 22.
8. "Electronic fact sheet," Social Security Online, http://www.ssa.gov/pubs/10003.html.
9. http://en.wikipedia.org/wiki/Medicare.PartD.
10. http://en.wikipedia.org/wiki/Medicaid.
11. Barbara Ehrenreich, "Nickel and dimed: Women, poverty, and work," *Mothering*, November/December 2001, p. 42.
12. "Children's Health Insurance Program," http://en.wikipedia.org/wiki/State_Children's_Health_Insurance. Accessed February 6, 2010.

13. Kevin Sack, "Expansion of clinics shapes a Bush legacy," *New York Times*, December 25, 2008, http://www.nytimes.com/2008/12/26/health/policy/26clinics.html.

14. Ibid.

15. Natonal Association of Community Health Centers, "Policy & Issues Forum," http://www.nachc.com/policy-and-issues-forum.cfm. Accessed February 6, 2010.

16. Food Research and Action Center, "In nearly half of the states, more than one in ten residents are on food stamps," http://www.frac.org/Press_Release/one_in_ten_nov2508.htm.

17. Randy Albelda, "Up with women in the downturn," *Ms.*, Spring 2009, p. 37.

18. Roger Thurow and Timothy W. Martin, "Boost in food stamp funding percolates through economy," *Wall Street Journal*, July 7, 2009.

19. http://www.en.wikipedia.org/wiki/Child_Nutrition_Act.

20. Crittenden, p. 197.

21. Albelda, "Up with women in the downturn."

22. Erik Eckholm, *New York Times*, August 2, 2009.

23. Steven Greenhouse, "Will the safety net catch the economy's casualties?" *New York Times*, November 16, 2008, p. 3.

24. Maurice Emsellem, "Testimony of Maurice Emsellem, National Employment Law Project, Hearing Before the U.S. Congress, House of Representatives, Committee on Homeland Security on the Transportation Worker Identification Credential, October 31, 2007 p. 12. 20071031111154-82971.pdf.

25. Ibid.

26. Jason DeParle, "For recession victims, patchwork state aid," *New York Times*, May 10, 2009, p. 16.

27. The Center on Budget and Policy Priorities, 2008, www.cbpp.org/eic2009.

28. Betty Reid Mandell and Marguerite Rosenthal, "Interview with Gwendolyn Mink," *New Politics*, Summer 2006, p. 79.

29. "Workers' compensation," Wikipedia, http://en.wikipedia.org/wiki/Workers%27_compensation.

30. Ibid.

31. Amina Hassan, "Shipyard day care centers of World War II: The Kaiser Experiment," http://wwiishipyarddaycare.tripod.com/intro.htm.

32. State Policy Documentation Project: Findings in Brief: Child Care Assistance, Center on Budget and Policy Priorities, September 02, 2005. http://www.spdp.org/tanf/childcare/childcaresumm.htm

33. Albelda, "Up with women in the downturn."

Advocacy Organizations Concerned with Caregiving and Social Justice

ACORN (Association of Community Organizations for Reform Now, Inc.)
http://www.acorn.org
ACORN is a nonprofit, nonpartisan social justice organization with national headquarters in New York, New Orleans, and Washington, DC. It is the nation's largest grassroots community organization of low- and moderate-income people with more than 400,000 member families organized into more than 1,200 neighborhood chapters in 110 cities across the country. Since 1970, ACORN has been building community organizations that are committed to social and economic justice, and it helps those who have historically been locked out become powerful players in our democratic system.

Unfortunately, ACORN filed for bankruptcy and closed most of its offices in March 2010 due to lack of funds. A right-wing group sent two people to an ACORN office who claimed to be a pimp and a prostitute, asking for advice on how to conceal the source of illegal income involving prostitution. The video they took was later found to be fraudulently edited, but national publicity resulted in Congress cutting off funds for ACORN.

American Association of Retired Persons (AARP) http://www.aarp.org
AARP is concerned with caregiving for elders. They believe "that a shift in corporate policy and culture must occur for workers to successfully balance the demands of work and family...Employers will have to have resources in place, like flextime and programs to help caregivers at a distance, or else productivity will go down."

The Carework Network http://www.carework-network.org
This is an "international organization of researchers, policymakers, and advocates involved in various domains of care work. Based in the social sciences, individuals from all academic disciplines and advocacy organizations

who take various approaches to the study of care work and care work policy are invited to participate in the Carework Network." The network does not have an official membership list or dues structure. Participation is through the listserv and annual meetings and conferences held in conjunction with meetings of the American Sociological Association.

Center for Community Change http://www.communitychange.org

Founded in 1968, the Center for Community Change (CCC) is a non-profit organization that recruits and trains activists to spearhead leftist "political issue campaigns" and promotes increased funding for social welfare programs by bringing "attention to major national issues related to poverty." CCC bases its training programs on the techniques taught by the famed radical organizer Saul Alinsky. Following Alinsky's blueprint for establishing "grassroots" organizations to agitate for social change, CCC states that it has "nurtured thousands of local groups and leaders" across the United States.

Center for Law and Social Policy (CLASP) http://www.clasp.org

CLASP's mission is to develop and advocate for policies at the federal, state, and local levels that improve the lives of low-income people. They seek policies that work to strengthen families and create pathways to education and work. Through careful research and analysis and effective advocacy, CLASP develops and promotes new ideas, mobilizes others, and directly assists governments and advocates to put in place successful strategies that deliver results that matter to people across America. They are working on TANF reauthorization.

Center on Budget and Policy Priorities http://www.cbpp.org

The Center on Budget and Policy Priorities is one of the nation's premier policy organizations working at the federal and state levels on fiscal policy and public programs that affect low- and moderate-income families and individuals. They are doing national research comparing SNAP (food stamps), TANF, and UI caseloads over time. They are working on TANF reauthorization, which is scheduled to take place by October 2010. They are reluctant to push for the abolition of time limits without there being services attached. They are also talking about an unemployment trigger, no time limits during high unemployment.

Children's Defense Fund (CDF) http://www.childrensdefense.org

CDF is the foremost national proponent of policies and programs that provide children with the resources they need to succeed. They champion policies that will lift children out of poverty, protect them from abuse and neglect, and ensure their access to health care, quality education, and a moral and spiritual foundation. The director is Marian Wright Edelman. Her husband, Peter Edelman, resigned from the Clinton administration when

President Clinton signed the welfare reform bill (Personal Responsibility and Work Opportunity Act) in 1996.

Coalition on Human Needs (CHN) http://www.chn.org

CHN is an alliance of national organizations working together to promote public policies that address the needs of low-income and other vulnerable populations. The coalition's members include civil rights, religious, labor, and professional organizations and those concerned with the well being of children, women, the elderly, and people with disabilities.

Direct Care Alliance, Inc. http://www.directcarealliance.org

This is "the advocacy voice of direct care workers, by direct care workers, and for direct care workers in long-term care. We empower workers to speak out for better wages, benefits, respect, and working conditions, so more people can commit to direct care as a career. We also convene powerful allies nationwide to build consensus for change."

Families and Work Institute http://familiesandwork.org

Families and Work Institute is a nonprofit research institute founded in 1989. They do research on the workforce and workplace, education, care and community, parenting, and youth development.

Families USA http://www.familiesusa.org

Families USA is a national nonprofit, nonpartisan organization dedicated to the achievement of high-quality, affordable health care for all Americans. They manage a grassroots advocates' network of organizations and individuals working for the consumer perspective in national and state health policy debates. They act as a watchdog over government actions affecting health care, alerting consumers to changes, and helping them have a say in the development of policy.

Family and Home Network http://www.familyandhome.org

This is a grassroots organization founded by 3 at-home mothers more than 20 years ago. It is based in Merrifield, VA. They "support and encourage mothers and fathers who choose to forgo or cut back on paid employment to be home with their children." They cite studies that claim to show that children need the intensive care of a mother. They say, "Our continued correspondence from mothers across the nation, which includes both those in and out of the paid workforce, strongly indicates that mothers want the establishment of economic incentives and social support for those parents who prefer to rear their own children, and the opportunity for flexible employment choices and later career reentry." They do not mention welfare as a possible support; instead they advocate tax relief, health insurance benefits, increased availability of part-time, job-share, and telecommuting positions, flextime jobs, and adequate leave policies.

Family Caregiver Alliance (FCA) http://www.caregiver.org
The main focus of FCA is on caregiving of older and disabled people. They operate on local, state, and national levels. They provide direct services to family caregivers in the San Francisco Bay Area and are the model of California's statewide system of Caregiver Resource Centers. They call upon the Obama administration to authorize and fund a National Resource Center on Caregiving; modernize Medicare and Medicaid to better support family caregivers; commission an Institute of Medicine study on family caregiving; provide adequate funding for programs that assist family caregivers; expand the Family and Medical Leave Act and other paid leave policies; promote policies that expand the geriatric care workforce; enact legislation providing refundable tax credits for family caregivers and employers; and strengthen Social Security by recognizing the work of family caregivers. They recommend that the Family and Medical Leave Act be expanded beyond the care of immediate family members to include care for siblings, in-laws, and grandparents. They also call upon Congress to enact legislation requiring employers to provide at least seven paid sick days annually for all employees.

Food Research and Action Center (FRAC) http://www.frac.org
The FRAC is the leading national nonprofit organization working to improve public policies and public-private partnerships to eradicate hunger and undernutrition in the United States. FRAC works with hundreds of national, state, and local nonprofit organizations, public agencies, and corporations to address hunger and its root cause, poverty. They provide coordination, training, and support on nutrition and antipoverty issues to a nationwide network of advocates, food banks, program administrators and participants, and policymakers.

Gray Panthers http://graypanthers.org
The Gray Panthers is an intergenerational organization that works for social and economic justice and peace for all people. Their vision is to create a humane society that puts the needs of people over profits, responsibility over power, and democracy over institutions. They seek to unify the generations, recognizing that generations are formed by different histories and cultures, but a common respect holds them together.

They honor maturity: The concept of aging takes into account an individual's growth during the entire life span, from birth to death, in personal development, social involvement, and self-fulfillment. They are actively engaged in civic participation to achieve goals of social and economic justice. They believe in participatory democracy. The members define the organization's values, purpose, and the issues in which they place collective energy.

Jobs with Justice (JwJ) www.jwj.org
JwJ engages workers and allies in campaigns to win justice in workplaces and in communities where working families live. JwJ was founded in 1987 with

the vision of lifting up workers' rights struggles as part of a larger campaign for economic and social justice. They believe in long-term multi-issue coalition building, grassroots base-building and organizing, and strategic militant action as the foundation for building a grassroots movement.

Journal of Progressive Human Services
Faculty at University of New England in Maine publish this journal. Haworth Press publishes it. They are eager for articles about progressive practice and policy.

League of Women Voters http://www.lwv.org
The League of Women Voters, a nonpartisan political organization, is a grassroots organization working at the national, state, and local levels. It encourages informed and active participation in government, works to increase understanding of major public policy issues, and influences public policy through education and advocacy.

LEARN—Labor Education and Resource Network
http://www.learnworkfamily.org
This is "a unique online education and resource network for labor unions on organizing and bargaining for contract provisions that help build a family friendly workplace culture."

Legal Momentum http://www.legalmomentum.org
This is the nation's oldest legal defense and education fund dedicated to advancing the rights of all women and girls. The issues they have worked on include the following: violence against women, equal educational opportunity for women and girls, sexual harassment, reproductive rights, gender bias in the courts, and the rights of immigrant women.

LIFETIME contact@geds-to-phds.org
LIFETIME is a nonprofit organization created by student mothers at the University of California, Berkeley, who completed college degrees while raising their families on welfare, and who are committed to helping others do the same. Their goal is to help low-income parents enroll in, continue, and successfully complete higher education and training—a long-term investment in poor families with lasting results.

Moms Rising.org http://www.momsrising.org
Joan Blades, cofounder with Wes Boyd of MoveOn, founded this organization online. It supports family-friendly policies, including maternity/paternity leave, flexible work, after school programs, health care for all kids, excellent child care, realistic and fair wages, and paid sick days. They have blogs and a film, and they encourage house parties in communities to talk about and take action on issues. There are many organizations that are

aligned with MomsRising.org. There is no mention of welfare on their Web site.

Ms. *Magazine http://www.msmagazine.com*
Founded in 1971, "Ms. continues to be an award-winning magazine recognized nationally and internationally as the media expert on issues relating to women's status, women's rights, and women's points of view." *Ms.* has had a few good articles about welfare, and it might be worthwhile to submit articles to it about welfare issues.

Multistate Working Families Consortium
http://www.valuefamiliesatwork.org
Founded in 2003, this is an organization of labor and community coalitions, started in 8 states and now encompassing 11. The consortium pools resources and information to support the introduction of state or local bills to guarantee paid family leave insurance, paid sick days, and other work-family supports.

National Alliance for Caregiving http://www.caregiving.org
"Established in 1996, the National Alliance for Caregiving is a non-profit coalition of national organizations focusing on issues of family caregiving. Alliance members include grassroots organizations, professional associations, service organizations, disease-specific organizations, a government agency, and corporations. The Alliance was created to conduct research, do policy analysis, develop national programs, increase public awareness of family caregiving issues, work to strengthen state and local caregiving coalitions, and represent the US caregiving community internationally." Forty pieces of legislation were introduced to the 110th Congress by the time it recessed in October 3, 2008. They included expanding the Dependent Care Tax Credit; doubling the child care tax credit to taxpayers that incur expenses for their parents or grandparents who do not live with them; helping individuals with functional impairments and their families to pay for services and supports (financed by payroll deductions); and bills related to Medicare, Social Security, end of life issues, family and medical leave, educational outreach/care coordination/ respite services; safety for senior and crimes against elderly or disabled; and veterans issues. http://caregiving.org/FederalLegislation.htm

National Association for the Advancement of Colored People (NAACP)
http://www.naacp.org
NAACP is the oldest, largest, and strongest civil rights organization in the United States. The principal objective of the NAACP is to ensure the political, educational, social, and economic equality of minority group citizens of the United States. NAACP is committed to achievement through nonviolence and relies upon the press, the petition, the ballot, and the courts, and

it is persistent in the use of legal and moral persuasion even in the face of overt and violent racial hostility.

National Association of Social Workers (NASW)
http://www.socialworkers.org
NASW has always been active in welfare rights. They opposed the 1996 PRWOA and since then have lobbied for more education and training for recipients. They have published information on TANF and lobbied for progressive change.

NASW recommends universal systems of support:

NASW believes that as a nation, we should concentrate on creating economic opportunity, strengthening families, and maximizing the ability of everyone—not just those on welfare—to contribute to society. We should develop universal systems of support for meeting basic needs, including health care, food, housing, child care, and education; create job opportunities that pay a living wage and provide a full range of benefits; and ensure economic security through adequate income support for individuals and families unable to support themselves.

National Coalition for the Homeless *http://www.nationalhomeless.org*
E-mail: info@nationalhomeless.org
The National Coalition for the Homeless is an advocacy organization that works on homelessness issues. One of their policy recommendations is a Universal Livable Income, which would be an annual wage or public income security assistance amount that is set at a level sufficient to obtain and maintain safe and decent permanent housing and other basic human needs. The livable income level should vary for individuals and families and be indexed to the cost of affordable housing in the geographic area in which they reside.

National Council of Churches USA *http://www.ncccusa.org*
The National Council of Churches has been very active on poverty issues in general, and on campaigning to improve TANF. They keep their membership informed on TANF, organize lobbying activities, and publish resource material on TANF, and on poverty. They have been particularly active in lobbying when TANF has been up for reauthorization in Congress.

National Council of La Raza (NCLR) *http://www.nclr.org*
The largest national Latino civil rights and advocacy organization in the United States, NCLR works to improve opportunities for Hispanic Americans.

National Council of Women's Organizations (NCWO)
http://www.womensorganizations.org
NCWO is a nonpartisan, nonprofit coalition that represents more than 11 million women across the United States. Their more than 200 member

organizations collaborate through substantive policy work and grassroots activism to address issues of concern to women, including family and work, economic equity, education, affirmative action, older women, corporate accountability, women and technology, reproductive freedom, women's health, younger women and global progress for women's equality.

National Council on Aging (NCOA) http://www.ncoa.org

NCOA is a nonprofit service and advocacy organization headquartered in Washington, DC. NCOA is a national voice for older adults—especially those who are vulnerable and disadvantaged—and the community organizations that serve them. NCOA brings together nonprofit organizations, businesses, and government to develop creative solutions that improve the lives of all older adults. They work for social and economic justice, and respect and caring for all.

National Employment Law Project (NELP) http://www.nelp.org

NELP works to restore the promise of economic opportunity in the twenty-first-century economy. In partnership with national, state, and local allies, they promote policies and programs that create good jobs, strengthen upward mobility, enforce hard-won worker rights, and help unemployed workers regain their economic footing through improved benefits and services.

National Law Center on Homelessness and Poverty (NLCHP) www.nlchp.org

NLCHP addresses the causes of homelessness, not just its symptoms. Its mission is to prevent and end homelessness by serving as the legal arm of the nationwide movement to end homelessness. The organization pursues three main strategies: impact litigation, policy advocacy, and public education. NLCHP strives to place homelessness in the larger context of poverty. By taking this approach, the organization aims to address homelessness as a visible manifestation of deeper causes, including the shortage of affordable housing, insufficient income, and inadequate social services.

National Organization for Women (NOW) http://www.now.org

The leadership of NOW was militant in their opposition to the 1996 welfare reform, but they were unable to bring along sufficient numbers of their members to make a difference. In fact, some members were quite hostile to the involvement of NOW in welfare reform issues, and believed that welfare recipients should be required to work. NOW has continued to be involved in welfare, but it does not seem to be a high priority. NOW's action agenda for 2009 covers nine issue areas: economic justice; reproductive rights and sexual health; equal rights and ending sex discrimination; health care for all; stopping violence against women; lesbian, gay, bisexual, and transgender rights; educational equity; promoting diversity and ending racism; and media fairness and accessibility.

The 2004 Women's March on Welfare included several groups and some speakers who focused on welfare and poverty. Betty Reid Mandell marched, and carried a sign saying, "Welfare reform kills babies." She got a lot of support from other marchers.

National Partnership on Women and Families
http://www.nationalpartnership.org

Founded in 1971, this organization "is dedicated to promoting public policies and business practices that expand opportunities for women and improve the well-being of our nation's families." They work with states and localities to develop and support legislation such as family and medical leave and prohibiting pregnancy discrimination. They drafted the Family and Medical Leave Act legislation and have been strong advocates for it since then.

National Women's Law Center (NWLC) http://www. nwlc.org

Since 1972, "the Center uses the law in all its forms: getting new laws on the books and enforced; litigating ground-breaking cases in state and federal courts all the way to the Supreme Court; and educating the public about ways to make the law and public policies work for women and their families." They pay special attention to the needs of low-income women and their families. They fight for strong enforcement of Title IX programs and removing barriers to girls' educational opportunities. They work on closing the wage gap and ensuring women are paid fairly; improving benefits for workers, including expanded family and medical leave; and expanding opportunities for women in nontraditional fields.

Their Family Economic Security program focuses on "helping economically vulnerable women—including single mothers, women of color, and elderly women—by promoting high-quality, affordable child and dependent care, strong income and work support programs, secure retirement programs, and a fair tax system that raises adequate revenues."

The center has put out several reports analyzing how the American Recovery and Reinvestment Act addresses women's needs.

Older Women's League (OWL)—The Voice of Midlife and Older Women
http://www.owl-national.org

OWL was founded in 1980 after a White House miniconference on aging in Des Moines, Iowa. OWL recognizes the value of women's work, paid or unpaid; focuses on the economic plight of women in later years; and attacks inequities inherent in public policy. OWL is a nonprofit, nonpartisan organization that accomplishes its work through research, education, and advocacy activities conducted through a chapter network. Now in its 23rd year, OWL provides a strong and effective voice for more than 58 million women aged 40 and over in America. OWL has created a grassroots network of more than 60 chapters nationwide composed of women and men of all ages. OWL leaders and members undertake national public education and advocacy campaigns, and work through forums, campaigns and coalitions to put those issues in the public spotlight and on the legislative agenda. They have focused on such issues as the health care coverage needs of midlife and older women, Social Security, pension reform, retirement security for women, caregiving, long-term care, housing, and domestic violence.

Sloan Work and Family Research Network http://wfnetwork.bc.edu

Based at Boston College, the Alfred P. Sloan Work and Family Research Network "targets the information needs of academics and researchers, workplace practitioners, state public policy makers, and interested individuals. It is the place to find high-quality research and reports, easy-to-read summary sheets and briefs, and work-family topic pages."

Social Welfare Action Alliance http://socialwelfareactionalliance.org

This is a group of radical social workers who try to implement progressive policies and action in the social work field. They are active in welfare rights and other poverty issues.

Urban Institute http://www.urban.org

The Urban Institute was founded in 1968 in response to President Johnson's initiative to charter a center to do independent nonpartisan analysis of the problems facing America's cities and their residents. They gather data, conduct research, evaluate programs, offer technical assistance overseas, and educate Americans on social and economic issues.

They work in all 50 states and abroad in more than 28 countries, and share their research findings with policymakers, program administrators, business, academics, and the public online and through reports and scholarly books.

In 2009, they published *Work-Life Policies*, edited by Ann Crouter and Alan Booth. It is a compilation of papers presented at the 2007 National Symposium on Family Issues at Penn State University. They have also published *Intergenerational Caregiving*, edited by Alan Booth, Ann Crouter, Suzanne Bianchi, and Judith Seltzer. In March 2009, they published an article, "A New Minimum Benefit for Low Lifetime Earners," by Melissa M. Favreault. It advocates an enhanced minimum benefit for Social Security that targets workers with long career with low lifetime earnings, along with a modest credit that compensates workers for up to three years out of the labor market due to caregiving, unemployment, or poor health.

Welfare Warriors http://www.welfarewarriors.org

A welfare rights group located in Milwaukee, Wisconsin, and led by Pat Gowens. They are in favor of a children's allowance. They are fighting the state child protection agency, which they claim is unnecessarily taking children from their parents and placing them in foster care or adoption.

Work-Family List Serve work-fam@list.msu.edu
This listserv, originally named takecarenet, was founded by Robert Drago, Department of Labor Studies and Industrial Relations at Penn State University. Drago directed the listserv for 16 years and is now working for the U.S. Congress. Ellen Kossek at Michigan State University now directs the list. It is a rich source of information about work and family issues.

CONTRIBUTORS

Randy Albelda is a professor of economics and senior research associate at the Center for Social Policy at University of Massachusetts, Boston. Her research and teaching covers a broad range of economic policies affecting women, especially low-income women and families. She has written dozens of articles and books on women's economic status. She is the coauthor of the following two books: *Unlevel Playing Fields: Understanding Wage Inequality and Wage Discrimination* and *Glass Ceilings and Bottomless Pits: Women's Work, Women's Poverty.*

Betty Reid Mandell is Professor Emerita, Bridgewater State College. She has coauthored *Introduction to Human Services: Policy and Practice,* 7th ed. She has also published *Welfare in America: Controlling the "Dangerous Classes,"* and *Where Are the Children? A Class Analysis of Foster Care and Adoption.* She is the coeditor of *New Politics.* She has been a social worker in child welfare, mental health, and welfare agencies. She has been a welfare rights activist since the 1960s.

Gwendolyn Mink writes and teaches about U.S. equality law, poverty policy, gender issues, and American politics. She was on the faculty of the University of California-Santa Cruz from 1980 to 2001 and Smith College from 2001 to 2009. She is author of *Welfare's End* (1998; rev. ed. 2002), a *Choice* magazine "Outstanding Academic Book"; *Hostile Environment* (2000); *The Wages of Motherhood* (1995), which won the 1996 Victoria Schuck Book Award of the American Political Science Association; and *Old Labor and New Immigrants in American Political Development* (1986). She is the editor of *Whose Welfare?* (1999); coeditor (with Wilma Mankiller, Marysa Navarro, Barbara Smith and Gloria Steinem) of *The Reader's Companion to U.S. Women's History* (1998); coeditor (with Rickie Solinger) of *Welfare: A Documentary History of Policy and Politics* (2003); and coeditor (with Alice O'Connor) of *Poverty: An Encyclopedia of History, Politics, and Policy* (2 volumes, 2004).

Marguerite G. Rosenthal, Ph.D., Professor Emerita, School of Social Work, Salem State College, MA. Dr. Rosenthal's areas of interest and research include social welfare history, comparative social welfare, child and family policy, and criminal justice. She is coeditor and contributor to *Diminishing Welfare: A Cross-National Study of Social Provision* (Praeger, 1992), currently serves as the co-book editor for the *Journal of Sociology and Social Welfare* and is a member of the Criminal Justice Committee of the National Association of Social Workers, Massachusetts chapter. Before beginning her academic career, she worked as a researcher/investigator and advocate in the N.J. Department of the Public Advocate, Office of the Public Defender, a state agency. Much of the focus of her chapter was stimulated by her sabbatical work with Grassroots Leadership, a justice organization working to end prison privatization.

INDEX